The Essex Genealogist

Index to Volumes 21-25

(2001-2005)

Essex Society of Genealogists, Inc.
Essex County, Massachusetts

HERITAGE BOOKS
2009

HERITAGE BOOKS

AN IMPRINT OF HERITAGE BOOKS, INC.

Books, CDs, and more—Worldwide

For our listing of thousands of titles see our website
at
www.HeritageBooks.com

Published 2009 by
HERITAGE BOOKS, INC.
Publishing Division
100 Railroad Ave. #104
Westminster, Maryland 21157

Copyright © 2009 Essex Society of Genealogists, Inc.

Other books by the author:

*Essex County Deeds, 1639-1678, Abstracts of Volumes 1-4
Copy Books, Essex County, Massachusetts*

CD: The Essex Genealogist, Volumes 1 and 2 (1981-1982)

The Essex Genealogist, Volumes 1-25 (1981-2005)

The Essex Genealogist, Index to Volumes 1-15 (1981-1995)

The Essex Genealogist, Index to Volumes 16-20 (1996-2000)

The Essex Genealogist, Index to Volumes 21-25 (2001-2005)

International Standard Book Numbers
Paperbound: 978-0-7884-4798-3
Clothbound: 978-0-7884-8067-6

The following guidelines have been observed for the indexing of these five volumes of The Essex Genealogist, 2001-2005:

All titles such as Dr. and Rev. have been eliminated except where there is no given name provided.

All variant spellings of given names have been consolidated under one common spelling (e.g., Rebeckah, Rebekah, Rebecka will appear as "Rebecca."

Wherever possible, married women have been listed under both their maiden names and under their married names, with maiden names in parentheses.

Names appearing in Society related articles and of no particular genealogical significance, have not been included.

Names with page numbers followed by an "a" will be found on the back covers of the original issues. They will be found on the last pages of the reprinted volumes.

The index was compiled and edited by Nancy Hayward and proofread by Barbara Bishop Poole.

Essex Society of Genealogists, Inc.
P. O. Box 313
Lynnfield, MA 01940
www.esog.org

SUBJECT INDEX

FAMILY GENEALOGIES

ESSEX COUNTY ARTICLES

SUBJECT INDEX

SUBJECT INDEX

SUBJECT INDEX

EVERY NAME INDEX

ABBE
Abigail, 21:37
Benjamin, 21:37
Ebenezer, 21:37
Elizabeth, 21:37
Hannah (Silsby), 21:37
Hepsibah, 21:37
John, 21:36, 37
Jonathan, 21:37
Mary, 21:36, 37
Mary (Allen), 21:37
Mary (Knowlton), 21:36, 37
Mary (Loring), 21:36, 37
Mary (Tryon), 21:37
Mercy, 21:37
Samuel, 21:36, 37
Sarah, 21:37
Thomas, 21:37
ABBOT/ABBOTT/ABOT, 22:42; 23:29;
    24:40, 86
___, Capt., 23:210
A., 21:102
Ada F., 25:195
Anna, 24:90
Anna (Peabody), 24:90
Charlotte Helen, 24:35, 45
Charlette V. (Stevens), 24:103
Christian (___), 25:181
Debora (Stevens), 24:87
Dorcas, 24:96
Dorcas (Whiting), 23:223, 224
Ebenezer, 24:99
Edward, 24:87
Elizabeth, 24:36, 39, 96
Elizabeth (Ballard), 24:84
Elizabeth (Tarbell), 24:176
Gabez, 24:84
George, 21:195, 199; 22:167, 24:37, 39
Gilbert R., 25:195
Hannah (Chandler), 24:37, 39, 55
Hephzibah (Stevens), 24:84
Ira A., 25:194, 195
Jacob, 24:84
James, 23:140
Joana (Parker), 25:84
John, 21:197; 24:37, 44, 86; 25:144,
    181
John Emery, 24:232a
John L., 24:96
Jonathan, 24:39, 96
Joseph, 24:90, 96; 25:84
Joshua, 23:223, 224
Josiah, 23:41
Lydia, 24:90
Lydia (Farrington), 24:99
Lydia (Stevens), 24:44, 84
Mary, 24:40, 176; 25:181
Mary (___), 24:96
Nathaniel, 24:84
Nehemiah, 23:238; 25:84
Obed, 24:176
Oliver, 24:104
Orlando, 24:103
Phebe (Hutchinson), 24:96
Sarah, 24:35, 37, 44, 88, 90, 96, 99;
    25:84
Sarah (Barker), 24:37
Sarah (Stevens), 24:37, 84
Stephen, 23:28; 24:37, 96
Susanne, 24:91, 99
Thomas, 24:84
Uriah, 24:85

William, 25:84
ABERCROMBY, 22:135
James, 22:139
ABORN see also EABORN
Catherine (Smith), 22:24
E., 23:155
John, 22:76
Mary, 22:24
Moses, 21:35
Saml, 22:79
Samuel, 22:24
Susannah (Trask), 22:24
ABOT see ABBOT/ABBOTT
ACARS see ACRES
ACKHURST
Lettice, 25:55
ACKLEY
Adam, 23:172
ACONS
Merriam, 22:221, 227
ACRES/ACARS see also AKERS
Benjamin, 22:89, 92
Daniel, 22:92
Hannah (Silver), 22:87, 89, 91, 92
Henry, 22:86, 89, 91, 92
John, 22:89, 92
Katherine, 22:89, 91
Martha, 22:89, 92
Mary, 22:89, 92
Mary (Marston), 22:92
Rebecca (Danforth), 22:92
ACY
Wm., 22:167
ADAM, 23:86
James, 21:180a
Robert, 21:180a
ADAMS, 21:154; 23:3
Abigail (___), 24:126
Abigail (Parker), 24:162; 25:39
Abigail (Smith), 24:114
Alice (___), 21:184
Andrew N., 24:158
Anna (Parker), 24:162
Benjamin, 22:78; 24:158, 159, 162;
    25:39
Charles Frances, 24:126
Deborah (___), 21:158
Elizabeth (Stevens), 24:83
Elkanah, 21:157
Esther, 25:83
Esther (Parker), 25:84
Esther (Sparhawk), 24:158
Frances Adelaide (Richardson),
    Frank, 21:184
Hannah, 23:57
Hannah, 24:232
Hannah (Riggs), 24:232
Hepsibah (Haven), 21:157
Israel, 24:83
James, 25:8
James Luther, 24:232a
Joel, 25:87
John, 21:136, 157; 22:69; 23:10, 11;
    24:42, 126, 135, 161, 162; 25:5
John Quincy, 24:126
Joseph, 23:140; 25:87
Josiah, 21:148
Lois/Louisa (Haven), 21:158
Mary, 24:232
Mary (Parker), 24:158
Maude, 25:82
Moses, 21:158

Nehemiah, 24:232
Rebecca, 21:145, 146
Rebecca (Potter), 21:145
Robert, 21:111
Ruth (Goodridge), 24:232
Samuel, 24:158; 25:83, 84
Thomas, 21:145; 23:140
ADKINS
John, 23:140; 25:104
ADKINSON
John, 25:105
AGASSIZ
Louis, 23:60a
AHERN/AHEM, 25:73
Annie, 25:63
Bertie, 25:65, 66
Catherine, 25:65
Catherine (Ahern), 25:65
David, 25:63
Dennis, 25:63, 66, 71
Johanna (Sullivan), 25:63
John, 25:65, 74
Kate, 25:67
Margaret, 25:72
Margaret (___), 25:70
Margaret (Lane), 25:66
Michael, 25:70
AITKIN
Margaret, 22:119
Margaret (Gibb), 22:120
Thomas, 22:120
AKELEY/AKERLEY
Aline Louis (Fuller), 21:53, 24:17
Ansel Davis, 21:53, 24:17
Archibald Douglas, 21:53
Archie, 24:17, 21
Archie Douglas, 24:17-20
Charlotte (Davenport), 21:53; 24:17,
    21
Effie Blanche (Grendell), 24:20
Geraldine Agnes, 21:53
Israel Thorton, 21:54
James William, 24:17-20
Lydia Violet (Davis), 24:17, 20, 53
Mary Ann (Mullin), 21:54
Obediah Robert, 24:18
Oliver Garrison, 24:21
Robert, 24:18, 21
Robert Obediah, 21:53
AKERS see also ACRES
Francis, 22:92
Hannah, 22:92
John, 22:92
Mary, 22:92
Moses, 22:92
Rebecca, 22:92
ALBACH
J. R., 23:48
ALBERT
Duke, 24:68
Prince, 24:69
ALCOCK
Francis, 21:46-48
Lewis, 21:48
Robert, 23:208
Ruth (Blaney), 23:208
ALCOTT
Amos Bronson, 22:148
ALDEN, 21:65
Anna (Brame), 21:30
John, 21:68
Nancy/Sally, 22:53

Priscilla (Mullins), 24:114
ALDERCHURCH
Edward, 23:15
ALDIS
Eunice, 21:160
John, 21:160
Mehitable (___), 21:160
ALDRICH
Huldah, 22:178
Huldah (Hill), 22:178
Huldah (Thayer), 22:161
Jacob, 22:161
Mary (___), 22:178
Peter, 21:44
Priscilla (Kenney), 21:44
Samuel, 22:178
Seth, 22:178
ALDRIDGE
Bertha, 25:198
ALFONSO
Lord Of Molina, 24:67
ALFORD
William, 21:240a
ALIN
James, 23:140
ALKINS
John, 23:140
ALLD
Hannah (Kent), 24:115
Sarah, 24:115
William, 24:115
ALLEN/ALLIN, 22:37, 42
Abigail, 22:55; 24:232; 25:203
Abigail (Hill), 22:55
Ambrose, 22:221, 233
Andrew, 21:195, 199
Ann, 23:101, 102, 106
Ann (Goodale), 25:203
Anna Briant, 21:105
Benjamin, 22:45; 24:189
Bethiah (___), 22:55
Carrie Hall, 25:195
Diantha (___), 25:192
Donna Murray, 22:80
Edward, 23:15
Frank G., 22:17
Gracie, 25:82
Hannah, 21:14
Helen C., 23:114
Jacob, 22:221, 227; 23:140
Joanna, 22:55
John, 21:145; 23:140
John Kermett, 21:213
John W., 21:105
Joseph, 22:55; 24:217; 25:181
Martha, 24:95, 103
Mary, 21:37, 39, 52
Mary (___), 24:189
Mary Wilson, 21:105
Myron O., 22:41
Nehemiah, 23:140
Rebecca (Wilson), 21:105
Robert, 21:240a
Ruth Smith (Roundy), 21:108
Sarah (Woodbury), 22:55
Solomon, 22:221
Solomon, 22:230
Thomas, 23:143
William, 21:240a; 23:160; 25:203
Zebulon, 22:55
ALLEY
Abigail (Killam), 22:88
Anna (Tarbox), 22:50
Benjamin, 22:50
Elizabeth (___), 22:91
Ephraim, 22:91

Hannah, 22:50; 25:147
Hannah Hicks (Atwell), 22:50
James, 22:50
John, 22:50, 91
Joseph, 22:50
Mary (Newhall), 22:50
Polly, 22:50
Rebekah, 25:147
Salley, 22:50
Samuel, 22:89, 91
Sarah, 22:89
Sarah/Sary (Silver), 22:87, 88, 91
Thomas, 22:88, 91; 23:215
ALLING, 22:135
James, 22:138
ALVAREZ
Teresa, 24:67
ALZO
Lisa, 25:186
AMBROSE
Alice, 21:142; 23:54
AMERIGE
Mary, 21:239
Morris, 21:239
Sally (Brown), 21:239
AMES see also EAMES, 24:39
Abigail (Spofford), 24:39
Abigail/Nabby (Stevens), 24:85
Benjamin, 24:93, 102
Dyer, 23:42
Elizabeth (Stevens), 24:44
Hannah (Stevens), 24:44
Nathaniel, 24:39
Phebe, 24:93, 102
Samuel, 24:39, 44, 85
AMESBURY
Phebe (___), 22:46
Stephen, 22:46
AMIDON, 23:47
ANDERSON
___, Mrs., 24:196
Benjamn, 24:196
Blake, 24:196
Eliza, 25:125
Eliza (___), 25:125
John, 23:140
R. C., 24:61, 72; 25:156a
Robert Charles, 21:211; 22:41, 99,
    109; 23:160, 221; 24:46, 65, 72,
    156; 25:16
Roberta Marie (Sidman), 21:18
S. Chris, 25:123
V. E., 24:61
W. J., 23:56
ANDERTON
Hannah (Anderton), 23:208
Hannah (Bessom), 23:207, 209
Thomas, 23:209
ANDRAS/ ANDRESS
Abigail, 24:34
C., Mrs., 24:34
N., 24:34
ANDREW
Abigail, 24:189
Alice Prince, 24:69
Jonathan, 24:189
Joseph, 24:189
Mary (___), 24:189
Nathaniel, 24:189
Prince, 24:69
Thomas, 25:174
ANDREWES/ANDREWS/ANDRUSE,
    25:172
___, Mrs., 21:151
Abigail, 25:156
D., Mrs., 24:34

E., 24:34
Elias, 24:34, 54, 139, 141
Frank DeWitte, 22:124
Grace (___), 23:120
H., 24:34
I., 24:34
J. P., 24:34
J., Mrs., 24:34
John, 21:149; 22:43, 117, 203, 204,
    209; 24:30, 33, 109, 146, 147;
    25:133, 134
Joseph, 24:30
M., 24:34
M., Miss, 24:34
Mary, 25:201
Rebecca (___), 23:120
Robert, 23:120
Ruth, 23:120
Sarah (Holyoke), 22:204
W., 24:34
William, 24:30, 115, 117, 151
ANDROS
___, Gov., 21:240a; 23:162
ANDRUSE see ANDREWS
ANNA
Queen, 24:68
ANNE
Empress, 24:68
Princess, 24:69
Queen, 22:123; 24:68
ANROS
John, 23:140
ANSON
Cap, 24:133
ANTONY
___, Mrs., 23:140
ANTROBUS
Joan, 25:201
ANTRUM
Thomas, 22:240a
APITZ
Joseph, 23:23, 34, 115
APPLETON, 22:21, 135
___, Gen., 23:113
___, Maj., 21:211, 212
___, Mr., 22:209
___, Pres., 23:114
F. H., 23:114
Francis Henry, 23:17
James, 22:220, 221, 231, 232
John, 21:96
Margaret (___), 21:156
Martha, 21:222
Mary (Phillips), 24:43
Mary (Russell), 24:43
Mary (Stevens), 24:42, 43
Mehitable, 21:156
Nathaniel, 21:156
Samuel, 23:116
Samuel, 24:42, 43, 166, 212
Tamesin (___), 25:125
W.S., 24:162
William, 25:125
William S., 22:109
William Sumner, 22:137
ARCHAMBAULT
Harry D., Mrs., 25:146
ARCHARD
Samuel, 21:149
ARCHBELL see ARCHIBALD
ARCHER, 22:159
Geo., 24:189
Henry, 22:153; 24:151
Judith, 24:189
Judith (___), 24:189
Samuel, 21:240a; 23:160

ARCHIBALD/ARCHBELL
  Janet, 21:52
  John, 25:8
ARENDS, 21:9
ARLEM
  Elizabeth Travis (Batten), 24:218
  Samuel, 24:218
ARMITAGE
  Godfrey, 21:210
  James, 22:203
  Jane (___), 22:203
  Jane, (Poole), 21:210
  Joseph, 21:149, 152, 209, 210
ARMSTRONG
  David, 25:191
  Rebecca White (Cottle), 25:191
ARNOLD, 22:135
  Abigail, 22:136
  Benedict, 24:82
  James, 22:185
  Joseph, 21:217
  William, 21:216
ARTHAUD
  John Bradley, 21:161, 238; 22:162;
    23:99; 24:217, 219, 221
ARTIOLI
  A., Mrs., 25:116
  Augusto, 25:116
ASH
  Betsy, 25:192
  Elizabeth (Brock/Knox), 25:197
  Margaret, 25:192
  Nathaniel, 25:192, 197
  Sarah, 25:188
  Sarah, 25:197
ASHBY, 21:10
  Esther (___), 22:173
  George, 22:173
  Jonathan, 23:93
  Mary Ann, 23:93
  Sarah (Skidmore), 23:93
  Sarah Elizabeth, 23:93
ASHLEY
  Mary (Hallowell), 21:71
ASHTON
  Ephrem, 23:140
ASLEBE/ASLEBEE/ASLET/ASLETT,
  21:93
  John, 21:92, 94, 195 199
  Mary, 24:40
  Rebecca, 21:94
  Rebecca (Ayer), 21:92
  Samuel, 21:92
  Sarah, 21:92-94
ASPINALL/ASPINWALL
  Mary, 25:53
  Willyam, 24:46
ATKIN/ATKINS, 24:126
  Ann, 25:19
  Elizabeth (___), 25:18, 22
  Hesther/Esther, 25:18, 19, 22, 58
  Malcolm, 25:6
  Mary, 21:237
  Rebecca, 25:18
  Sarah, 25:19
  Thomas, 25:18
ATTEAUX
  F. E., 23:56
ATTKINSON
  John, 25:104
ATTWILL
  Amos, 22:48
  Anna (___), 22:52
  Betsey, 25:147
  Bridgit (___), 22:52
  James, 22:52

  Joseph Sanger, 22:48
  Lydia (___), 22:52
  Mary (___), 22:52
  William, 22:52
  Zachariah, 22:52, 53
ATWELL/ATWILL, 22:240
  ___ (Mains), 22:43
  "Daughter", 22:48
  Addie, 22:50
  Alfred, 22:51
  Alice (Lewis), 22:43
  Amos, 22:43, 47-49, 54
  Amos Main, 22:48
  Andrew, 22:43, 45
  Anna, 22:48, 50, 52
  Anna (Breeden), 22:49
  Anna (Ramsdell), 22:46, 47, 54
  Anna/Nancy, 22:53
  Anne, 22:46, 48
  Benjamin, 22:43, 46
  Benjamin F., 22:45, 46
  Benjamin Franklin, 22:51
  Beth/Betsey (Searle/Searl), 22:47, 54
  Betsey, 22:48
  Betsey/Betsy F., 22:49, 51
  Betty, 22:48
  Betty Charlotte, 22:48
  Bridget, 22:51, 52
  Bridget (Cummings), 22:47, 51, 54
  Charles, 22:52, 53
  Charles Rufus, 22:48
  Charlotte, 22:48
  Chase W., 22:51
  Chase Whitcher, 22:51
  Chloe, 22:48
  Cynthia, 22:51
  Dolly (Whitcher), 22:47, 51, 54
  Dorothy (___), 22:43
  Druzilla (Doane/Dane), 22:49
  Ebenezer, 22:51, 52
  Edwin, 22:51
  Elizabeth/Betsy, 22:46, 51-53
  Elizabeth (Breed), 22:49
  Elizabeth (Maine), 22:44, 54
  Eunice, 22:46
  Francis, 22:51
  Franklin, 22:52
  George, 22:49
  George Lovell, 22:48
  George Rufus, 22:48
  Gustavus, 22:51
  Hannah, 22:46, 47
  Hannah (Bowland), 22:52
  Hannah (Palfrey), 22:51
  Hannah (Smith), 22:51
  Hannah Hicks, 22:50
  Hollis, 22:51
  Horatio Nelson, 22:48
  Ichabod, 22:48
  James, 22:51-53
  Jesse Lee, 22:49
  Joanna, 22:50
  Joanna (___), 22:49, 50
  Joanna (Mansfield), 22:50
  John, 22:43-48, 51, 52, 54
  John Daggett, 22:51
  Jonathan, 22:51, 52
  Joseph, 22:43, 45, 46, 54
  Joseph Warren, 22:51
  Josiah, 22:52
  Lucy (Rhodes), 22:49
  Lydia, 22:43, 50
  Lydia (Felt), 22:43, 44, 46, 54
  Lydia (Hunkins), 22:51
  Lydia Daggett (Hicks), 22:47, 48, 54
  Lydia Hicks, 22:50

  Margaret (___), 22:43
  Margaret (Maxe), 22:44, 45. 54
  Margaret/Peggy, 22:46
  Martha, 22:46
  Martha (Ingalls), 22:51
  Martha/Patty, 22:51
  Mary, 22:48, 51
  Mary (___), 22:48, 54
  Mary (Bacheler), 22:49
  Mary (Fuller), 22:48, 54
  Mary (Lawrence), 22:47, 48
  Mary (Stone), 22:47, 52, 54
  Mary (Stone), 22:54
  Mary/Polly, 22:48, 51, 53
  Mary/Polly (Young), 22:48
  Mehitable (Wilson), 22:48, 54
  Mehitable/Hattie (Wilson), 22:47
  Micheson, 22:49
  Miranda, 22:52
  Miriam (Cass), 22:46, 54
  Nancy (Nichols), 22:51
  Nancy (Roberts), 22:51
  Nancy/Sally (Alden), 22:53
  Nathan, 22:46-48, 51-54
  Nelson Reed, 22:51
  Ozios, 22:46
  Parm/Pamerla/Perm/Pearm (Cowell),
    22:54
  Paul Pritchard, 22:51
  Phebe (___), 22:46
  Philip, 22:43
  Polly, 22:49, 51, 53
  Polly (Atwell), 22:51
  Rebecca, 22:46, 51
  Rebecca (Lawrence), 22:51
  Rebecca (Woodbury), 22:49
  Richard, 22:43, 44, 46-48, 54, 81
  Richard A., 22:43, 180
  Richard Ingalls, 22:51
  Rufus, 22:48
  Russell, 22:51
  Ruthe/Ruthy, 22:49
  Sally, 22:51
  Sally (Burrill), 22:53
  Sally (Diamond), 22:49
  Samuel, 22:51
  Sarah, 22:43-45, 47
  Sarah (Balkom/Bolcom/Bolkum),
    22:46, 47, 54
  Sarah (Joslen), 22:46, 54
  Sarah (Nichols/Nickol/Nickols), 22:46,
    47, 54
  Sarah (Rhodes), 22:45, 46, 54
  Sarah B., 22.51
  Sarah B. (Atwell), 22:51
  Sarah G. (Smith), 22:52
  Sarah/Sally, 22:48, 50
  Sarah/Sally (Lawrence), 22:52
  Susanna, 22:51
  Tabitha, 22:46
  Thomas Hicks, 22:49, 50
  Thomas Page, 22:51
  Welthea (Woodcock), 22:48
  William, 22:46-48, 50, 51, 54
  William Augustus, 22:51
  William Burroughs, 22:50
  William Cummings, 22:51
  William Lawrence, 22:48
  Zachariah, 22:47-49, 51
ATWOOD
  Apphia (Bangs), 25:22
  Henry, 25:22
  Joanna (Strout), 25:18
  Jonathan, 25:22
  Joshua, 25:22
  Martha (Pike), 25:22

Stephen, 25:22
AUCHMUTY
Robert, 23:8-11, 16
AUGER
Mercy (Haven), 21:157
Timothy, 21:157
AUGUSTA
Duchess, 24:68
AUSTIN
Benjamin, 21:116; 24:38, 39
Daniel, 24:39
Deborah, 22:175
Eliazer, 22:173
Hannah (Foster), 21:116
James, 22:174
John, 24:100; 25:21
Jonah, 22:175
Joseph Frothingham, 22:175
Josiah, 22:171, 173-175
Mary, 21:116
Mary (Stevens), 21:116; 24:38, 39
Patty (Stevens), 24:100
Priscilla (Stevens), 24:39
Sally, 22:171
Sarah (___), 22:171, 173-175
Thomas, 21:116; 24:40
AVELING
Henry, 23:56
AVEREL/AVERELL
James, 23:151
Sarah, 23:237, 238
AVERY
Hannah, 21:176
Lillian Drake, 24:218
AXEY
Frances (___), 22:206
AYER/AYERS/AYRES/EYRES
Ann Elizabeth, 25:194
Elizabeth, 25:56
Elizabeth (Hutchins), 21:46
Elizabeth (Palmer), 25:56
Hannah (Errington), 23:175
John, 24:43
Mary, 21:85, 86, 93; 24:55
Rebecca, 21:92
Rebecca (___), 24:217
Richard H., 24:169-171
Robert, 25:56
Thomas, 21:46, 217; 23:175

BABBIDGE
Lydia, 24:189
Susannah (___), 24:189
BABBIT
Thomas, 23:140
BABCOCK
Abigail, 21:155
BABSON, 22:113; 23:164; 25:11
Anna (Rogers), 21:238
David, 22:221, 228-234
Dorcas (Elwell), 21:238
John, 21:238
John J., 23:159, 164, 194; 24:218,219;
  25:13
John James, 21:238
Martha (Haraden), 21:238
Mary (Butman), 21:238
Mary (Dolliver), 21:238
Mary (Griffen), 21:238
Richard, 21:238
Sarah, 21:238
T.E., 24:152
Thomas, 25:14
William, 21:238; 22:221, 227-233
Zebulon, 22:221, 231

BACH
Rebackah, 25:45, 139
BACHELDER see also BATCHELDER
David, 21:212
Elizabeth, 25:55
John, 21:214
Phebe, 24:89
BACHELER
Mary, 22:49
BACON, 23:218; 24:32, 48, 49
Freeman, 21:239
George Allen, 21:239
Hannah (Higgins), 21:239
Hulda (Holbrook), 21:239
Isabella, 21:239
Joanna (Lanman), 21:237
John, 21:237, 239
Louisa Jane (Lynde), 21:239
Michael, 25:4
Saml., 23:89
BADGER
Joseph, 25:187
Judith, 25:187
BAGLEY, 22:99
BAGNALL/BAGNELL
Elizabeth (Whitehouse), 23:117
Florence (___), 21:20
Jane, 22:218
Nelson, 21:20
Samuel, 23:117
BAILEY/BAILY/BAYLEY, 25:44
___, Goodwife, 24:106
Abigail, 25:89
Eleanor (Emery), 22:239
Elizabeth (Stevens), 24:39
Isaac, 22:239
James, 21:180; 22:87, 167
John, 22:87, 239
Jonathan, 22:87
Joseph, 23:140
Josiah, 24:39
Mary, 24:164
Mary (Carr), 21:180
Miriam, 21:158
Moses, 24:164
Nathaniel, 22:87; 24:39
Rebecca, 22:239
Ruth (Bradshaw), 24:164; 25:44
Samuel, 25:38
Sarah, 22:120, 239; 24:89, 98
Sarah (Clark), 24:39
Sarah (Emery), 22:239
William, 24:98
Thomas, 25:38
BAKER, 21:165, 167; 22:212
Abigail, 25:201
Alice C., 22:96
Charles A., 21:22
Elisabeth, 23:92
Hephzibah, 24:43, 88
Jabez, 22:112; 23:165
John Wales, 22:237
Mary, 24:208
Mary Waters, 22:237
Richard, 22:237; 25:53
Samuel, 23:89
Sarah, 21:52; 23:140
Susana Whitney, 25:53
Susanna (___), 22:237; 25:53
Thomas, 22:36, 221, 228
Wm Pearley, 23:140
BALBONI
Adella (___), 25:116
BALCH, 21:24; 22:20
Benjamin, 22:57, 58
Deborah, 22:57

John, 21:24
Mary (Leech), 22:57
Miriam, 22:40
Rebackah, 25:140, 141
Sarah (Gardner), 22:58
BALDWIN
Bernard R., 23:17
Hannah, 21:159
James, 21:159
Loammi, 25:188, 189
Mary (___), 21:159
Ruth, 21:159
Thomas, 24:52
Thomas W., 21:38
William, 24:104
BALKOM/BOLKUM
Alexander, 22:47
Sarah, 22:47
Sarah (Woodcock), 22:47
BALL see also BALLE
Emma Eliza (Thrasher), 24:115
Gertrude Frances, 24:115
Isaac, 23:140
John Nichols, 24:115
Mary, 25:5
William T. W., 23:56
BALLARD, 23:161
Elisha, 23:140
Elizabeth, 24:84
Elizabeth (___), 21:92
John, 21:149; 22:203, 204, 213
Joshua, 24:96
Mary, 21:31, 152, 155, 157, 160
Nathaniel, 21:35, 158
Phebe, 24:96
Rebecca (Hudson), 21:158
Sarah, 21:150
William, 21:153, 195; 23:109
BALLE see also BALL
Isaac, 23:140
Jacob, 23:140
BALSH
Martha (Newmarch), 22:58
Samuel, 22:57
BANCROFT
___, Ens., 21:93
Abigail (Eaton), 21:213
Alice Alvira 'Vera' (Swanback), 24:21
Ebenezer, 21:94, 212, 213, 220
Elizabeth (Metcalf), 21:212
Emily H., 23:115
George, 22:120a
John, 21:95
John E., 24:21
Jonathan, 21:212, 213
Judith, 21:212, 213
Mary, 22:76
Mary (Webster), 21:212
Mary (Wiley), 21:214
Mehitable, 21:213
Mehitable (Fitch), 21:213
Moses, 21:214
Raham, 21:212, 213
Ruth (Kendall), 21:213
Samuel, 21:212, 213
Sarah, 21:212, 213, 222
Sarah (Lampson), 21:213
Sarah (Leathe), 21:213
Sarah (Poole), 21:212
Thomas, 21:212, 219
BANGS
Apphia, 25:22
BANK/BANKE/BANKS, 24:96
John, 25:8
Charles, 23:234, 235; 25:6
Charles E., 23:109, 234

Charles Edward, 21:89; 24:46

BARBER
Abigail, 21:155
Abigail (Babcock), 21:155
John, 21:155, 240a

BARBOUR, 22:162, 163, 184

BARCLAY
John E., Mrs., 25:18, 19, 22

BARDE
Abigail, 21:160

BARDEN
James, 21:187

BARDES, 25:28
Bruce, 25:19, 25
Eleanor, 25:19, 25

BAREFOOTE/BARFOOTE
Walter, 25:96, 104

BARHAM
___, Mrs., 24:120

BARKER see also PARKER
Alice, 21:59
Benjamin, 24:36
Deborah, 24:36, 40, 86
Ebenezer, 24:39
Elizabeth, 24:36, 40, 83, 93
Elizabeth (Lovejoy), 24:93
Esther, 24:35, 36
Hannah, 24:43, 89, 91
Jacob, 24:85
James, 22:167
Joan (___), 24:35, 36
John, 24:35
Lucy, 25:191
Mary, 24:36, 43, 95; 25:19
Mary (___), 22:165
Mary (Abbott), 24:40
Mary (Frye), 24:40, 44
Mary (Stevens), 24:35
Molly (Stevens), 24:84
Phineas, 24:84
Richard, 21:195, 199; 24:35, 36
Robert, 21:195
Samuel, 23:117
Sarah, 24:37
Sarah (Bessom), 23:207, 208
Stephen, 24:40, 44
Susanna, 22:238
Susanna (Foster), 23:117
Thomas, 22:167
Timothy, 24:85
William, 24:36
Zebediah, 24:93

BARLOW
Claude W., 22:107

BARN
Elizabeth (___), 23:140
John, 23:140

BARNABEE
H. C., 23:56

BARNARD
Dorothy, 22:178
Edward, 21:196
Elizabeth, 24:96
Francis, 23:42
Hannah, 24:35, 36, 116
James, 21:109
Joan (Harvey), 24:36
John, 21:196-198; 24:44
Naomi (___), 24:44
Rebecca, 24:39, 44
Robert, 24:36
Sarah Lucy (Bennett), 21:109
Thomas, 21:195, 196, 198; 24:37, 56a, 232a

BARNES
Abigail, 22:191

Enoch B., 24:171
Sarah, 22:55
William, 22:56

BARR
Archibald, 23:140
James, 25:125
Priscilla (___), 25:125

BARRAT/ BARRATT/
BARRIT/BARRET/BARRETT/
BARROT
___, Rev., 21:158
Anna, 25:45
Anna (___), 25:144
Elizabeth, 21:211
George T., 22:221, 234
Hannah, 22:174
Hannah (___), 22:174, 175
John, 21:210, 211, 222; 23:140
Jonathan, 22:175; 24:214
Joseph, 22:174
Lucy, 24:206, 214
Lydia, 21:222
Lydia (___), 24:214
Marah, 25:45, 142
Mehitable, 23:87
Patty, 22:174
Sarah, 25:86
Sarah (Poole), 21:211
William, 21:210, 211, 222; 23:140

BARRINGTON
Francis, 22:164
Jane (Cromwell), 22:164

BARRIT see BARRAT

BARRON
Jonathan, 25:41
Lucy (Parker), 24:162, 163
Mary (Learned), 21:188
Moses, 24:163, 188

BARROT see BARRAT

BARRY, 21:154
Horatio Newhall, 25:152
John, 22:236, 237; 25:52-54, 152
John M., 25:107
Joseph, 22:47, 48
Martha, 22:237
Mary, 22:236
Mary (___), 22:236, 237; 25:52-54, 152
Nathan Frye, 25:53
Samuel Stidman, 25:52
William, 21:151
William J., 23:17
William Luther, 25:54

BARSTOW
Elizabeth Joanna, 22:201, 202
Michael, 25:163

BARTHOLOMEW
Elizabeth, 22:190, 191, 193
Enos, 22:191
John, 22:190, 191
Sarah, 22:191
William, 21:29

BARTLET/BARTLETT
Elizabeth, 22:172
Edward O., 22:79
Gershom, 25:168
Hannah (Philbrick), 21:240
Henry, 25:19
Joane, 21:49
Lucy W., 25:195
Mary E., 25:197
Perley, 21:240
Richard, 21:49, 185

BARTON
John, 24:189
Lydia (___), 24:189

William, 22:47
Zacheus, 24:189

BARZ-SNELL
Jeffrey, 24:232a

BASKEN
Virginia, 25:95

BASS
Joseph, 21:31
Lois, 21:31

BASSETT, 21:156
Elizabeth, 21:87; 23:105, 169
Esther, 22:184
Isaac, 23:140
James, 22:49
William, 21:30; 23:169

BASTO
Sarah, 22:162

BATCHELDER see also BACHELDER
___, Sister, 24:105
Anna, 22:175
Elizabeth (___), 24:106
Hannah, 22:175
Hannah (___), 22:175, 176
James, 21:214
John, 22:103
Joseph, 24:106
Mark, 22:38; 24:107
Mary, 22:176
Nathaniel, 22:175, 176
Roscoe, 21:21

BATES, 21:10
Charles F., 21:11
Henry, 23:140
John, 22:44
Lydia (___), 25:83
Robert, 25:83
Roberts, 23:174
Sarah (___), 23:174
Sarah (Forbes), 21:11
William, 21:11

BATSON
Elizabeth (Sanders), 23:233
John, 23:233

BATT
N., 21:114

BATTEN/BATTING/BATTIN/
BATTON
"Child", 24:220
Abigail (Carney), 24:217
Abraham, 24:217-221
Ann, 24:218
Anna, 24:220
Anne (Elwell), 24:217, 218
Benjamin G., 24:221
Bethia, 24:218
Catharine, 24:221
Clarence, 24:221
Daniel, 24:221
Dorcas, 24:219
Dorcas (Stanwood), 24:220
Ebenezer, 24:218-221
Eliza A. (Kenton), 24:221
Elisabeth, 24:219
Elizabeth Travis, 24:218
Elizabeth/Betsy (Clarke), 24:220, 221
George M., 24:221
Hannah (Stanwood), 24:218- 220
Henry S., 24:221
John, 23:141; 24:217-221
Joseph, 24:218
Judith, 24:219
Loisa Maria, 24:221
Lydia Witham, 24:219
Martha Ann, 24:221
Mary, 24:218, 219, 239
Mary (___), 24:220, 221

Susannah (Estey), 23:117
Tholomiah, 21:11
Thomas/Tholomiah, 21:11
BERSON
Eliot L., 24:62
BERTOCCHI
Frank, 25:116
BESSEL
Paul, 23:170
BESSOM/BEASOM/BEZUNE
"Child", 23:214
Abbie Ellen (Stone), 23:211
Abigail, 23:210
Abigail Lewis, 23:210
Anna, 23:211
Anna/Nancy M. (Harris), 23:209, 211
Annie Rachel, 23:211
Annis O. (Kelley), 23:211
Betsy (Martin), 23:211
Betsy L., 23:210
Charlotte C. W., 23:210
Earl Albert, 23:211
Edmund L., 23:210
Edmund Lewis, 23:210
Elizabeth/Betsy, 23:208-210, 214
Elizabeth/Betsy (Lewis), 23:209, 210
George W., 23:210
George Washington, 23:211
Grace, 23:207-210
Hannah, 23:207-210
Hannah (Blaney), 23:211
Hannah (Laskey), 23:213
Jane/Jean, 23:207-209
John, 23:207-211, 214
John Russell, 23:211
Joseph, 23:207-209, 211
Leonard Curtis, 23:211
Margaret, 23:207, 208
Margaret (Furness), 23:214
Martha, 23:210
Mary, 23:207-209, 214
Meriam, 23:210
Nicholas, 23:214
Persis (Fletcher), 23:208, 209
Philip/Phillip, 23:207-212
Rachel (Gill), 23:211
Rebecca, 23:211, 214
Rebecca (Bowden), 23:214
Rebecca (Chin/Chinn), 23:209, 211
Rebecca (Dutton), 23:210
Rebecca Cleaves (Smith), 23:210
Richard, 23:209
Richard VanBlunk, 23:211
Robert Harris, 23:211
Ruth/Ruthy, 23:207, 208, 210
Ruth (Collier), 23:209, 210
Sarah, 23:207, 208, 210, 211
Sarah (Bubier), 23:207
Susanna, 23:207, 209
Sydney Edward William, 23:211
Tabitha, 23:210
William, 23:207
William Blaney, 23:211
William Bubier, 23:209, 211
William G., 23:210
William Gray, 23:211
William H., 23:211
BETHELL
Hannah (___), 24:190
Richard, 24:190
BETIT
Kyle J., 25:121
BICKFORD
Anna (___), 22:171, 172
Benj'a, 23:141
David, 22:171, 172

Nancy, 22:171
**BICKNER/BICKNOR/BICKNAL/
   BICKNELL/BICKNOLL**
"Child", 23:52
Benjamin, 23:52
John, 23:52
Joseph, 23:52, 59
Martha (Metcalf), 23:52, 59
Samuel, 23:52
Sarah, 23:52, 59
Sarah (Ingalls), 23:52
William, 23:51, 52, 59
BIDFIELD
Elizabeth, 21:49
Elizabeth (___), 21:49
Samuel, 21:49
BIGELOW
Jacob, 25:170
Phebe (Rand), 21:34
Samuel, 21:34
BIGSBEE
Benjamin, 22:44
BIGWOOD
A. Rosemary, 23:85, 86
BILL
Phillip, 25:132
BILLIAS
George Athan, 24:79
BILLINGHAM
___, Gov., 21:214
BIRKNER
Ann M., 23:113, 115
BISCO
Leonard, 23:141
BISHOP
___, Goodman, 22:152
___, Goody, 25:95, 104
___, Mrs., 25:102
Anne (Kenney), 21:44
Benj, 23:141
Dinah, 22:109
Elizabeth, 22:109; 25:52
Elizabeth (___), 25:52
Elizabeth (Phillips), 22:109
Hanah, 22:109
Henry, 22:109
James, 22:109
Job, 22:109
John, 21:44; 23:54, 141; 25:52, 102,
   103
Margaret, 25:52
Margaret (___), 22:109
Mary, 25:52
Mary (___), 22:109
Nancy Sione, 25:52
Nathaniel, 22:109
Paul, 22:109
Rebbecca (___), 25:98
Rebecca, 24:176
Sarah, 22:109; 25:98
Thomas, 22:109, 110; 25:52
BISSEN/BISSOM/BISSON/BESSOM
Benjamin, 23:207
Elizabeth, 23:213
Elizabeth (Lasky), 23:213
Elizabeth LeGros, 23:213
Hannah, 23:213
Hannah (___), 23:213
James Laskey, 23:214
Jean//Jeanne/John LeCras/LeGros,
   23:211, 213, 214
Jeanne (Cabot), 23:207
Jeanne (LeSeeleur), 23:213
Josue LeGros, 23:213
Margaret (Grant), 23:214
Nicholas, 23:213

Nicholas LeGros, 23:213
Phillip, 23:210, 211
Philippe LeGros, 23:207, 213
Polly, 23:214
Richard Hawley, 23:214
Richard LeGros, 23:213
Sarah (Bubier), 23:211
Susanne LeGros, 23:213
BISTRON
Lydia, 21:197, 198
BITNAR/BITNER/BICKNER
Sarah (Ingalls), 23:51
William, 23:51, 59
BIXBY
Abner, 21:156
Eleanor Edwards (Johnson), 21:120;
   22:238
Gideon, 22:238; 23:117
Hannah, 21:157
Joseph, 21:156
Mehitable, 21:157
Mehitable (Rugg), 21:156
Rebecca (Foster), 23:117
Samuel, 21:120; 22:238
Sarah (Haven), 21:156
Sarah (Wood), 22:218
Sarah Ellen, 21:120; 22:238
Tabitah (___), 25:83
Thamezin (Nurse), 21:156
Thomas, 25:83
BLACK
"Daughter", 23:179
Daniel, 25:9
Elizabeth, 23:179
Freeborn (Wolf), 23:179
George Fraser, 23:86
John, 23:141, 160, 161, 179
Lydia, 23:159-164, 179
Moses, 23:16
Persis, 23:179
Rosanna, 25:165
Susanna (___), 23:160
Tom, 21:166
BLACKER
Ruth, 23:210
BLACKLEACH
___, Mr., 22:102
BLACKMER
Jemima (Kenney), 21:44
John, 21:44
BLACKNEY
Elizabeth, 25:152
BLAIR
Margaret, 21:169; 22:36
BLAKE
Francis, 24:125
Jas. A., 23:56
Richard, 21:195
William, 23:141
BLANCA II
Reyna, 24:68
BLANCHARD
Bradford Briant, 21:109
David, 25:91, 92
Elbert Phillips, 21:109
Elinor (Stevens), 24:83
George Freeman, 21:109
James Freeman, 21:109
John, 24:83; 25:92, 137
Joseph, 24:170, 172
Sarah A. (Bryant), 21:109
Walter Ernest, 21:109
BLANCHE, 25:172
Queen, 24:68
BLANCHFORD
John, 23:141

BLANEY
"Daughter", 23:208
"Son", 23:208
Asa, 23:141
Bethia, 23:208
Bethia (___), 22:240
Betsey (Grant), 23:208
Christopher, 23:208
Grace Bessom, 23:208
Hannah, 23:211
Hannah (King), 23:169
Hannah (Rand), 21:33
Henry, 21:31, 33
Jedediah, 22:240
John, 23:169
Jonathan, 23:208
Lois, 21:31
Lydia, 21:33
Nancy (Williston), 23:208
Philip, 23:208
Ruth, 23:208
Ruth (Bessom), 23:207, 208
Sarah, 23:208
Stephen, 23:208
Susannah M., 23:208
William, 23:208
BLASDEL/BLAISDELL
Henry, 25:36, 37
Lydia (Parker), 25:36, 37
BLATCHFORD
John, 23:141
BLATT
Warren, 23:134; 25:123
BLESSING
Joanna, 22:215; 23:236-8
Margaret, 22:215
BLINMAN
Millicent, 25:202
Richard, 25:202
BLITHEN
John, 21:27
BLOCKSON
Charles H., 25:121
BLODGETT/BLODGETTE
Elizabeth, 24:205, 213
George Brainard, 24:222
William, 24:213
BLOOD
Anna (Parker), 25:84
C. O., 22:78
Lois, 25:85, 146
Nathaniel, 25:84
Richard, 21:29
Robert, 22:206
Ruth, 25:40, 84
BLOOMFIELD
Esther (Rolfe), 21:146
Ezekiel, 21:146
Hope (FitzRandolph), 21:146
Margaret (Van Galen), 21:146
Mary, 21:144-146
Thomas, 21:144
BLOUNT
Alice Eliza (Richardson), 22:119
Dorothea, 22:119
Gardner, 22:119
Gertrude May (Palmer), 22:119
John Gardner, 22:119
Mary Jane (Bragg), 22:119
BLUE
Uriah, 22:130
BLUEBEARD, 25:82
BLUNT
Ephraim, 22:119
Lydia (Boynton), 22:119

Martha (Ordway), 22:119
Mary, 24:100
Moses, 22:119
BLYNMAN, 24:147, 148
BLYTH
Benjamin, 22:172
Mehitable (___), 22:172
Samuel, 22:172
BOADE
Henry, 23:233
BOARDMAN
Ivery, 23:141
Moses B., 22:78
BODEN, 21:10
Edward, 23:141
Sam'a, 23:141
BODGE
George Madison, 21:152, 211; 22:42,
124, 205
BODWELL
Beth (Emery), 24:83
Henry, 24:83
Phebe, 24:40, 83
BOISSON
Victor, 23:141
BOLCOM
Sarah, 22:46, 54
BOLTON, 22:135
Charles K., 22:137; 23:85
Ethel Stanwood, 24:219, 220
BOND, 22:136; 24:148, 149
___, Goodwife, 25:97
Abigail/Nabby (Rogers), 21:239
Charles Henry, 21:239
Charles Lawrence, 21:239
Charles Milton, 21:239
Charles William Milton, 21:239
Frances, 23:150
Henry, 21:170
Hester, 25:98, 101, 102, 105
Isabella (Bacon), 21:239
John, 21:239
Jonathan, 21:239
Joseph, 23:141
Judith (Dow), 21:239
Mary, 23:150
Mary (Amerige), 21:239
Nathaniel, 21:239; 25:202
Sally (Sweetser), 21:239
BONNER, 21:9
BOOTH
Agnes, 23:56
J. B., 23:56
BOOZ
Peter, 25:168, 169
BOSWORTH
Helen, 21:134
BOTHWAY/BOTHWAYS, 24:28, 30
BOTTOLPH
Mehitable, 21:71
Thomas, 21:71
BOUDREAU
Dennis M., 25:122
BOUND
Ruth, 21:43
BOUTAL/BOUTALL/BOUTEL/
BOUTELL/BOUTELLE/
BOUTWELL/BOWTALL/
BOWTELL
Abigail (Edwards), 21:211
Catherine, 21:215
Elizabeth, 21:213, 215, 221
Elizabeth (Frothingham), 21:215
Elizabeth (Smith), 21:215
James, 21:211, 214, 215, 219, 221
Judith, 21:215

Judith (Poole), 21:215
Kendall, 21:215, 221
Mary, 21:221
Mary (Wilder), 21:215
Persis (Hubbard), 21:215
Rachel (Lincoln), 21:215
Rebecca, 21:213, 221
Rebecca (Kendall), 21:221
Sarah, 21:215, 221
Tabitha, 21:221
Thomas, 21:211, 216, 217, 219, 221
Timothy, 21:215
William, 21:215
BOW
Joseph, 24:190
BOWDEN/BOWDENS, 23:141, 207
Mary (___), 23:214
Rebecca, 23:214
Samuel, 23:214
William Hammond, 21:37
BOWDITCH
___, Mrs., 25:181
Charles Ingersoll, 25:125
Ebenezer, 22:236; 25:125, 126
Elizabeth (___), 25:125, 126
Habakkuk, 25:125
Joseph, 25:125, 126
Mary (___), 25:125, 126
Nathaniel, 21:82; 25:125
Rebekah, 22:236
Rebekah (___), 22:236
Sarah, 25:126
Sarah (___), 24:190
William, 25:126, 181
BOWDOIN
E. Seavey, 22:195
Seavey, 22:170
BOWEN see also BROWN, 21:154
Charles, 22:190
Clarence Winthrop, 21:148
John, 25:167
Judith, 21:97
Margaret, 23:40-2, 44-46
Nathan, 21:31; 23:207
BOWERS
Ann, 25:92
Caroline Elliot, 25:92
Elizabeth, 25:35, 92
Horatio, 25:92
Josiah, 25:137
Margaret, 25:92
Priscilla, 21:93
Samuel, 25:92
Sarah, 25:92
Sarah (Parker), 25:92
BOWLAND
Hannah, 22:52
BOWLER
Elizabeth (Collins), 21:33
James, 21:33
BOWLEY
Dorothy (Elliott), 25:192
Ebenezer, 25:191
Edwin, 25:190
Mary (Nichols), 25:191
BOWMAN
Jonathan, 24:78
BOWN
___, Miss, 22:185
BOWTALL/BOWTELL see BOUTAL
BOWYER
Frances, 25:202
BOYCE
Benjamin, 22:24
David, 21:10, 13, 14; 22:27
Dorothy, 21:180; 22:239

Joseph, 21:27; 22:24
Sarah (Meachum), 22:24
BOYD see also BOYT
A., 24:34
Adam, 23:15; 24:139
James, 23:13, 14, 16
BOYDEN
Roland W., 21:230
BOYER
Paul, 21:37, 88
Paul S., 23:137
BOYES
Matthew, 22:167
Samuel, 21:180; 22:239
BOYINTON/BOYNTON
Eleazer/Eliezer, 22:221, 227-230
Elizabeth, 24:136
John, 22:119, 167
Lydia, 22:119
Lydia (Dow), 22:119
William, 22:167
BOYT see also BOYD
John, 25:26
Rebeckah (Peak), 25:26
BRABROCK/BRABROOK/
BRABROOKE see also
BRAYBROOK, 24:151
Joan (___), 24:147; 25:134, 135
Mehitable, 22:156; 24:147; 25:134, 135
Richard, 22:152, 154, 156; 24:109, 111, 146, 147; 25:134, 135
BRACKETT
Peter, 24:47
Sarah (Parker), 24:47
BRADBURY, 23:234
Mary (___), 23:54, 55
Sally, 25:192
Sarah (Pike), 23:54
Wymond, 23:54
BRADDUE
Rebecka, 23:141
BRADEEN/BREDING
Hannah (Rucke), 25:8
James, 25:8
BRADFORD, 21:69, 22:167, 23:225
___, Gov., 24:232a
Andrew, 21:66
Ebenezer, 23:141
Elizabeth, 21:65, 66
Hannah, 21:66, 104
Hannah (___), 21:66
L. H., 25:14
Mary (___), 21:66
Robert, 22:105
William, 22:187
BRADLEY, 24:61
Martha, 22:162
BRADSHAW
Ruth, 24:164, 204; 25:44, 45
BRADSTREET see also
BROADSTREET, 22:167
___, Mr., 22:152
Ann/Anne (___), 21:85, 195; 22:21
Anna (Price), 24:35
Anne (Dudley), 21:88
Dudley, 21:196; 24:35
Elizabeth, 25:38, 44
Moses, 23:141
Simon, 21:85, 105, 199, 209; 22:21; 23:236; 24:42
BRADY
Mathew B., 22:132
BRAGDON
Arthur, 24:217
Mary (Moulton), 21:88

Ruth, 21:88
Samuel, 21:88
BRAGG
Dolly (Ingalls), 24:88, 95
Edmond, 22:159; 24:28
Edward, 22:152; 23:141, 177
John, 22:119
Mary, 23:177
Mary (Wittrege), 23:177
Mary Jane, 22:119
Nicholas, 22:119
Sally (Gilman), 22:119
Susann, 24:88, 95
Thomas, 24:85, 88, 95
BRAHAM
John J., 23:56
BRAINERD, 24:33
BRAKS
Marsha Ann (Wiiknikainen), 21:18
BRAME
Anna, 21:30
BRANDT
Edward R., 25:123
BRANT
Joseph, 24:71
BRASHEAR
Benois, 23:240
Mary, 23:240
Mary (Richford), 23:240
BRAVENDER/BRAVAND/BRABANT
Alexander, 25:8, 10
BRAY
Charlotte, 22:240, 23:57
Cornelia Eliza, 23:93
Daniel, 23:93; 25:127
Ebenezer, 23:57; 24:16, 175, 231
Eleanor/Elinor (Dodge), 24:16, 175, 231
Elisabeth, 25:127
Ellen Maria, 23:93
Hannah (Adams), 23:57
Humphrey, 23:176
John, 23:176
Judith (Sargent), 24:16, 175, 231
Lucy, 21:120; 23:57, 176
Lydia (Woodbury), 23:176
Mary (Emerson), 21:240; 23:176
Mary (Wilson), 21:240; 23:176; 24:16, 136, 175, 231
May (Emerson), 24:16, 175, 231
Phebe/Phebea F. (Skidmore), 23:93
Richard, 22:43, 44
Susanna (Woodbury), 23:176
Thomas, 21:240; 23:176; 24:16, 136, 175, 231
BRAYBROOK see also BRABROCK
Joanne (___), 25:203
Mehitable, 25:203
Richard, 25:203
BREAN see also BREEN
Mary, 21:32, 151
BREED, 25:94
Aaron, 22:49, 50
Allen, 21:210; 22:44
Amos, 22:49, 50
Anna, 22:50
Benjamin Newhall, 22:49
Ebenezer, 25:93
Elizabeth, 22:49
Elizabeth (Parker), 25:92, 93
Ephraim, 21:32, 52
Frederick, 25:147
Fullerton, 22:50
Harriet Almira, 22:50
Hermione, 22:50
Horace Anson, 22:50

Isaac, 22:50
Jabez, 22:49
James, 25:93
James Edwin, 22:50
John, 21:35; 22:44, 45
Joseph, 21:214; 22:44; 23:37
Lydia, 22:50
Lydia (___), 22:49
Lydia Miria, 22:50
Martha (Mansfield), 21:32
Mary, 25:147
Mary (___), 22:50
Mary/Polly, 25:94
Nabby Burrill, 22:50
Phebe (Trumbull), 25:93
Ruth (___), 22:50
Ruth (Newhall), 22:49
Ruth/Ruthy, 22:50
Samuel, 22:47
Sarah/Sally, 22:50, 52; 25:147
Sarah/Sally (Atwell), 22:50
Susannah (Mansfield), 21:32
Timothy, 22:44
Warner, 22:50
BREEDEN
Anna, 22:49
BREEN see also BREAN
Helen, 23:109
BRENTON
Hannah, 21:240a
BREWER
Elizabeth, 21:28
Margreat (Weld), 23:219
Nathaniel, 21:28; 23:219
Priscilla, 24:186
BREWSTER
___, Elder, 24:232a
BRIANT see also BRYANT
"Son", 21:103
Albert, 21:104
Alice Augusta, 21:104
Alice Dalton, 21:107
Ann T. (Goldsbury), 21:103
Anna, 21:99-101
Anna (___), 21:98
Augustine, 21:103
Augustine B., 21:107
Benjamin, 21:98, 100, 101, 103, 163; 23:117
Benjamin Franklin, 21:103, 106, 107
Betsey, 21:100, 102
Brown, 21:101
Caroline (Johnson), 21:102
Charles H., 21:107
Charlotte Ward, 21:106
Cynthia A. (Nelson), 21:107
Daniel, 21:103
Daniel H., 21:103
Daniel Wallis, 21:107
Delia (Dalton), 21:107
Delia Ann, 21:104
Edward Payson, 21:102, 166, 168
Elizabeth, 21:98, 99
Elizabeth (Obear/Ober), 21:100, 163; 23:117
Ella Maria, 21:104
Ellen Ingersoll, 21:106
Emily Judson, 21:102, 166
Emma A., 21:107
Evaline Hubbard, 21:107
Evelyn (Ober), 21:103
George William, 21:103, 107
Hannah Parsons (Wiley), 21:104
James, 21:15, 100, 102, 110, 115, 163-168, 218
John, 21:98, 99, 101, 103; 22:79

John Groves, 21:100
John Ober, 21:103, 167
John Warren, 21:103,107
Jonathan, 21:98-101, 103, 104, 106
Lydia, 21:98, 99
Lydia (English), 21:100
Lydia (Herrick), 21:102, 165, 167
Lydia Ellen, 21:106
Lydia Nichols, 21:101, 104
Margaret (Smith), 21:98
Maria, 21:101
Martha Bigelow, 21:106
Mary, 21:98, 99
Mary (Herrick), 21:103, 167, 168
Mary Elizabeth, 21:106
Mary Elizabeth (Pedrick), 21:106
Mehitable, 21:212
Parker, 21:104
Rebecca, 21:100, 102
Rebecca (Richardson), 21:103
Rebecca Hubbard, 21:106
Roland Safford, 21:106
Sally, 21:101
Sally (Brown), 21:101
Samuel Ingersoll, 21:98, 102, 103, 110,
   163, 167, 168, 227, 229
Sarah, 21:98, 99
Sarah (Bancroft), 21:212
Sarah (Hoyt), 21:103
Sarah (Norwood), 21:99
Sarah (Strickland), 21:102, 115, 163,
   164; 22:218
Sarah A., 21:106
Sarah Ellen, 21:102, 106, 164, 226,
   230, 238
Sarah Ellen (Danforth), 21:104
Sarah Frances, 21:104
Sarah H., 21:103
Sarah Parker (Spokesfield), 21:104
Sidney Brown, 21:104
Susan Emerson (Thompson), 21:104
Susan J. (Herrick), 21:107
Susan W., 21:107
William, 21:100, 214, 216, 217

BRICKETT
Harry L., 22:76, 79
James, 24:108; 25:197

BRICKFORD
Nehemiah, 23:141

BRICKLEY
Bartholomew A., 23:17

BRIDGE/BRIDGES
___, Capt., 22:212, 206, 208
Alice (Parker), 25:137
Benjamin, 21:156, 158
Bethiah, 21:156
Ebenezer, 25:84
Edmund, 22:167
Elizabeth, 21:160; 24:86
Elizabeth (___), 21:152, 156, 158;
   24:94
Hackaliah, 21:149
Henry G., 24:94
James, 21:197; 24:85
Joana (Parker), 25:84
John, 24:36, 86, 88
Matthew, 25:137
Robert, 22:208, 209; 25:9
Sarah, 21:156, 160
Sarah (Stevens), 24:88

BRIDGHAM
Henry, 21:148

BRIGHAM
Lincoln F., 24:232a
Mercy (___), 25:5
Sebastian, 22:167

BRIMBELCOME/BRIMBLECOM
John, 25:20
Philip, 25:20
S., 23:155
Tabitha (___), 25:20

BRINDLEY/BRINDLY
George Bowditch, 25:52
John, 25:52
Mary, 25:52
Sarah, 25:52
Sarah (___), 25:52

BRINKLEY
Robert, 21:80

BRINLEY
Mary, 25:200

BRINNOCK
James, 23:141

BRINTNALL
___, Mr., 22:45
Benjamin, 24:208
John, 22:45
Rebecca (Emerson), 24:208

BRITTON
Edward, 22:175
Polly, 22:175
Polly (___), 22:175

BROADHEAD
Eleanor, 24:195, 196

BROADSTREET see also
   BRADSTREET
___, Gov., 25:19

BROCK/BROCKES see also KNOX
___, Mr., 21:210
Elizabeth, 25:197
Isaac, 21:212
John, 21:210

BROCKLEBANK
Jane, 22:167
John, 22:166
Samuel, 21:152; 22:166

BROMLEY
___, Dr., 24:63
William C., 24:62

BROOKE
John, 21:222

BROOKHOUSE
___, Mrs., 21:166; 24:195
Jn. F., 21:166
R., 21:164-167
Robert, 24:195

BROOKS
___ Mr., 23:30
"Daughter", 24:190
Alfred Mansfield, 25:14
David, 22:221, 227-234; 23:165
Elizabeth (___), 22:119
George, 22:119
Harriet/Harriot (___), 25:152, 153
Harriot, 25:152
John, 21:99; 25:152, 153
Josiah, 22:112
Lucy Ann (___), 24:190
Luke, 24:190
Maria, 25:152
Maria (___), 25:153
Mary, 22:119
Peter C., 23:29
Reuben, 22:221, 227-233
Samuel, 25:153
Sarah Maria, 25:153

BROOKSBY, 22:23; 23:183

BROUGHTON
Nickelos/Nickoles, 24:80

BROWN see also BROWNE, BOWEN,
   21:70, 96, 220; 22:185; 23:35, 215;
   25:120
___, Capt., 22:48
Abigail, 23:99
Abraham, 23:141
Ann (Pendleton), 21:175
Ann T. (Goldsbury), 21:103
Anne, 25:20
Benjamin, 23:141, 172, 189
C. A., 25:179
Caleb, 23:99, 100
Clark, 23:99, 100
Cornelius, 21:95; 23:99
Daniel, 21:239
David, 23:100
Deborah, 25:21
Ebenezer, 23:100
Edward A., 21:221
Edward R., 24:105
Eleazer, 21:175
Elisebath, 24:104
Elisha, 23:141
Elizabeth, 23:99, 155, 156, 178, 223;
   24:35, 37, 38
Elizabeth (Jewett), 23:99, 100
Emine, 23:177
George, 21:114; 23:141, 223
Gilbert, 21:209
Hannah, 23:99; 24:41
Hannah (Collins), 21:175
Hannah (Ramsdell), 21:239
Hannah (Spofford), 24:89
Hepsibah, 23:99, 100
Humphrey, 22:179
Isaac, 21:239
James, 21:114; 22:186; 23:35
Jemima (Quarles), 21:51
John, 21:64, 65, 67, 69, 71, 94, 186,
   211, 212; 22:37, 171, 186; 23:124,
   141; 24:150, 190
Jonathan, 23:141
Joseph, 21:34, 239; 23:155
Josiah, 21:95
Lucy (Davis), 23:100
Lydia, 24:95
Margaret (Smith), 21:239
Martha, 23:174
Mary, 21:175; 22:239; 23:99, 100;
   24:16, 175, 231, 232
Mary (___), 21:64, 65, 69
Mary (Newhall), 21:175, 176
Maximillian, 23:100
Mercy, 24:41
Mercy (Southwick), 23:155
Moses, 21:135, 136
Nathan, 22:171, 190
Nehemiah, 23:141
Nicholas, 21:210, 211
Oliver, 24:89
Polly (Alley), 22:50
R., 21:114
R. H., 23:114
Rachel, 21:180
Rebecca (___), 22:171; 24:190
Rebecca (Bailey), 22:239
Rhoda (Stevens), 24:95
Richard, 21:111, 114
Ruth, 22:239
Sally, 21:101, 239; 24:219
Samuel W., 22:221, 233, 234
Sarah, 22:98, 221, 228; 23:99
Sarah (Batting), 24:219
Sarah (Kidder), 23:223
Stephen, 24:219
Susannah, 21:94; 23:100

Tabitha, 22:179
Tabitha (Holdrige), 22:179
Thomas, 21:111, 114, 150, 175, 176; 24:73
Tom, 21:64
William, 22:39, 50; 23:142; 24:95
BROWNE see also BROWN
Benjamin, 21:240a
Elizabeth, 21:177
Francis, 21:240a
Hannah, 21:240a
Hannah (Brenton), 21:240a
Hugh, 21:240a
James, 21:240a; 22:57
Jemima, 22:57
Jemima (Quarles), 22:57
John, 21:95, 117, 214, 240a; 23:177, 231
Joseph, 21:148, 240a
Margaret (Hayward), 23:177
Mary, 21:240a
Mary (___), 21:93
Mary (Newhall), 21:148
Mary (Young), 21:240a
Samuel, 21:240a
Sarah, 21:240a; 22:178
Sarah (Smith), 21:240a
Susanna (Dutton), 21:117
Susannah, 21:116
William, 21:10-12, 92, 240a
BRUCE
Adelbert Melvin, 21:19, 22, 110, 224, 227-229
Grace (Lefavour), 21:19
Grace Strictland (Lefavour), 21:110, 224, 227-229
Harvey Eugene, 21:19, 110, 227, 229
Martha, 21:33, 34
BRUNO, 25:112, 113, 120
BRUNSWIG, 25:171
BRYANT see also BRIANT
___, Mr., 22:75
Abraham, 21:211, 213, 216
Alice Augusta (Hardy), 21:107
Anna, 22:78
Caroline Louise, 23:157
Charles Augustus, 21:107
Delia Anne, 21:107
Ella N., 21:107
Evaline Hubbard, 21:109
Fannie Edson, 21:107
Frederick Smith, 21:107
George, 22:188
John Vilas, 21:107
Laurie Moore, 21:107, 109
Lydia Ellen, 21:109
Maurice Albert, 21:107
Nattie Hamilton, 21:107
Parker, 21:107
Parker Hardy, 21:107
Peris, 23:26, 27
Sally, 21:104
Sarah (Bancroft), 21:213
Sarah A., 21:109
Sarah Frances, 21:107
Susan E. (___), 22:77
Thomas, 21:216, 219
William, 21:220
BUBIER/BOOBIER/BUBYER/BUBE, 23:212
Christopher, 23:207, 211, 142
Margaret (LeVallier), 23:207
Sarah, 23:207, 211
BUCHAN
George, 24:89

BUCK
Elra, 24:20
Frances (March), 23:52
Stephanie, 23:139, 219; 25:11
BUCKMAN
Rebekah (Parker), 24:157
BUCKMINSTER
Joseph, 21:154
BUCKNAM
Benjamin, 24:160, 161
Rebecca (Parker), 24:160
BUFFINGTON/BUFFINTON
Betsy (___), 24:190
Daniel, 24:190
Elizabeth Gould, 24:190
John, 24:190
Lydia, 22:235
Mary, 22:235
Zadack, 22:235
BUFFUM
Caleb, 22:215, 217
Damaris (Pope), 22:216
Deborah, 22:215, 217
John, 21:93
Joshua, 21:90, 215-217
Lucretia, 21:33
Marcy, 25:148
Margaret, 22:215, 216
Margaret (Blessing), 22:215
Robert, 22:215-217
Tamosin (Ward), 22:216-218
BUGBY
Judith/Jude (___), 24:46
Richard, 24:46
BUGNON
James, 24:81
BULKELEY, 23:224
John, 23:226
Joseph, 23:226
Peter, 23:226
Rebecca, 23:226, 227
Rebecca (Wheeler), 23:226
Sarah, 23:219
BULL
John, 25:167
BULLARD
Benjamin, 21:159
Ebenezer, 21:159
Elizabeth (Haven), 21:159
Lydia (Haven), 21:159
Mary, 21:158
Maudlin, 24:54
Sarah (___), 21:159
Seth, 21:159
Tabitha (___), 21:159
BULLOCK
___, Gov., 22:60a
Benjamin, 22:173
Elizabeth (___), 22:173, 174
Isaac, 21:25
Nathaniel, 22:173, 174
Steven C., 23:137
William, 22:174
BUNKER
Clareann H., 24:63
BUNNELL
Ruth Ann, 22:189
BURBANK
Adeline D., 21:108
Betsey, 25:190, 193, 194
Caleb, 24:171, 172
Elizabeth/Betty (Palmer), 25:193, 195
Jane, 25:190
Jane/Jenny, 25:190, 195, 196, 200
John, 22:167
Lydia, 22:91

Moses, 24:171
Nathan, 25:193, 195
BURBECK
Elizabeth (Butler), 21:59
James, 21:59
BURCHAM
Edward, 21:29
BURCHSTEAD/BURCHSTED
Anna (Brame), 21:30
Henry, 21:30
John, 21:30
John H., 21:30
John Henry, 23:224
Mary (Rand), 21:30
Mary (Whiting), 23:221, 224
Sarah (James), 21:30
Winthrop Alexander, 23:224
BURDE
Samuel, 23:142
BURDETT
Hannah, 23:142
BURDICK
Abbey, 24:72
Abigail (Sage), 24:72
D.S., 24:72
Isaac, 24:72
Robert, 24:72
BURDITT
Jemima, 21:237
BURDOCK
Benjamin, 23:10
BURGE
John, 24:154; 25:41
BURGES/BURGESS
Alexander, 25:8
Bartholomew, 23:142
John, 21:188; 24:154
Mary (Learned), 21:188
BURILL
Anna, 22:211
BURKE
Alan, 21:79
Charles T., 23:17
John H., 23:16
Michael, 23:126
BURLEIGH/BURLEY
Charles, 22:162
Lydia, 22:235
Lydia (___), 22:235
William, 22:235
BURMAN
Hannah, 23:117
BURNAM
Elizabeth, 23:142
Elizabeth (___), 23:142
Jonathan, 23:142
Nehemiah, 23:142
Susanna, 23:142
BURNAP/BURNAPP see also BENNETT, BURNETT
Benjamin, 21:156, 217
Elizabeth, 21:214
Hannah, 21:156; 24:40, 84
Hannah (Haven), 21:156
John, 21:156
Joseph, 21:213, 214, 219
Lois, 21:156
Mehitable, 21:156
Robert, 21:210, 211
Sarah, 21:156
Sarah (Nichols), 21:213
Tabitha, 21:214
Thomas, 21:211, 213, 219, 220
BURNELL
Cassandra, 22:22-24
Katherine (___), 22:240

Robert, 22:240
BURNETT see also BURNAP
  Joseph, 21:155
BURNHAM/BURNUM, 22:156; 24:148,
  150
  ___, Col., 23:27
  ___, Mrs., 24:34
  A., Mrs., 24:34
  Abraham, 24:32, 34
  B., 24:34
  B., Mrs., 24:34
  Benjamin M., 22:221, 231
  C., 24:34
  Clarissa (___), 24:32
  Daniel, 23:142
  David, 21:59, 180; 23:57, 142; 25:201
  E., Mrs., 24:34
  Ebenezer, 24:33; 25:131, 133, 136
  Elizabeth (Marshall), 21:59, 180; 23:57
  Elizabeth (Perkins), 25:201
  Elizabeth (Wells), 25:201
  F., 24:34
  J. C., 24:34
  Jacob, 25:155
  Jeremiah, 23:142
  Jesse, 22:221, 231, 232
  Joanna (Lull), 25:155
  John, 22:110, 114, 115, 117, 153,
    154, 157, 159, 160; 23:142;
    24:28, 29, 31, 109, 110-112,
    141-143, 146-148, 151, 152;
    25:133, 134, 136, 201
  Jonathan, 23:142
  Lucy, 23:142
  Marie (Lawrence), 25:201
  Martha, 23:57
  Martha (Lufkin), 22:240; 23:57
  Mary (Andrews), 25:201
  N., 24:34
  Parker, 22:240; 23:57
  Robert, 25:201
  Roderick, 24:33
  Roxana, 21:45
  Samuel, 25:136
  Tabitha (Goldsmith), 24:31
  Thomas, 22:152, 153; 24:111, 140;
    25:133, 201
  W., 24:34
  William, 24:31-33; 25:136
BURNS
  Amy Stechler, 24:186
  George, 25:82
  John, 22:222, 228-231
  Ken, 24:186
BURNUM see BURNHAM
BURR
  Aaron, 21:180a; 23:13
BURRAGE see also BURRIDGE
  Elizabeth, 21:31
BURRELL see BURRILL
BURRIDGE see also BURRAGE
  Hannah, 24:48
BURRILL/BURRELL
  Abraham, 21:153
  Coll., 21:215
  Ebenezer, 21:31; 24:120
  Elizabeth, 21:33
  Isaiah, 22:50
  John, 21:149, 150, 214; 22:204
  Joseph, 21:150, 153
  Lydia, 21:153
  Mary, 22:45
  Mary (Tarbox), 22:50
  Mary Breed, 25:147
  Sally, 22:53
  Sally (Breed), 25:147

Sally Mansfield, 25:147
Samuel, 22:52, 53
Theophilus, 21:31, 32, 35, 153, 214;
  22:77
BURROS/BURROUGHS, 23:142
  Elizabeth/Betsey (Atwell), 22:51
  George, 21:40, 44
  Tony, 25:121
  William, 22:51
BURRUM
  Tamosin/Thomasine/Tomasin
BURT
  Abagial, 23:142
  Edward, 25:4
  Hugh, 21:30, 186, 209
  Sarah, 21:30
  Thomas, 21:214
BURTON
  John, 23:142
BUSH
  Grace (Sanders), 23:232
  John, 23:232
BUSHNELL see also RUSSELL, 24:99
  John, 21:240a
BUTERFEILD/BUTERFIELD see
  BUTTERFIELD
BUTLER, 23:215
  Elizabeth, 21:59
  James, 23:142
  John, 21:59
  Mary (Daniels), 21:59
  S., 24:34
  Sarah, 21:175
  Sarah (___), 22:59
  William, 25:132
  William O., 23:186
BUTLERS, 22:140
BUTMAN/BUTTMAN
  Asa, 25:153
  Asa Oliver, 25:153
  Bradstreet, 23:142
  Caleb, 25:153
  Elizabeth, 25:153
  Elizabeth (___), 24:73; 25:153
  J., 24:34
  John, 22:222, 230, 231
  Mary, 21:238
  Mary (___), 23:142
  Seecomb, 25:153
  Susah Dodge, 25:153
  William, 24:73
BUTTERFEILD/BUTTERFIELD/
  BUTERFEILD/BUTERFIELD
  Joanna, 25:41, 87
  Joanna (Butterfield), 25:87
  John, 24:159
  Louisa, 21:104
  Lucy, 24:102
  Rachel, 24:159, 206; 25:145
  Rebecca (Parker), 25:83
  Robert, 25:87
  Roger, 21:194
  Sarah, 25:83
  William, 25:83, 84
BUTTERWORTH
  Mary, 22:161
BUTTMAN
  A. H., 24:34
  John, 22:230
BUXTON
  Anthony, 21:40
  Elizabeth, 21:40
  Elizabeth (___), 21:40
  Henry, 23:142
  Isaac, 21:42
  John, 21:40

Margaret (Chick), 21:40
Mary, 21:39, 40, 43
Mary (Small), 21:40
Priscilla (Lynn), 21:40
Rachel, 21:42
Ruth, 24:97, 98
Susanna (Putnam), 21:42
BYAM
  George, 24:106
  Thomas, 24:162
BYER
  Mary, 22:179
BYERS
  Paula K., 25:121
BYRAM
  E. R., 23:56
  Sarah, 21:104
BYRD
  Minot, 24:19

CABOT, 22:135; 25:48
  ___ (Jackson), 23:8
  Andrew, 21:135, 136; 25:47
  Elizabeth (Perkins), 22:148
  George, 21:135, 136; 25:47
  Jeanne, 23:207
  John, 21:136; 25:47
  Samuel, 22:148
CADMAN
  Paul F., 23:135
CADY
  Elijah, 23:39
CAESAR, 25:169
CALFE
  John, 21:77, 191
CALL
  Elizabeth/Betsy (Bessom), 23:208, 209
  Henry, 23:208
  Henry P., 23:207, 209
  Henry Payne, 23:209
  Joanna, 24:155, 156
  Lydia (Shepardson), 24:156
  Miriam (Russell), 23:209
  Paul A., 23:209
  Philip, 23:209
  Sarah Bessom, 23:209
  Thomas, 24:156, 157
CALLAGHAN
  William, 23:142
CALLAHAN
  Michael T., 23:17
CALLENDER
  George, 21:71
  Joanna, 21:71
  Sarah, 21:71
CALLER
  James M., 24:108
CAMERON
  Allan, 23:117
  Anne, 22:218
CAMPBELL
  Ann, 22:238
  Anne (Cameron), 22:218
  Annie Wilson, 21:16
  Dorothy, 23:114
  Dorothy Montfort, 23:115
  Elisabeth Bancroft, 23:115
  Emily B., 23:113
  Emily H. (___), 23:114, 115
  George, 22:218
  Herman H., 23:115
  Jane, 23:76
  Virginia, 22:170
CANE
  John, 23:142

CANN
R.L., 24:71
Rebecca, 24:70
CANNELL
John, 25:4
CAPEN
___, Parson, 22:18, 21, 137
Joseph, 23:237, 238
CAPONE
Al, 22:198
CARD
Rachel, 22:222, 229, 230
William, 22:222, 228
CARDER
Mary, 25:35
CAREY
Emily (Dennett), 24:103
Frank, 24:103
Susannah/Sukey, 23:93
Thester, 24:103
William, 24:103
CARKIN
Alice (Barker), 21:59
Jonas, 21:59
Joseph, 21:59
Lydia (Gutterson), 21:59
Moses, 21:59
Sybil (Littlehale), 21:59
CARLETON see also CARLTON
Betsey (___), 25:140
Betsy, 24:89, 97, 102
Christopher, 24:83
Elizabeth (Stevens), 24:83
Enos, 25:190
Enos G., 25:140
Isaac, 24:86
Joanna (Stevens), 24:95
Phineas, 24:95
CARLOS III
Rey, 24:68
CARLSON
Stephen P., 23:109
William, 24:73
CARLTON see also CARLETON, 21:10
Dudley, 25:139
Edward, 22:167
John, 25:181
Joseph, 25:181
Mary (___), 25:181
Mary (Parker), 25:138
Samuel, 21:10
Thomas, 25:138
CARLYLE
Elizabeth (Peak), 25:26
John, 25:26
CARMACK
Sharon DeBartolo, 25:122, 123
CARNEGIE
Andrew, 21:79
CARNES
Elizabeth Derby, 22:174
John, 22:174
Lydia (___), 22:174
Mark C., 23:137
Nabby, 22:174
CARNEY
Abigail, 24:217
Alice, 21:53
Ann (___), 24:217
Hugh A., 23:17
James H., 23:17
Joseph, 24:217
CAROLINE
Countess, 24:68
CARR, 22:21
Ann, 23:54

Anna, 21:116
Anne (___), 21:117
Bernice A., 23:120; 24:116, 230
Dorothy (Boyce), 21:180; 22:239
Elizabeth, 22:120, 239
Elizabeth (Dexter?), 22:239
Elizabeth (Oliver?), 22:239
Elizabeth (Pike), 23:54
George, 21:117, 180; 22:120, 239
James, 23:55
Mary, 21:180
Richard, 21:180; 22:120, 239; 23:55
Samuel, 21:180
Sarah (Bailey), 22:120, 239
William, 23:54
CARROLL
Benjamin, 21:158
David, 21:156
George, 21:158
Martha (Haven), 21:158
Mary (___), 21:156, 158
Michael J., 23:17
Paula, 23:18
Susanna/Susannah, 21:156, 160
Thomas, 23:113
CARRS, 22:160
CARRUTH, 24:98
CARTER
Abigail, 21:28
Anna, 22:222, 229, 230
John, 23:142
Judith, 23:240
Margaret (Whiting), 23:218
Mary, 21:28
Mary (Parkhurst), 23:240
Richard, 23:218
Samuel, 21:28
Thomas, 23:240
CARTERET
Philip, 21:144
CARTWRIGHT
___, Goodman, 22:152
CASABURI
Victor F., 23:135
CASE
Margaret, 23:88
CASH
Alice (Smalley), 25:20
Ann, 25:21
Anne (Brown), 25:20
Patience (Pike), 25:20
Samuel, 25:20
Stephen, 25:20
CASS
Lewis, 23:186
Mary, 21:44
Miriam, 22:54
Miriam, 22:46
CASWELL, 23:212
Arthur, 23:142
Samuel, 22:222, 232, 233; 23:142
CATERSON
Bill, 23:57, 58, 176, 177, 239, 240;
   24:16, 54, 175, 231, 232; 25:55-57,
   156, 201-203;
CATHERINE
Countess, 24:68
CATHOMER
John, 21:29
CATON
Daniel, 22:96
Elizabeth, 22:96
Mary (Liscomb), 22:96
CAULFIELD
Ernest, 25:204

CAWLEY
Norman B., 22:76, 79
CENTER
Eleanor, 24:222
John, 24:222
Ruth (Todd), 24:222
CHADMAN
___, Chm., 23:142
CHADWELL
Anna, 22:47
CHADWICK
___, Mrs., 22:76
J. Raymond, 22:76, 77, 79
John, 21:96
Joseph, 25:141
Mary, 25:141
Mary (Parker), 25:141
CHALLIS
Gideon, 23:142
Mary, 25:187
Philip, 23:54
CHAMBERLAIN/CHAMBERLANE/
   CHAMBERLINE
Benjamin, 24:162; 25:39
Daniel, 23:215
John, 24:51
Lydia, 24:49, 51, 52
Mary (Parker), 24:162; 25:39
Phinehas, 24:215
Rebeckah, 21:117
Thomas, 24:46
CHAMBERS
Charles, 25:165
CHAMPLAIN, 22:113
Samuel, 22:18, 20, 21
CHAMPNEY
Bethiah (___), 23:225
Daniel, 23:225
CHANDLER, 22:135, 136, 164; 24:42
___ (Miss), 24:85
___ (Stevens), 24:42
___, Mrs., 22:77
Annis (Bayford), 23:240
Daniel, 24:87
Elizabeth, 24:38, 43
Elizabeth (Cook), 21:59
Hannah, 23:240; 24:37, 39, 55
Henry, 24:36
Hephzibah, 24:45
Isaac, 22:136
James, 21:196
Joamia (Stevens), 24:87
Joanna, 24:93
John, 23:142
Joseph, 21:59
Joshua, 21:197; 24:98
Josiah, 22:136
Lydia, 24:90
Mary, 22:136; 24:100, 176
Mary (Dane), 23:240
Mary (Stevens), 24:38
Philemon, 22:136
Polly Mehitabel, 24:93, 102
Sarah, 21:116; 22:136
Thomas, 21:195; 22:136; 24:38, 42
Timothy, 22:136
Willard, 22:77
William, 21:199; 22:136; 23:240
CHAPIN
Howard Miller, 22:124
CHAPLIN
Ann Theopold, 21:238
Hugh, 22:167
CHAPMAN
Abigail, 25:151
Benjamin, 25:52

Grover, 22:148
CLIFFORD, 21:9
CLIMBER
  Alice (Wise), 22:188, 189
  Charley, 22:188
  David, 22:188
  Ezra, 22:188
  Richard, 22:189
  "Richard" (Wise), 22:188
CLINE
  ___, Rev., 23:32
CLOON
  John C., 23:210
  Tabitha (Bessom), 23:210
CLOSE
  John, 23:143
CLOUD
  Peach Dull, 23:143
CLOUGH
  Abigail (___), 21:180
  Caleb, 22:171
  David, 21:180
  Ephraim, 22:163
  Jacob, 22:172
  James, 22:49
  John, 22:163
  Jonathan, 22:163
  Joseph, 22:171, 172
  Lois, 21:180
  Lois (Clough), 21:180
  Mary (Goodwin), 21:180
  Mary (Johnson), 22:162, 163
  Noah, 21:180
  Olive, 21:180
  Polly (Atwell), 22:49
  Ruth, 22:171
  Ruth (___), 22:171, 172
  Sue Mary, 22:171
  Sumner, 21:59
  Thomas, 22:162
  William, 21:180
CLOYCE
  Mary, 21:42
  Mary (Preston), 21:41
  Peter, 21:41
  Rebecca, 21:42
  Sarah, 21:42
  Sarah (Towne), 23:238
COAL see COLE, 21:89
COAS
  Samuel, 24:219
  Sarah (___), 24:219
  Sarah (Batting), 24:219
COATE/COATES/COATS
  Abigail, 22:210
  Alden, 21:207
  Elizabeth, 22:211, 214; 23:37
  Jane, 22:210
  Jane (Sumner), 22:211
  Joseph, 22:45, 47
  Martha, 23:37, 40
  Martha (Atwell), 22:46
  Robert, 22:210, 211
  Thomas, 21:29
COBAM, 24:89
  Lydia (Stevens), 24:89
COBB
  Mary, 25:149
COBBET/COBBETT/COBBITT/
  COBET
  ___, Mr., 24:111, 112
  Samuel, 22:206
  Thomas, 21:210; 24:109, 112
COBORN/COBURN
  Jonathn, 21:77, 189, 191
  Stephn, 21:77, 191

COCHRON
  Bridget (Atwell), 22:51
  Thomas, 22:51
COCKLING
  Michael, 23:143
CODDINGTON
  William, 21:195
CODMAN
  Ogden, 24:133
CODNER
  William, 25:166
CODRY
  William, 21:212
COE
  Adam S., 21:66
  Benjamin T., 21:66
  Ezra, 21:66
  Katherine M. (___), 21:66
COFFEN/COFFIN, 22:69
  Anne, 24:162
  Benjamin, 24:162
  Charles, 24:215
  Dorcas, 24:162
  Dorcas (Parker), 24:215
  Gayer, 24:161, 162
  Judith (Greenleaf), 25:56
  Katherine, 24:162
  Mary, 24:162; 25:56
  Peter, 22:222, 227
  Rebecca, 24:157, 162
  Rebecca (Parker), 24:161, 162
  Tabitha, 24:162
  Tristram, 22:88; 25:56
  Ursula, 24:161, 162
COFFREN
  William, 23:143
COGGESHALL
  Elizabeth, 25:167
COGGIN/COGGINS
  Elizabeth W., 24:196
  Lydia (Stevens), 24:97
  Thomas, 24:97
COGSEL
  John, 24:147
COGSWELL, 22:114, 159; 23:212;
  24:32-34, 143, 151
  Abigail, 24:31
  Darious, 24:139, 141
  Francis, 23:23
  Gifford, 24:30, 31; 25:133
  Hannah, 21:151
  Jo., 22:117
  John, 24:27-31, 109, 142-144, 146,
    148, 151; 25:26, 28, 131-133
  Joseph, 21:151
  Judith (Badger), 25:187
  Margaret, 24:31
  Mary (Tainor/Taynor), 25:26, 28
  Nathaniel, 21:151; 25:187
  Robert, 21:151
  Samuel, 21:151; 24:29, 30
  Sarah (___), 24:31
  Susanna (Haven), 21:151
  Susanna (Hearn), 21:151
  Susannah, 21:151
  Thomas, 25:188, 189
  Westol, 21:150, 151
  William, 24:29, 143, 144, 151; 25:132,
    133
COHEN
  Brian, 22:161
COHER
  Sarah, 21:98
COIL
  Henry, 23:137

COKER
  Catherine (___), 22:86
  Robert, 22:86
COLBROOK
  ___, Judge, 24:80
COLBURN
  Hannah, 21:36
  Lucy, 22:51
  Lucy C. (Tyler), 21:101
  Sarah, 21:237
COLBY, 22:20; 23:212
  Anthony, 22:90, 155
  Betsy (George), 25:198
  Charles H., 25:192, 198
  Dorothy, 21:177
  Elizabeth (Carr), 22:120
  Hezekiah, 24:116
  Isaac, 22:90
  John, 22:120
  Judith, 22:161; 25:187
  Lot, 22:120
  Martha (Parratt), 22:90
  Mary, 24:116; 25:200
  Moses, 22:120
  Rebecca, 22:89
  Samuel, 25:197
  Sarah, 22:90, 97, 98
  Sarah (Ash), 25:188, 197
  Sarah (Cole), 24:116
  Susanna (___), 22:155
  Zaccheus, 25:198
COLDAM/COLDHAM/COLDUM
  Clement, 22:204, 213
  Elizabeth, 22:202, 203, 206, 210-212
  Peter Wilson, 21:48; 22:100
  Thomas, 21:152
COLE/COAL/COALE/COALL/
  COLES see also NICHOLAS,
  21:89
  "Daughter", 21:95
  Abijah, 21:97
  Abraham, 21:89-93, 97
  Ann, 21:93
  Ann/Anne (___), 21:89-92
  Anna, 21:94
  Azor, 23:143
  Daniel, 21:96, 97
  Elizabeth, 21:92; 24:155
  Eunice (___), 21:89
  Frank T., 21:89
  George, 21:89
  Grace, 25:156
  Hannah, 21:94-97
  Hepzebah, 21:95-97
  Isaac, 21:89, 92
  Jedediah, 21:97
  John, 21:89-93, 95, 97
  Jonathan, 21:95-97
  Judith, 21:97
  Judith (Brown/Bowen), 21:97
  Marcy (Vealy), 21:92
  Martha, 21:95, 97
  Mary, 21:94, 96, 97
  Mary (Eaton), 21:94-96
  Mary (Knight), 21:92-94
  Mary (Wedgwood), 21:89
  Rebecca (Aslebee), 21:94
  Robert, 21:89
  Ruth, 25:21
  Samuel, 21:89, 92, 93, 95
  Sarah, 21:92; 24:116
  Sarah (Aslebee), 21:92-94
  Sarah (Davis), 21:89, 92
  Susanna, 21:92
  Susannah (Brown), 21:94
  Thomas, 21:89-92, 94

Trafford, 25:123
Weden, 23:143
William, 21:89
COLEMAN see also COLMAN
Thos., 21:114
COLER see COLLIER
COLLETTA
John Philip, 25:123
COLLIER/COLER /COLYER, 23:212
Elizabeth (Poole), 21:222
Gershom, 21:222
John, 23:210
Ruth, 23:209, 210
Ruth (Blacker), 23:210
COLLINS, 24:61
Barnard, 25:153
Benjamin, 22:44
Caleb, 21:33
Elizabeth, 21:33
Hannah, 21:175
Hannah (___), 25:153
Henry, 21:29, 33, 175
Isaac, 22:222, 231
Jacoby, 21:33
John, 21:12, 29; 25:199
Joseph, 21:34, 35; 25:19, 22
Lucretia (Buffum), 21:33
Lydia (Blaney), 21:33
Martha, 22:222, 230
Mary, 21:33, 238
Mary (___), 21:175
Mary (Norwood), 21:33
Mary (Rand), 21:33
Patrick A., 23:16
Rebecca (Phillips), 21:33
Samuel, 22:217
Sarah Ingraham, 25:153
Stanley Newcomb, 25:22
William, 21:35
Zachariah Rand, 21:33
COLLSON
David, 21:216
Lydia, 21:216
COLMAN see also COLEMAN,
MONTANA
Anne, 21:142; 23:54
Roberta (Pandolfini), 24:223
Roy, 24:223
COLSON
___, Mr., 21:217
David, 21:217
Elizabeth, 21:93
COLTON
Abby, 21:101
Eliza, 21:103
Lydia, 22:119
COLWELL
Amey, 21:52
Amey (Downing), 21:52
Robert, 21:52
COLYER/COLER see COLLIER
COMBS
John, 23:140, 145
COMEE/COMEY, 25:7
David, 25:4
Esther (___), 25:4
John, 25:4
Martha (Munro), 25:4
Peter, 25:9
COMINGS/COMINS/COMMINGS see
also CUMMINGS
Bridget, 25:143
Reuben, 24:207
William, 21:240a
COMONO, 24:146, 149

COMPTON
Anna Mary, 21:16
CONAN
___ (More), 24:190
Joshua, 24:190
CONANT, 21:24; 22:20
Bethia, 24:116
Bethiah (Mansfield), 21:100
John, 21:100; 24:116
Lot, 21:100
Martha, 24:116
Martha (Dodge), 24:116
Mary, 23:177
Rebecca, 21:100
Richard, 21:100
Roger, 21:24, 33, 58, 100, 226
Roger, 23:240a
Sarah, 22:58
Sarah (Horton), 22:58
CONDIT
W. W., 22:78
CONDY
Ann (___), 25:18, 25, 28
Anna (___), 25:17
Elizabeth, 25:25
Hannah (McGowan), 24:116
John, 24:116
Samuel, 25:17, 18, 28
CONERY
Benjamin, 21:213
CONKLING
Hannah (___), 25:126
James, 25:126
CONNAUGHTON
William, 23:18
CONNELL
Sarah (Goen), 21:102
CONNLEY
Mary, 21:137
CONNOLLY
Paul K., 23:17
CONVERS
Augustus, 25:152, 153
Emma, 25:152
Emma (___), 25:152,153
Mary Elizabeth, 25:153
Wm Mansfield, 25:152
CONVERSE
Edward, 24:153; 25:33
James, 24:153
Samuel, 22:45
Sarah (___), 22:45
Sarah (Atwell), 22:45
Sarah (Parker), 24:153; 25:33
COOK/COOKE
Alice, 23:222, 223; 24:37, 42
Benjamin, 22:176
Caleb, 25:181
Catherine Cornelia, 23:119
Charles, 22:120
Daniel, 22:173
Deliverance, 22:191
Elizabeth, 21:59; 22:174, 176; 23:223;
25:181
Elizabeth (___), 22:120, 171-176, 235
Francis, 22:172-174
George, 22:174-176, 235
Haines, 23:223
Hannah, 22:120
James, 22:171
John, 22:172
Jonathan, 22:172
Joseph, 23:222, 223; 25:5
Lucy, 22:171
Martha (Stedman), 23:222
Mary, 22:120; 24:116

Mary (Mireck), 22:120
Moody, 22:120
Nancy, 25:151
Nathan, 22:172
Norman, 22:235
Patience, 21:36
Samuel, 22:25, 27, 60a, 120, 171
Sarah, 22:60a, 120; 23:223
Stephen, 22:171-173
Susanna (___), 22:172-174
Susannah, 21:144
Thomas, 25:5
Timothy, 22:174
William, 23:143
COOLIDGE
Elisha, 21:215
Sarah (Boutel), 21:215
COONEY
Frank, 21:207, 208
COOPER
John, 23:120
Mary, 23:45
Peter, 22:167
Sarah (Salmon), 23:120
COPLEY, 21:69
John Singleton, 22:69; 23:7, 11
Mary (Singleton), 23:7
William, 24:3
CORBEN
Lydia (Atwell), 22:43
Robert, 22:43
CORCORAN
John G., 21:21, 224
CORDIN/CORDING, 25:96, 97
___, Mr., 25:101, 102
Richard, 25:95, 103
COREY/CORY
Abel, 25:46
Abiel, 25:87
Deloraine-Pendre, 24:153
Giles, 21:100
Kathleen B., 23:85; 25:124
Lucy (Parker), 25:46
Margaret, 21:100
Martha, 21:44
Mary, 24:51, 52
Stephen, 25:46
CORLETT
John, 21:179
Letitia, 21:179
Letitia (Craine), 21:179
CORNELL, 22:69
CORR
Bernard, 23:16
CORRIVEAU
Elsie Briant (Cunningham), 21:227
CORSER
Jane (Nichols), 22:180
John, 22:180
CORTIS
Sarra, 23:143
CORWIN
___, Sheriff, 21:87
George, 22:157
Jonathan, 21:91, 143; 23:55
CORY see COREY
COSGRIFF, 21:9
COSWELL
John, 24:147
COTTON see COTTON
COTTER
James E., 23:17
COTTLE
Abigail (Eaton), 25:191
Dolly (Nichols), 25:187, 188, 191
Hannah (Lowell), 25:191

Joseph, 25:187, 188, 191
Rebecca White, 25:191
Rhoda, 25:191
Thomas, 25:191
Woodbridge, 25:188, 191
COTTON/COTTEN
___, Mr., 21:200
Addam, 23:143
John, 21:115; 23:226
Mary, 23:226
COULTER
Donald Henry, 21:18
Nelda Virginia (Haszard), 21:18
COURSER
John, 24:154
COUSINS
Elizabeth, 21:36
Frank, 22:32
John E., 21:230
COVING
James, 21:71
Mary (___), 21:71
COWAN
Elianor, 22:235
Elisabeth (___), 22:235, 236
James, 22:235
John, 22:235
Mary, 22:235
Robert, 22:235, 236
William, 22:236
COWDREY/COWDRY
Tabitha (Boutall), 21:221
William, 21:210-212, 221
COWELL
Parm/Pamerla/Perm/Pearm, 22:46, 54
COWLES
Sidney, 23:178
COWLEY
Barbara Lucille (Fowler), 24:115
Marion Lindsay, 24:115
William E., 24:115
COX, 21:209; 22:160; 24:27, 29, 30, 33, 141, 144
Allyn, 24:32
Benjamin, 22:171, 174, 237; 25:52, 53, 151
Betsy, 22:174
Edward Smith, 25:53
Eliza, 22:237
Elizabeth (___), 22:171, 174
Francis, 25:151
Hyde, 25:14
Mehitable Smith, 25:53
Moses, 23:143
Samuel, 24:210
Sarah (___), 22:237; 25:52, 53, 151
Sarah Smith, 25:52
COY/COYE
___, Mr., 23:142
Elizabeth (Edwards), 22:105
John, 22:105; 23:143
M., 24:34
COZZENS
Isaac, 21:156
Martha, 21:156
Martha (Haven), 21:156
Mary, 21:156
Rebecca, 21:156
CRADOCK
Matthew, 23:180a
CRAIGAN
John, 22:187
Sarah (Dawes), 22:187
CRAINE see also CRANE
Letitia, 21:179

CRAM
Mary, 21:44
CRANDALL
John, 23:168
CRANE see also CRAINE
___, Gov., 23:114
James, 24:210
Mary (Parker), 24:210
CRAVEN
John T., 23:56
CREIGHTON/CRIGHTON
Ann, 23:66
Anna (Pearson), 22:180
George, 22:180
CRESSEY/CRESSY
Mary, 24:166
Mehitabel, 24:122
CRESSWELL
Florence, 24:174
Grace (Farnum), 24:173, 174
John, 24:174
CRESSY see CRESSEY
CRIERIE
Archelaus, 24:122
CRIGHTON see CREIGHTON
CRIPPEN
William, 23:143
CRISPIN
Charles David, 21:109
David Golt, 21:109
David T., 21:109
Florence Lefavour, 21:109
Marjorie, 21:109
Martha Bigelow (Bennett), 21:109
Maud Estelle, 21:109
Sarah Lucy, 21:109
William Bennett, 21:109
CRISTIE
John, 23:143
CROAD/CROADE
Richard, 21:91, 92
CROCKER
Elesabeth/Elizabeth, 23:143
CROCKETT
___, Miss, 24:166
CROFTS
William, 22:208
CROMWELL, 21:38; 25:5, 6, 135
Adelaide M., 23:135
Henry, 22:164
Jane, 22:164
Oliver, 22:164; 23:4, 110; 25:3
Phillip, 21:90
CRONAN/CRONIN
Arlene Ryder (Haszard), 21:18
Jeremiah, 24:122
John F., 23:17
Theodore Michael, 21:18
CROOM
Emily Anne, 25:121
CROOS
George, 23:143
Patience (___), 23:143
CROSBEY/CROSBY
Abigail (Whittaker), 24:50, 51
Anah/Hannah (Parker), 25:37
Anna/Anne (Tarbell), 25:88
Constance, 22:167
Dorothy, 23:224
Francis, 24:50
James, 24:50
Joseph, 21:117
Mary, 24:50; 25:52
Nancy, 25:52
Nathan, 23:224; 24:49, 50; 25:88
Nicholas, 24:73

Peggy (___), 24:73
Rebecca, 24:50
Sarah, 23:224
Sarah (___), 24:50
Sarah (French), 21:117
Sarah (Shed), 23:224
Simon, 24:50, 154
Susannah, 21:116
Susannah (Browne), 21:116
Thomas, 21:116; 25:37
William, 24:49, 51
CROSS, 24:111, 147, 151
Ann (Jordan), 24:55
Anna (Wilson), 21:102
Gorge, 23:143
John, 23:189, 207; 24:24, 55
Joseph, 21:12
Martha, 24:87, 95
Mary, 21:12, 44
Rebecca (___), 21:12
Richard, 23:143
Robert, 24:55, 109-112, 139, 142, 143, 146, 147, 149, 152; 25:135, 136
Stephen, 25:136
Wm. Henry, 21:102
CROUCH
David, 23:99, 100
Hannah (Brown), 23:99
John, 23:99
Mary (Brown), 23:99, 100
CROUSE
Edna, 22:129
CROW
___, Mrs., 21:149
Christopher, 21:149
CROWELL, 24:140, 142, 150, 152
___, Rev., 24:29, 144, 146
Harriet, 25:152
Robert, 24:139, 147, 150; 25:132, 152
Saml, 25:152
Samuel Filmore, 25:152
CROWINSHIELD see
CROWNINSHIELD
CROWLEY
John C., 23:16
Patrick H., 23:17
CROWNINSHIELD/
CROWINSHIELD, 21:180a
John, 25:180
Sarah (Hathorne), 24:190
CROWNWELL
John, 25:4
CRUISE
Tom, 21:80
CUE
Elizabeth (Kimball), 22:57
Huldah, 22:57
Mary (Porter), 22:57
Robert, 22:57
CULLEN
James, 24:19
CULLINANE
Michael, 25:74
CULVER
Mary (Miller), 21:100
CUMBS
William, 23:143
CUMMINGS/CUMMINS see also
COMINGS, 22:159; 23:237
___, Lawyer, 22:84
Abbott Lowell, 22:160
Asa, 24:96
Bridget, 22:47, 51, 54; 25:45, 146
Hannah, 24:95
Hannah (Peabody), 24:96
Isaac, 23:237

John, 23:143
Lucy (Colburn), 22:51
Martha, 21:240
William, 22:51
CUNINGHAM/CUNNINGHAM
___, Mr., 21:33
Abigail (Rand), 21:33
Andrew, 21:216
Anna, 23:179
Edith/Edythe LeFavour, 21:110, 228
Effie Fettyplace (Lefavour), 21:110,
    223, 226, 227, 229, 234, 236
Elsie Briant, 21:110, 227, 228
John, 23:143
Louise Kilbourn, 21:110, 227
Richard, 21:110
Richard LeFavour, 21:228
Roy Adrian, 21:110, 227, 229, 235
Sarah Alice, 21:110, 227
CURREY see also CURRY
Elizabeth (Jones), 22:179
Mary, 22:179
Richard, 22:179
CURRIER
Anne, 22:98
Daniel, 22:98
Edward, 22:222, 234
Hannah, 22:98
John, 22:98
Joseph, 22:98
Josiah, 23:143
Mary (Parker), 25:138
Mehitable (Silver), 22:98
Nathan, 22:98
Reuben, 25:187
Ruth Lucretia, 21:18
Sarah, 21:144; 22:98
Sarah (Brown), 22:98
Seth, 22:98
Stephen, 22:98
CURRY see also CURREY, 21:232
CURTICE see also CURTIS
Henry, 23:143
CURTIN
J., 25:64
Mary (___), 25:64
CURTIS/CURTISS see also CURTICE
___, Miss, 23:143
___, Mrs., 23:143
Abbey (Burdick), 24:72
Almira, 24:72
Amos, 23:108
Betsey (___), 23:108
Elijah, 24:72
Franklin, 23:190
Hannah, 21:45, 177
John, 21:45; 25:90
Lydia, 23:59, 119
Mary, 25:53
Mary (Looke), 21:45
Molly (Parker), 25:90
Sam'l, 23:143
William, 22:213
CURWEN
George, 22:160
CURZON, 21:173
CUSHING, 22:106, 135
___, Cardinal, 23:195
___, Mr., 22:93
Caleb, 22:138; 23:186
John, 21:95
Polly, 23:143
Zenas, 23:143
CUSHMAN
Rebecca, 21:178
Sarah, 21:153

CUTKOMP
Kent, 25:123
CUTLER
Anna, 25:161
Elizabeth (___), 21:41
H., 21:231
Hannah, 21:41, 42
Samuel, 21:41
CUTTER
John, 25:167
Rebecca, 23:175
Richard, 21:39
CUTTING
Nathan, 25:161
CUTTS
John, 23:233

DABNEY
Abigail (___), 24:195
DACEY
Timothy J., 23:16
DADE
Isaac, 23:143
DAFFERN
Mary (___), 22:44
DAGGETT see also DOGGETT
Arnold, 24:224
Lydia, 22:48
William, 25:9
DAGUERRE
Louis, 23:19
DALAND
Benjamin, 22:25, 27, 171
Elizabeth, 22:171
Geneva A., 21:32
Hannah (___), 22:171
DALE
Ebenezer, 24:219, 220
DALEY see also DALLY, DALY
John A., 23:16
DALLY see also DALEY, DALY
Joseph, 21:147
DALTON, 22:21; 24:169
Delia, 21:107
Tom, 21:11
DALY see also DALEY, DALLY
Augustine J., 23:17
Edward, 25:74
Marie, 25:67
Marie E., 25:122
DAMMON
Ebenezer, 21:219
John, 21:212
Thomas, 21:219
DAMON, 22:31
Ebenezer, 21:219
John, 21:212
DANE, 21:136
___, Mr., 21:210
Abigail, 21:87
Anne Stainton, 25:11
Eleanor (Clark), 23:240
Elizabeth, 21:88
Elizabeth (Ingalls), 25:202
Frances (Bowyer), 25:202
Francis, 21:195, 199; 25:202
Hannah, 25:202
Jno., 22:159
John, 23:240; 25:202
Joshua, 22:222, 227-233
Mary, 23:240
Nathan, 23:135, 136
Nathaniel, 23:143
Sarah, 25:55
DANEL, 23:143

DANFORD
Betty, 25:44
Betty (Parker), 25:138
Stephen, 25:138
DANFORTH
___, Mr., 24:159
Elizabeth, 24:155
Jacob, 24:155
John, 24:155
Jonathan, 24:47, 154, 155, 159; 25:35
Joshua, 21:239
Kezia (Reed), 21:239
Lucy, 21:239
Mary (Withington), 23:225
Mary/Mare, 22:92; 24:37; 25:34-36
Nicholas, 23:223; 24:155
Rachel, 24:88
Rebecca, 22:92; 24:155, 157, 159, 160
Rebecca (Parker), 24:154, 155, 159
Samuel, 24:50, 155
Sarah, 23:220, 225; 24:155
Sarah Ellen, 21:104
Thomas, 21:154; 23:161, 163, 225;
    24:155
DANIEL see also DANIELSON
James, 25:8
DANIELS, 22:25
Mary, 21:59; 25:52
DANIELSON see also DANIEL
William, 23:38, 40
DAOUST
Arsene, 24:227
DAREN
Elizabeth (Bartholomew), 22:191
Joseph, 22:191
DARLING, 23:163
Elizabeth, 25:155
George, 25:8, 9
DARWIN
Abigail (Barnes), 22:191
Anna (Parrett), 22:191
Anna (Perry), 22:190
Charlotte (Morrisey), 25:58
Deliverance (Cook), 22:191
Deliverance (Hall), 22:190
Deliverance (Hills), 22:191
Elizabeth (Bartholomew), 22:190, 191
Joseph, 22:190, 191
Lucina, 22:191
Sabrina, 22:191
William, 25:58
DASEY
Charles V., 23:17
DAVENPORT
Abigail, 21:179
Amos, 24:19
Arletta, 24:19
Arletta 'Letta', 24:20
C. M., 24:62
Charlotte, 24:17-22, 53
Charlotte (Gray), 21:19, 20, 54
Ethel, 21:109
John, 23:221
Martha, 24:20
Samuel, 24:19, 20
Samuel B., 21:54
Villa, 24:20, 21
DAVID
William H., 21:227
DAVIS, 21:36; 23:35; 24:168
A. H., 21:105
Abigail, 23:163
Abigail (___), 22:188
Abigail (How), 23:163, 164, 179
Abigail (Medcalf), 23:163, 179
Amassa, 21:69

Ann, 22:94; 23:179
Ann (Robinson), 23:164, 179
Anna (Cunningham), 23:179
Anne, 22:97
Beleys, 23:143
Benjamin, 22:97; 23:143
Betsy, 22:222, 232, 233
Betty, 22:97
Cornelius, 24:166, 167
David, 23:143
Deborah (Harris), 23:165, 179
Dorothy, 24:220
Ebenezer, 23:161-163, 165, 179
Edward, 23:144
Eliphalet, 22:222, 228
Elisabeth (Batten), 24:219
Elizabeth, 23:163, 165, 179
Elizabeth (___), 23:163-165, 179
Elizabeth (Bachelder), 25:55
Elizabeth (Jewett), 24:166, 167
Elizabeth (Tarr), 23:165, 179
Elizabeth Washington (Ellis), 21:53
Enoch, 22:97
Ephraim, 23:144
Gartret, 22:178
George, 21:210
Hannah, 22:93; 23:179; 25:55, 57
Hannah (Hanson), 21:54
Helaine, 23:136
Horace, 21:53
Isaac/Isaak, 21:240a; 23:159-164, 179
Israel, 23:161, 164, 179
Jacob, 23:159
James, 21:238; 22:222, 233, 234; 23:159, 161, 163, 164, 179; 25:55
Jemima, 21:116
Jemima (Eastman), 22:97
Jenkin, 21:29
Job, 24:219
John, 21:54; 23:144, 159, 161-166, 179
John N., 22:222, 234
Joseph, 22:97; 23:179
Joseph E., 22:222, 234
Lawrence, 25:18
Lucy, 23:100
Lydia, 23:163, 179
Lydia (Black), 23:159-164, 179
Lydia Violet, 21:53; 24:17, 20
Martha (Emins), 23:164, 179
Mary, 21:30, 31; 22:44, 97, 188; 23:161-164, 179
Mary (Finson), 23:179
Mary (Stanwood), 23:179
Mary (Tucker), 21:116
Mehitable, 22:97
Nathaniel, 22:97
Nellie (Richardson), 21:105
Rebecca, 23:163
Rebecca (Atkins), 25:18
Reuben/Ruben, 22:97
Samuel, 22:112; 23:161, 163, 164, 166, 179; 24:170
Sarah, 21:89, 92; 22:97; 24:35, 37
Sarah (Babson), 21:238
Sarah (Silver), 22:97
Stephen, 21:116
Susanna, 23:163, 165, 179
Sylvanus, 23:162
Sylvester, 23:162
Tobias, 24:37
Walter Goodwin, 21:36; 22:43, 99, 110; 23:160; 24:217; 25:22
William, 23:143

DAVISON
Daniel, 25:8, 10
DAVNEY
Nathaniel G., 24:94
DAWES, 22:160
Sarah, 22:187; 25:4, 5
William, 23:90
DAY, 24:92
Aaron, 23:144
Benjamin, 23:144
Betsy B., 22:222, 231-234
Daniel, 24:100
David, 22:222, 231-233
Delia Anne (Bryant), 21:107
Edith Ella, 21:107
Elizabeth, 23:144
Elizabeth (___), 23:144
Hannah, 25:52
James, 22:222, 227, 228
James A., 21:107
John, 23:140, 144; 25:52
Marsha Ann (Wiiknikainen), 21:18
Martha, 24:101
Martha (Stevens), 24:92
Mary, 22:222, 230
Nancy (Stevens), 24:100
Ruth (___), 25:52
Stephen, 23:240a
Thomas Whitemore, 25:52
William, 22:222, 227-230, 234; 23:144; 25:52
DeAZAGRA
Alvar P., 24:67
Marguerite (Navarra), 24:67
DeCHAMPLAIN
Samuel, 22:64, 111
DeGRAVE
Anthonetta, 21:10
DeLaCERDA
Blanca, 24:68
Ferdinand, 24:67
Joanna (___), 24:67
DeRHODE
Hugh, 22:201
Michael, 22:201
Willemus, 22:201, 202
DeRIVERE
Immanuel, 21:32
DeSCUDAMORE see SKIDMORE, 23:87
DEACON
John, 21:210
DEAN/DEANE
George, 21:93
James, 21:52
John, 21:52
Joshua, 22:222, 228
Lydia (___), 24:191
Marcy, 21:52
Marcy (Fenner), 21:52
Prudence (Page), 21:52
Sarah (Browne), 21:240a
Sarah (Smith), 21:52
Sarah (Tisdale), 21:52
Seth, 21:52
Thomas, 21:240a; 24:191
William, 21:52; 25:8
DEARBORN
David Curtis, 23:63, 85
DEE
Benjamin, 24:40
John H., 23:56
Mary (Stevens), 24:40
DEETZ
James, 22:160, 161
DELANEY, 22:190

DELAWARE
Anna, 23:117
DELOREY
Janet Ireland, 21:46; 22:23
DEMMING see DENNEN
DEMOS
John Putnam, 21:88
DENCH
Edward Bradford, 22:177
Marie Antoinette (Hunt), 22:177
Marie Catherine, 22:177
DENING see DEMMING
DENISON see DENNISON
DENNEN/DENNIN/DENNING/ DEMMING/DENNING/ DENING
Emine (Brown), 23:177
George, 23:177
Hannah (Dike), 23:177
Job, 23:141
Joseph, 22:222, 230, 231; 23:57, 177
Mary, 21:120; 23:57
Mary (Eveleth), 23:177
Mary (Haskell), 23:57
Nicholas, 23:177
DENNETT
Eliza, 24:103
Emily, 24:103
Hannah (Stevens), 24:103
James, 24:103
John, 24:103
Maria (Lowell), 24:103
Mary, 24:103
Thomas, 24:103
DENNIN/DENNING see DENNEN
DENNIS, 23:212
___, Mrs., 24:196
Benjamin, 23:210
Charlotte C. W. (Bessom), 23:210
Edwin W., 24:196
Elizabeth, 25:156
Grace (Cole), 25:156
John, 22:222, 228, 229
Susannah, 22:40
Thomas, 25:156
DENNISON
___, Gen., 21:152
Ann, 21:176
D., 22:39
Daniel, 21:47; 22:103; 24:26; 25:96, 101, 103
Dorothy/Dorothy (Weld), 23:219
Isaac, 22:222, 231, 232
Jemima, 22:222, 227
William, 23:219
DENSLOW
William R., 23:137
DERBY, 21:180a; 22:32
John, 21:99, 163; 24:56a
Lucreatia (___), 22:25
Richard, 24:56a
Roger, 22:25
Sarah (Norwood), 21:99
DERESLEYE
Margaret, 23:219
DeRHOADES see RHOADES
DERING
Elizabeth (Packer), 24:136
Henry, 24:136
DesJARDINS
Edward, 22:166
DESRANLEAU
Maryann, 21:54
DEVEREUX, 23:191, 192
___, Capt., 22:48
Samuel, 23:208

DEVLIN
  James H., 23:17
DEWREN
  Moses, 23:151
DEXTER
  Bridget, 24:160
  Catharine, 21:159
  Catherine (___), 21:159
  Elizabeth, 22:239
  Joanna (Parker), 24:157, 160
  John, 24:160, 212
  John Haven, 23:134
  Rebecca, 24:160
  Richard, 24:160
  Samuel, 21:159; 24:160
  Sarah, 24:160
  Thomas, 23:109, 110, 144
  William, 22:222, 230, 231; 23:144
DiVITO
  Rose, 25:113
DIAMOND
  Sally, 22:49
DICER
  Elizabeth Austin, 22:111
DICKERMAN
  John, 21:211
  Sarah (Edwards), 21:211
DICKERSON
  Philemon, 23:240a
DICKINSON
  Jennet (___), 23:120
  Thomas, 22:167; 23:120
DICKSON
  Marion, 22:120
  R. J., 23:85
DIKE, 23:177
  Agnes (Tibbetts/Tybbot), 22:56;
    23:177
  Anthony, 22:37
  Elizabeth, 22:55
  Hannah, 23:177
  Rebecca (Doliver), 23:177
  Richard, 23:177
DILLINGHAM
  ___, Mr., 21:210
DIMOND
  Abigail (Eastman), 23:117
  Israel, 23:117
  Molly, 22:218
DIVAN/DIVEN
  John, 21:214; 22:209, 210
DIX
  Abigail, 21:59
  John, 21:216, 217
  Polly (Childs), 21:59
  William, 21:59
DIXEY/DIXY
  William, 23:111; 25:108a
DIXON
  James, 23:42
  John, 23:38
DIXSON
  James, 23:43
DIXY see DIXEY
DOANE/DANE
  Druzilla, 22:49
  John, 21:187
DOBSON
  David, 23:85; 25:124
DODD
  Charity, 25:55, 57
  Charity (Woodroffe), 25:55, 57
  George, 25:55, 57
  William, 23:144
DODEY
  Michael, 23:144

DODG/DODGE, 21:10; 22:108
  ___, Goodwife, 22:38
  Abigail, 22:218
  Abigail (Porter), 23:117
  Benjamin, 22:222, 230, 231
  Bethia (Conant), 24:116
  Catharine Elizabeth, 25:54
  Charles, 23:117
  Cornelius, 22:57
  David, 23:144
  Deborah (Balch), 22:57
  Edith (___), 22:58; 24:16, 175, 231
  Edward, 22:38; 24:16, 175, 231
  Elinor, 24:16, 175, 231
  Elizabeth (___), 22:55, 56, 58
  George, 24:191
  Hannah, 22:41, 55, 57; 23:176
  Israel, 24:191
  Jerusha (Woodbury), 22:57
  John, 22:38, 39, 57, 104, 105;
    23:176; 24:116
  Jonathan, 22:57; 23:144
  Joseph, 22:38
  Josias, 22:38
  Lucia, 24:191
  Lucy Pickering, 25:54
  Lydia (___), 24:191
  Lydia (Poland), 22:57
  M., Mrs., 24:34
  Martha, 23:119; 24:116
  Mary, 23:119
  Mary (Haskell), 24:16, 175, 231
  Mercy, 22:57
  Nath'el, 23:144
  Pickering, 25:54, 60a, 152
  Rebecca (___), 25:54, 152
  Rebecca Ann, 25:152
  Richard, 22:58, 102, 103, 107; 24:16,
    175, 231
  S., 24:34
  Samuel, 23:144
  Sarah, 22:57; 24:116
  Sarah (___), 22:103, 104
  Sarah (Proctor), 22:57; 23:176
  Tabitha, 22:41
  William, 22:55, 56, 58, 103
  Zachariah, 23:141
DOGETT/DOGGETT see also
    DAGGETT
  Thomas, 22:43
  William, 23:144
DOHERTY
  Cornelius, 23:16
  Michael, 23:16
  William W., 23:16
DOLAN
  Thomas, 23:16
DOLBEARE see also DOLIBER
  Barnard, 24:191
  Edmund, 24:191
  Sarah (___), 24:191
DOLE/DOLES
  Daniel, 21:114
  G. T., 21:106
  Richard, 25:97, 102, 103
DOLIBER see also DOLBEARE
  Donald, 23:183
  John Harris, 23:191
DOLIVER/DOLLIVER
  ___, Capt., 23:210
  Grace (Bessom), 23:210
  Margaret, 24:94
  Mary, 21:238
  Mary (Elwell), 21:238
  Rebecca, 23:177
  Samuel, 21:238, 23:177

  William P., 22:222, 234
DONAHUE see also DONOGHUE
  Joseph Joyce, 23:17
  Patrick, 23:16
  William F., 23:17
DONNELLY
  Charles F., 23:16
  E. C., 23:56
  H. V., 23:56
DONNY, 23:149
  John, 23:144
  Mary, 23:144
DONOGHUE/DONOHOE see also
    DONAHUE
  Ralph Leo, 23:17
  Michael T., 23:16
DOOLITTLE
  Sarah, 24:155
DORAND, 23:180
DORE
  John B., 23:17
DOREN
  Elizabeth (Bartholomew), 22:190
  Joseph, 22:190
DORMAN, 23:237
  Eliza (___), 25:192
  Jesse, 25:192
  Thomas, 23:236
DORRANCE
  Samuel, 23:37
DORSEY
  James A., 23:17
DOTY
  Abigail (Davenport), 21:179
  Betsey Elizabeth (Tuttle), 21:179
  Harmon Francis, 21:179
  Louise Mary (Harris), 21:179
  Lyman, 21:179
  Maria Louisa, 21:179
  Martin, 21:179
DOUGHTY
  Evaline Hubbard (Bryant), 21:109
  Henrietta, 21:109
  Mabel R., 21:109
  William, 21:109
  William D., 21:109
DOUGLAS/DOUGLASS/DUGLAS,
    21:78
  Althea, 25:121
  Frederick, 23:185
  Helen (Schlinting), 24:55
  John, 21:6; 23:39, 144
  Thomas, 23:144
  William, 23:144
DOVE, 23:65
DOW, 21:10; 22:135; 23:234
  Benjamin, 23:38
  Bertha (Martin), 21:240
  Ebenezer, 23:38
  Ednah (Parker), 25:139
  George, 21:90; 22:154
  George Francis, 22:137, 160; 23:237;
    24:26
  Georgina Margaretta, 24:227
  Hannah, 22:178
  Jeremiah, 25:139
  John, 21:240; 22:178
  John Henry, 21:240
  Joseph, 22:177; 23:234
  Judith, 21:239
  Lydia, 22:119
  Mary, 21:59
  Mehitable (Haynes), 22:178
  Reuben, 22:51
  Samuel, 24:227
  Sarah (Browne), 22:178

Thomas, 23:38
DOWD
James E., 23:17
DOWN
Elizabeth (Silver), 22:87
Joseph, 22:87
DOWNEY
Maurice J., 23:17
DOWNING/DOWNY, 22:21, 23
Amey, 21:52
Emanuel, 25:203
John, 21:35; 24:109, 112; 25:135, 203
Lucy (Winthrop), 25:203
Malcolm, 25:8
Mehitable (Brabrook), 24:147; 25:135, 203
Sarah, 25:203
DOWSE
Lawrence, 21:28
Margery (Rand), 21:28
DOWSETT
Peter, 23:144
DOYLE
William, 22:222
William, 22:233
DRAPER
Nicholas, 21:240a
DRESSER, 23:164
John, 22:167
DREW
___, Capt., 21:166
DRISCOLL
Daniel M., 23:17
Jeremiah, 23:144
DRIVER
Elizabeth, 25:181
Thomas, 25:153
DRUMMOND
William, 23:15
DRURY
John, 21:158, 159
Susannah, 21:159
Susannah (___), 21:159
Susannah (Goddard), 21:158, 160
Thomas, 23:144
DUBE, 23:192
DUBOIS
Dominique, 21:50
Marie Ann (Peradeau), 21:50
DUDLEY, 24:52
___, Capt., 21:196
___, Gov., 21:87
___, Mr., 24:47
Anne, 21:88
Joseph, 22:95
Mercy, 21:113
Sarah, 21:32, 34
Thomas, 21:113, 209; 24:46
DUFFY
Mark, 23:124
DUGLASS see DOUGLAS
DUGLE
Allester, 25:8
DUKE
Edward, 23:144
DUMAS
Alexandre, 25:106
DUMENIL
Lynn, 23:137
DUMMER, 21:48; 25:8, 9
David, 22:47
R., 21:114
Richard, 21:46, 112, 113
DUMPHY
William, 25:155

DUNBAR
Benjamin, 23:144
Cyrus, 22:184
Esther (Bassett), 22:184
Jonathan, 22:184
Lucy, 24:207
Sarah, 24:207
Sarah (___), 22:184
DUNCAN
Robert, 23:15
DUNCH
Deborah, 23:168
DUNHAM
Benajah, 21:145
Benjamin, 21:146
David, 21:146
Esther (Rolfe), 21:146
Eunice, 21:146
Joanna (Thornell), 21:146
Jonathan, 21:144-147
Mary (___), 21:146
Mary (Bloomfield), 21:146
Mary Singletary, 21:146
Nathaniel, 21:146
DUNKCUM, 25:9
DUNKIN
George, 23:144, 148
DUNKLE
Bob, 23:123
Robert J., 24:161
DUNLAP
Andrew, 23:16
Sarah, 23:139; 25:11
DUNN
David, 22:178
Henry, 22:178
Huldah (Aldrich), 22:178
Huldah Aldrich, 22:178
Lydia (Parker), 22:178
DUNNELL
Jonathan, 21:44
Mehitable (Kenney), 21:44
DUNNEWAY
Daniel, 23:144
DUNSMOORE see MOORE, 25:9
DUNSTER
Faith, 21:52
DUNTON
Samuel, 21:216
DURANT
Hannah (Alley), 22:50
Reuben, 22:50
DUREN
Charles N., Mrs., 25:146
Polly/Mary, 25:93
DURGIN
Samuel, 25:192
DURHAM
Jane, 23:46
Jane, 23:50
DURKEE
Elizabeth (Parsons), 23:228
John, 23:228
Mary (Hankey), 24:55
Pearl, 24:55
DUSTIN
Josiah, 21:216
Lydia, 21:93
Sarah, 21:93
DUTCH/DOUCH
Betsy, 22:175
Ezra Jones, 22:173
Fanny, 22:171
Fanny (___), 22:171-175
George, 22:172
Grace, 25:156

Grace (Pratt), 22:110; 25:156
Harriet, 22:175
John, 22:171-175
Joseph, 22:174
Mary, 22:171
Osmund, 22:110; 25:156
Sally, 22:171
Samuel, 22:36, 172
Sophia, 22:174
Susanna (More), 22:36
DUTTON
Benjamin, 25:192
Hannah, 24:212, 213
Rebecca, 23:210
Susannah, 21:117
DWIGHT
Mary (Poole), 21:211
Timothy, 21:211
DWINNELL
Jacob, 21:45
Kezia (Gould), 21:45
DWYER
Emily (Swanback), 24:20
Mary L., 24:21
Michael J., 23:17
Timothy, 24:21
DYAR/DYER
Mary, 22:203
Thomas, 25:163
Frederick H., 22:125

EABORN/EABOURNE/ABORN, 22:24
EAKLE
Arlene H., 23:85
EAMES see also AMES
Anthony, 23:38
Hanna (Stevens), 24:39
Mary, 21:33, 155
Nathan, 21:96
Samuel, 21:155; 24:39
Sybillah (Haven), 21:155
EARLE
Mattie, 23:56
EASTMAN
Abigail, 23:117
Jemima, 22:97
Mehitable (Merrill), 23:117
Obadiah, 23:117
Sarah, 21:120; 22:218
EASTON
John, 21:111
N., 21:114
Nicholas, 21:111, 112
EASTY
Mary (___), 21:42
EATON
Abigail, 21:213; 25:191
Anna (Rand), 21:32
Benjamin, 21:32
Charlene S., 25:195
Charles, 22:220, 231
Daniel, 21:93, 94, 95, 97
Elizabeth, 21:32, 220
Elizabeth (Burnap), 21:214
Ellen Eliza (Emerson), 23:157
Eunice (Singletary), 21:144
Florence, 23:157, 158, 178
Hannah, 22:162
Hannah (Cole), 21:96, 97
Hannah (Johnson), 22:162, 163
James, 21:32; 23:158
James L., 23:157
Jeremiah, 23:144
John, 21:212, 217
Jonas, 21:210, 211
Jonathan, 21:214

Joseph, 22:38
Joshua, 21:216
Lilly, 21:209
Lucy Ann (Emerson), 23:157, 158
Lucy Ellen, 21:224
Mary, 21:94-96
Mary (___), 21:95
Noah, 21:216
Priscilla, 21:36; 22:22
Ruth, 22:98
Sarah, 21:214, 219, 220; 25:141
Theophilus, 23:180a
Thomas, 21:144
Urssilla, 24:157, 161
William, 21:32, 94, 95, 211

EBBEN/EBEN/EBENS, 22:115, 118, 156; 24:28, 30, 32
Mary Jean, 22:150

EDENDEN
Edmund, 21:28
Eliza (Whitman), 21:28
Sarah, 21:28

EDGCOMB
Hannah, 24:115
Levi, 24:115
Sarah (Alld), 24:115

EDMONDS/EDMUNDS
Abigail, 21:153
Joseph, 21:149; 22:44, 212
Samuel, 22:212
William, 21:29, 149

EDNEY
James, 22:222, 230, 231

EDSON
Ebenezer, 21:71
Jane (___), 21:71
Samuel, 21:71

EDWARD/EDWARDS
___, Mr., 24:98
Abigail, 21:211
Abraham, 22:106
Benjamin, 22:102, 104-108
Bethia, 22:105, 107
Duke, 24:68
Eleanor, 22:102; 23:117
Eleanor (___), 22:104
Elizabeth, 21:210, 211, 222; 22:105, 106
Elizabeth (___), 22:106
Ellena, 22:102
Ellena (___), 22:104
Elnor, 22:39, 103
Elnor (___), 22:101, 104, 106
George Hortense, 22:106
Hannah (___), 22:102
Joan/Joannah (___), 22:101, 102, 104
Johannah, 22:101
John, 22:38, 39, 100, 101, 104-106
Jonathan, 22:107
Joseph, 22:102, 106
Joshua, 22:106
Martha, 22:105
Mary, 21:210, 211; 22:105
Mary (Poole), 21:210, 211, 222
Mary (Solart), 22:106
Matthew, 21:210-212, 222
Nathaniel, 22:106
Rice/Rise/Rhys/Rhyc/Reece, 22: 38, 39, 100-107
Sarah, 21:210, 211, 222; 22:105-107; 23:180
Susan, 22:100
Tabitha, 21:211
Thomas, 22:100, 105-107

EGAN
James, 23:16

EGART
James, 23:15

EHRICH
Louis R., 23:115

EICHOLZ
Alice, 24:228

ELA
Enos, 24:169, 170

ELDERKIN
John, 22:204
Roland D., 21:36

ELEANOR
Countess, 24:68
Queen, 24:68

ELIOT see ELLIOT

ELITHROP
Thomas, 22:167

ELIZABETH II
Queen, 24:67, 69

ELKINS
Thomas, 25:126

ELLENWOOD
Israel, 21:32
Susanna (Rand), 21:32

ELLERY/ELLRY
Benjamin, 22:222, 230, 231
William, 22:222, 232-234

ELLINGWOOD/ELLINWOOD
Benjamin, 22:55
Eleanor, 22:55
Ellen (Lynn), 22:55
Martha (Rowlandson), 21:88
Mary (___), 22:55
Ralph, 21:88; 22:55
Returne, 21:88

ELLIOT/ELLIOTT/ELIOT
Abigail, 21:40
Andrew, 23:239
Betsey (George), 25:192, 198
Betsy (Nichols), 25:189
David, 25:192
Deborah, 22:179
Dorothy, 25:192
Elizabeth/Betsy (Nichols), 25:190, 192, 193
Elizabeth P., 25:193, 199
George, 25:192
George C., 25:82
Grace (Woodier), 23:239
John, 25:192, 193, 199
Judith, 25:192
Judith (___), 25:192
Mercy, 23:239
Mercy (Shattuck), 23:239
Phineas, 25:192
Samuel, 25:192
Simon, 23:16
Thomas, 25:189, 190, 192, 193, 198, 199
William, 21:200; 23:144

ELLIS
Alice, 25:134
Ansgard, 24:55
Betsey, 21:160
David, 22:82
Elizabeth Washington, 21:53
Eunice (Witbee), 21:54
Florence M., 21:108
Freeborn, 21:54
S., 22:77
Susanna, 25:168

ELLISON
Mary (Dunham), 21:146
Mary (Singletary), 21:146
William, 21:146

ELLRY see ELLERY

ELLWELL see ELWELL

ELSLY
Barbery, 25:104
Barbri, 25:98, 100

ELVINS
Richard, 24:191
Samuel, 24:191
Sarah (___), 24:191

ELWELL/ELLWELL/ELWELLS
Anne, 24:217, 218
Benjamin, 22:222, 233
Dorcas, 21:238
Ebenezer, 24:217
I., 23:151
Jean, 24:217
Jean (Elwell), 24:217
Josiah, 21:238
Mary, 21:238
Mary (Collins), 21:238
Payn/Payne, 22:222, 228-230
Robert, 21:238
Samuel, 22:222, 231-234
William, 23:144, 151

EMERI/EMERIE/EMERY
___, Goody, 25:98
___, Mrs., 25:96
Elen, 25:98
Elizabeth, 25:96-98
John, 25:96, 97

EMERSON, 23:35
___, Capt., 22:51
___, Mrs., 22:84
Adeline D. (Burbank), 21:108
Arthur Irving, 21:108
Benjamin, 22:93
Bent., 21:105
Brown, 21:226; 22:237; 25:52-54, 150, 152
Bryant, 21:101, 104
Caroline Louise (Bryant), 23:157
Catharine Buffinton, 25:53
Charles, 22:93
Charles F., 21:104
Daniel, 23:155, 158
Daniel Hopkins, 25:52
Daniel Putnam, 23:155
Edward Brown, 25:53
Eliza (Weston), 23:156, 158
Elizabeth, 21:101, 105
Elizabeth (___), 22:180
Elizabeth (Briant), 21:99
Elizabeth (Brown), 23:155, 156, 178
Ellen (Swan), 23:157
Ellen Eliza, 23:156
Emily, 21:104
Esther, 25:83
Esther (Parker), 25:84
Eva, 23:157, 178
Forestus D., 21:105
Forrest, 23:158
Forrest Fayetts, 23:156
Frank Augustus, 21:108
Franklin, 21:101, 105
George Edgar, 21:105
Grace, 23:157, 178
Hannah (Bradford), 21:104
Hannah Eliza, 21:104
Harriet, 25:152
Henry H., 21:105
Henry Pendexter, 23:156, 168
Herbert H., 21:104
Howard, 23:158
Howard Malcolm, 23:156
James P., 21:105
John, 21:99; 23:176; 24:16, 175, 191, 231

John Bryant, 21:104
John Owen, 21:104
Joseph, 21:99, 101, 102; 23:158
Joseph Bradford, 21:104
Joseph Brown, 23:155
Joseph L., 21:104
Justus, 23:157, 178
Justus Weston, 23:156
Louis Francis, 21:108
Louisa (Butterfield), 21:104
Lucy (Pratt), 23:155
Lucy Ann, 23:155, 157, 158
Lucy Ella, 23:157
Martha (Parkhurst), 21:104
Mary, 21:101, 240; 22:237; 23:176
Mary (___), 22:237; 25:52-54, 152
Mary (Boutall), 21:221
Mary (Packard), 21:105
Mary (Spaulding), 21:101
Mary R., 21:104
May, 24:16, 175, 231
Obadiah, 25:83, 84
Oliver, 23:155-158, 178
Oliver P., 22:78
Owen, 21:99, 101, 104, 105
Peter, 21:220
Ralph Waldo, 22:148
Rebecca, 23:155, 156, 158; 24:160, 208
Rebecca (Poole), 21:220
Rebecca Adams (Kittredge), 21:105
Rebecca Wiley, 23:155
Robert, 22:93; 23:158, 178
Robert Robinson, 23:155
Rufus, 21:101
Rufus Franklin, 21:105, 108
Rufus Webster, 21:104
Ruth (Symonds), 24:16, 175, 176, 231
Ruth (Warren), 21:99
Sarah, 22:93
Sarah (Byram), 21:104
Sarah (Silver), 22:93
Susan Hopkins, 25:54
Susannah, 22:93
Susie May, 21:108
Thomas, 22:180
William, 23:156, 157
William E., 23:155
William Willis, 23:155, 157, 158
EMERY/FMERY/EMERYES/
EMORY
___, Goodman, 25:98, 99, 104
___, Goody, 25:100
___, Mrs., 21:173; 25:101
___, Goodwife, 25:97
Agnes (Northend), 21:171
Alice (Grantham), 21:171
Ann, 21:171; 22:239
Anthony, 21:171
Beth, 24:83
Ebenezer, 21:171-173, 198; 25:101
Eleanor, 22:239
George, 21:90
J., 21:114
Jo., 25:101
John, 21:171, 172, 198; 22:239; 23:54; 25:98, 101-103
Jonathan, 21:171, 173
Mary (___), 21:172, 198; 22:239; 25:98
Mary (Shatswell), 21:198
Mary (Webster), 21:172
Mary (Woodman), 21:173
Ruth, 22:178; 24:164
Ruth (March), 24:164
Sarah, 22:239

Stephen, 21:171, 173
Thomas, 24:164
EMINS see also EMMONS
Martha, 23:164, 179
EMMET see also EMMOTT
Richard S., 23:17
EMMONS see also EMINS
Hannah, 25:155
Marinda (Miller), 21:100
Peter, 23:159
Thos. J., 21:100
EMMOTT see also EMMET
James, 21:145
EMORY see EMERY
ENDECOTT/ENDICOT/ENDICOTT,
21:10; 22:18, 20, 240a
___ (Endicott), 24:107
___, Gov., 21:40; 22:216; 23:240a; 24:193
___, Miss, 24:107
___, Mrs., 24:176a
Fidelia (___), 24:94
John, 21:24; 22:101; 23:167, 236; 24:94, 107, 176, 176a, 232a
Zerubbabel, 24:107
ENGLAND
Abigail (Pillsbury), 25:188
John, 21:209
Sarah (Nichols), 25:188
Stephen, 25:188
ENGLISH
'Twins', 21:105
Betsey B. (Foster), 21:102
Eliza T. (Jamieson), 21:106
Elizabeth Obear, 21:102, 106
Hannah Patten, 21:102
James Briant, 21:102
John Wilson, 21:102
Lizzie Briant, 21:106
Lydia, 21:100
Lydia Alice, 21:106
Lydia M. (Hildreth), 21:105
Lydia Obear, 21:102, 106
Maria Louise, 21:105
Mary Elizabeth, 21:105
Mary Ella (Healey), 21:108
Nattie E. (Hatch), 21:106
Philip, 21:102, 106; 23:215
Philip Augustus, 21:102
Philip Ernest, 21:106
Philip Faunce, 21:108
Rebecca (Briant), 21:102
Rebecca Briant, 21:102
Susan Ingersoll, 21:102
Thomas, 23:16
William, 21:105, 108
William Alvin, 21:105
William Groves, 21:102, 105
William Townshend, 21:106
ENNIS see also EVANS
Alexander, 25:8
ENRIQUE I
Juana (Nunez), 24:67
ENRIQUE II
Rey, 24:68
EPES
Elizabeth, 23:102-104, 106, 107; 24:201, 204
Symonds, 22:107
ERARIS
John, 25:98
ERICKSON
Sven A., 25:200
ERLENKOTTER
Donald, 21:215

ERRINGTON
Abraham, 23:175
Hannah, 23:175
Rebecca (Cutter), 23:175
ESKILDSON
George, 23:144
ESTABROOK/ESTEBROOK
Elizabeth (Parker), 24:54
Olive (Townsend), 24:54
Robert, 24:54
Sarah, 23:57; 24:54
Sarah (Temple), 24:54
Thomas, 24:54
ESTEY/ESTY
Mary (Towne), 22:215; 23:238
Susannah, 23:117
EVANS/EVENS see also ENNIS
___, Capt., 21:168
Catherine (Hoskins), 22:150
Charles, 22:150
William, 21:208; 22:150
EVELETH
Hannah, 23:144
Isaac, 23:144, 177
Jacob, 23:144
Joseph, 23:177; 24:73
Mary, 23:177
Mary (___), 24:73
Mary (Bragg), 23:177
Sarah (Parkman), 23:177
Silvester, 23:177
Susan (Newbury), 23:177
EVENS see EVANS
EVERETT
Ebenezer, 24:41
Joanna (Stevens), 24:41
John, 24:41
Mercy (Brown), 24:41
EVERTON
Sarah (Callender), 21:71
William, 21:71
EVETT
I., 24:69
EYRES see AYRES

FABISZEWSKI
Mary, 24:125, 130
FAIRBANK
Grace, 25:163
Martha (Gates), 25:200
Mary (Brinley), 25:200
Polly (___), 25:200
Zacheus, 25:200
FAIRBANKS
Clarissa, 25:190, 196
Comfort, 21:175
Jonathan, 21:175, 176
Lydia (Holbrook), 21:175
Maria Parker, 25:196
Martha (Gates), 25:196
Sarah (___), 21:176
Zaccheus, 25:196
FAIREFEILD/FAIRFEILD/
FAIRFIELD, 22:42, 104
___, Dr., 24:192
John, 22:36
Sally, 24:192
Walter, 22:36, 38-40, 103
William, 21:12
FAIRSERINCE
Robert, 23:144
FAISSLER
Bill, 24:33
FALCONER
Deliverance (Cook), 22:191

FALLEY
  Margaret Dickson, 23:85
FALLON
  Joseph D., 23:16
FALZONE
  Mark V., 22:195
FARBER, 25:176
  Dan, 25:204
  Jessie (Lie), 25:204
FARGASON
  John, 25:8
FARINGTON
  Mathew, 22:209
FARLEY
  Benjamin, 24:156
  Geo. E., 24:27
  Mary, 23:113, 235
  Nathaniel R., 24:26
FARLOW
  Charles Frederick, 21:158
FARMER
  Mary (Emerson), 21:101
  Oliver, 21:101
FARNAM/FARNHAM see also
      FARNUM, 24:28, 150
  Elizabeth (Stover), 21:59
  Hannah, 24:36
  J.M., 24:170
  Jedediah, 24:103
  Nathaniel, 21:59
  Rebecca, 24:103
  Rebecca (Poor), 24:103
  Russell C., 24:169
FARNSWORTH
  Mary (Farr), 23:168
  Matthias, 23:168
FARNUM see also FARNAM
  Addison, 24:174
  Angeline, 24:172
  Benaiah, 24:170-172
  Benjamin, 23:88; 24:172
  Bennie/Beniah C., 24:172
  Charles, 24:173, 174
  Clinton, 24:173, 174
  Eliza, 24:172
  Ellen, 24:174
  Ezra, 24:170
  Ezra M., 24:169
  Fred/Frederick, 24:169-174
  Frederick M., 24:172, 173
  Gertrude, 24:174
  Grace, 24:173, 174
  Hannah, 24:37, 41
  Hannah (Mitchell), 24:170, 171
  Hannah (Morse), 24:169
  Hannah L. (Mitchell), 24:169, 172
  Harriet E., 24:174
  Ida, 24:172
  Isaac, 24:100
  Jacob, 24:169-173
  Jacob M., 24:172
  Jacob Marsh, 24:169
  James, 24:86
  Jedediah, 24:86
  Joanna, 24:41, 87
  John, 24:39, 85-87, 170, 174
  John M., 24:169
  Josephine, 24:172
  Kate, 24:172
  Keziah (Skidmore), 23:88
  Lelita (___), 24:172
  Lucy J. (Harrington), 24:174
  Margaret, 24:38
  Mary Ann (Saddler), 24:173, 174
  Mehitable, 24:41, 87
  Persis (Stevens), 24:100

Phebe, 23:88
Ralph, 24:169, 173, 199
Rebecca, 24:95
Roxena, 24:173, 174
Samuel, 24:86
Stephen, 23:88; 24:169, 173
Tabitha, 24:41, 85, 86
Waty M., 24:174
William, 24:169, 170, 173; 25:82
William Marsh, 24:169
FARR see also TARR
  David, 22:222, 227
  Elizabeth, 23:168
  George, 21:29; 23:167-169
  Joseph, 21:34; 22:45; 23:169
  Martha, 23:169
  Mary, 23:168
FARRAR
  Samuel, 24:96
FARRINGTON, 21:148
  Abigail, 21:154
  Anna, 22:52, 53
  Lydia, 24:99
  Mary/Polly (Atwell), 22:53
  Mathew, 21:149
  Polley (Atwell), 22:53
  Sarah, 24:95
  Sarah (Stocker), 22:53
  Theophilus, 21:214
  Thomas, 22:50-53
  William, 22:50, 53
FAULKNER
  Abigail (Dane), 21:87
  Daniel, 24:36
  Edmond, 21:195, 199
  Hannah, 24:102
  John, 24:44
  Joseph, 24:44
  Rebecca (Barnard), 24:44
  Sarah (Abbott), 24:44
FAVOR/FAVOUR see also
      LEFAVOUR, 21:223
  Cutting, 22:59
  John, 22:59
  Mary (Osgood), 22:59
  Mary (Wells), 22:59
  Penelope, 22:59
  Philip, 22:59
FAWNE
  Elizabeth, 25:56
FEARS
  John, 21:208
FEATHERSTONE
  Phebe, 21:237
FELCH
  Ebenezer, 24:90
  Lydia, 24:43, 90, 91
  Lydia (Chandler), 24:90
FELLOWS
  Amanda M. (Gardner), 22:179
  Chloe (Turner), 22:179
  David, 22:179
  David Harvey, 22:179
  Elbert Gardner, 22:179
  Ephraim, 22:179
  Hannah (Warner), 22:179
  Hopestill (Holdridge), 22:179
  Nathaniel, 22:179
  Susannah (Rathbun), 22:179
  Ward J., 22:77, 79
  William, 22:179; 24:150
FELT, 21:26; 23:111; 24:146, 148
  Aaron, 22:47
  Elizabeth, 22:43
  Elizabeth (___), 22:43
  George, 22:43, 45; 23:161; 25:181

Hannah (Atwell), 22:47
Hannah (Mains), 22:43
Joseph, 21:90
Joseph B., 21:10; 22:161; 23:118;
      24:152
Joshua, 22:45, 46
Lydia, 22:43, 44, 46, 54
Lydia (Maine/Mains), 22:46
Moses, 22:43, 45, 46
FELTON, 23:183
  David, 22:27
  Elisabeth (Baker), 23:92
  Francis, 24:80
  Mary (Skelton), 22:23
  Nathaniel, 22:23; 23:92, 94
  Phebe, 23:92, 94
  Samuel, 21:40
  Sarah (Goodale), 21:40
  Stephen, 23:89, 92
FENNER
  Amey (Colwell), 21:52
  Arthur, 21:52
  John, 21:52
  Marcy, 21:52
  Mary (Smith), 21:52
FERDINAND
  Archduke, 21:192
FERDINAND I
  Rom Ks, 24:68
FERDINAND II
  Emperor, 24:68
FERDINANDA
  Countess, 24:68
FERGUSON
  Archibald, 25:9
  Charles W., 23:137
  Joan P. S., 23:86
FERNANDEZ
  Alfonso, 24:67
  Blanche (___), 24:67
FERRET
  Daniel, 23:144
FERRIS
  Mary Walton, 22:160
FIANDACA
  Alfred, 22:169
FIELD
  Sarah, 25:126
FIELDING
  R., 21:114
FIELDS
  Catherine, 22:179
  Samuel, 24:83
  Sarah (Stevens), 24:83
FIENNES
  Susan, 23:167
FIFIELD
  Deborah, 23:240
  Giles, 23:240
  Judith (Carter), 23:240
  Mary (Perkins), 23:240
FILEBROWN
  Mary (___), 22:50
FILLMORE
  Millard, 23:185, 186
FILMINGHAM
  Francis, 24:105
FINCH
  Caroline (Johnson), 21:102
  Will, 21:102
FINSON
  Mary, 23:179
FISCHER see also FISHER
  David Hackett, 22:160
FISH
  Mary (Mycrist), 22:187

Steven, 22:187
Theron, 25:173
FISHER see also FISCHER, 25:171
Joshua, 21:135, 136
FISK/FISKE, 22:42, 104
___, Capt., 22:103
___, Mr., 25:150
Anne, 24:106
Anne (___), 24:105
Benjamin, 24:86
Elizabeth, 21:154
Hannah (Haven), 21:159
Isaac, 21:159
John, 21:169; 24:105-107, 155, 156,
  159; 22:102; 25:34
Lydia (___), 21:159
Lydia (Fletcher), 25:42
Mary, 23:93
Phineas, 24:106, 107
Sarah (___), 24:106, 195
Shirley (___), 21:59
Simeon, 21:59
Thomas, 22:37-39, 103, 104; 24:107
William, 22:39; 24:106, 107
FITCH
___, Dea., 21:216, 217
Benjamin, 21:217
Bridget, 21:213, 216, 217, 219
Jeremiah, 21:33
Joseph, 21:219
Mary, 21:217
Mary (Rand), 21:33
Mehitable, 21:213
Mehitable (Poole), 21:219
Zachary, 21:212
FITTS
James Hale, 22:42
James Hill, 21:238
FITZ
Moses, 23:145
FITZGERALD
Benedict, 23:17
D., 21:16
Paul H., 23:17
T. J., 21:84
William T. A., 23:17
FITZPATRICK, 25:65-67, 73
Bernard, 23:16
John Bernard, 23:135
Marilyn, 21:169; 23:174, 218,
  227; 24:164, 176, 205; 25:16,
  33, 35, 44, 83, 137
Marilyn L., 25:90
Marilyn R., 22:109; 24:46, 104, 153,
  222
FITZRANDOLPH
Hope, 21:146
FLAG/FLAGG
Charles Alcott, 24:80
Eleazer, 21:219
Esther, 21:219
Esther (Green), 21:219
John, 22:47, 48
Mary, 21:157
Molly/Mary (Hart), 23:59, 119
Theodore, 23:59, 119
FLAKE
Marian, 24:173
FLANDERS
Mary, 24:103
FLEMING
William, 23:125
FLETCHER
Abraham, 23:145
Ada F., 25:193, 195
Benjamin, 25:85, 86

Betsey, 21:179
Bridget, 25:144
David, 25:87
Dorothy, 25:45, 142
Elizabeth, 25:91
Elizabeth (___), 25:43
Ester/Esther, 25:35, 40, 42
Ezekiel, 25:83
Frances P. (Nichols), 25:193, 195
Francis, 25:143
Hannah, 25:85, 86, 88, 143
Hannah (___), 25:40, 45, 85
Hannah (Parker), 25:86
Harriet E., 25:193, 195
Hattie E., 25:195
Jeptha, 25:86
Jim, 22:169
Joseph, 23:54; 25:39
Joshua, 25:40, 143
Josiah, 25:42; 83
Lucy W., 25:193
Lydia, 25:42
Mary, 24:155, 157, 158; 25:39, 86
Mary (___), 25:83
Persis, 23:208, 209
Rebecca, 24:206; 25:39, 83, 86, 146
Samuel, 25:40
Sarah, 25:45, 86, 143
Sarah (___), 25:40, 83
Stephen, 25:83
Stillman, 25:195
Thankful, 25:83
Timothy, 25:144
William, 23:41; 24:157; 25:40, 83
FLEWELLING
Lois, 22:168
FLINDAR
Richard, 25:126
FLINT, 22:31
Abigail, 22:57
Ann (___), 22:58
Ebenezer, 21:213
George, 21:35
Hannah (Moulton), 22:57
Judith (Bancroft), 21:213
Samuel, 22:29, 30
Thomas, 21:214; 22:57, 58
William, 23:59
FLOOD
Daniel, 22:92
Elizabeth, 22:92
George, 22:92
Hannah, 22:92
Joseph, 22:92
Mark, 22:92
Martha (Acres), 22:92
FLOWERS
Louisa, 24:98
FLOYD
Abigail, 24:156
C. Harold, 24:156
George W., 22:220, 234; 23:56
Jacob, 24:156
Joanna, 24:156
John, 22:212; 24:154-156
Noah, 24:156
Rachel, 24:156
Rachel (Parker), 24:154, 155
Sarah (Doolittle), 24:155
Tabitha, 24:156
FLUREY/FLORIE/FLORENCE,
  23:214
Charles, 23:214
David, 23:214
Elizabeth, 23:214
Elizabeth (Bessom), 23:214

FLYNN
Edward J., 23:17
FOLGER, 22:69
FOLLANSBEE
Susan, 25:198
FOLLETT
Persis (Black), 23:179
Robert, 23:179
FOLSOM
Charles, 22:161
FONTAINE
Genevieve, 22:200
FOOTE
Arthur, 24:232a
Caleb, 24:232a
FORBES
Allan, 23:135
F. Murray, 23:17
Harriette Merrifield, 25:204
Sarah, 21:11
FORBUSH
John, 25:9
John, 25:10
FORD, 22:135
Dennis, 22:201; 23:37
James, 25:132
Worthington, 22:137
FORGET
Robert, 21:199
FORNESS
Mary A., 23:115
FORREST
James, 23:9, 10
FORRESTOR
Elizabeth, 24:74
Rachel (___), 24:74
Simon, 24:74
FOSTER
___, Capt., 21:163, 164
Aaron, 23:145
Abigail (Smith), 23:117
Abraham, 22:91
Amos, 22:237
Andrew, 21:195, 199; 24:35
Anna, 24:206, 216
Anna (___), 25:164
Betsey B., 21:102
Charles Samuel, 21:120; 22:238
Constance Louise (Stevenson), 21:18
Daniel, 22:91
David, 23:145
Dolly V., 25:190
Elizabeth, 22:236
Ephraim, 24:36, 38
Evelyn Virginia, 21:18
Grace Pearl (Webster), 22:238
Hannah, 21:116; 22:44; 24:44, 92
Harriet (___), 25:152
Harriet (Berry), 22:238
Harriot Maria, 25:152
Huldah, 21:45
Isaac, 25:152
James, 21:83; 25:164, 166, 167
Jemima, 21:156
Jeremiah, 23:145
John, 24:85
John B., 22:222, 231, 232
Joseph, 24:155
Joshua, 24:85
Linda Lee (Wiljanan), 21:18
Lucy, 22:222, 227
Lydia (Burbank), 22:91
Lydia H., 21:225
Margaret (Van Galen), 21:146
Marsha Ann (Wiiknikainen), 21:18
Martha, 24:213

FURNESS
Margaret, 23:214

GABEL/GABLE
Clark, 25:108
Laurel, 25:204
Laurel K., 25:159
GAFFNEY
Michael, 23:145
GAGE
___, Gen., 23:90
___, Gov., 21:60a
Aaron, 24:41
Hannah (Stevens), 24:41
John, 24:110
Thomas, 24:56a
GALE
Anna Coffin, 22:235
Betsy, 22:176
Bradford, 24:232a
Edmond/Edmund, 22:173, 174-176, 235; 23:112
James, 22:175
Joanna Coffin, 22:176
Lucena, 22:180
Margaret (___), 22:173-176, 235
Patty, 22:235
Polly, 22:173
Samuel, 22:174, 235
GALEUCIA see also GALUCIA
Daniel, 22:48
GALLAGHER
Celia, 23:101, 106
GALLAWAY see also GALOWAY
Thomas, 23:145
GALLE
Joseph, 23:145
GALLISON
William, 21:60a
GALLOP
E. K., 21:167
GALOWAY see also GALLAWAY
Hugh, 23:145
GALUCIA see also GALEUCIA, 23:35
GALVIN
Edward L., 25:122
GAMLIN
Ed, 21:235
Emma G., 21:235
GANNON
Ann (Keough), 21:240; 23:180
Elizabeth, 21:240
John, 21:240; 23:180
Mary, 21:240
Sarah, 21:240
Thomas, 21:240
William, 21:240
GARBO
Greta, 25:106, 108
GARDINER/GARDNER, 22:69
Abel, 21:27; 22:175, 176; 235, 237
Abiel (___), 23:225
Amanda M., 22:179
Amos, 23:117
Annah, 24:191
Benony, 22:179
Bertha (___), 22:237
Bethia (___), 22:175, 176, 235
Caleb, 23:225
Elizabeth, 24:191, 218
Elizabeth (___), 24:191
Eunice Haszard, 22:218
Elizabeth (Smith), 22:179
George, 22:179
Hannah, 25:30, 182
Henry, 23:145

John, 22:179, 218; 24:217
Jonathan, 24:191, 192
Joseph, 23:145
Joseph Pitman, 22:176
Ludia (Dodge), 24:191
Lydia, 24:97
Marcy (Spencer), 22:179
Martha, 24:218
Mary (___), 24:192, 217
Mary (Byer), 22:179
Mary Chandler, 22:237
Nathaniel, 22:179
Priscilla, 22:235
Sally (___), 24:191
Sally (Fairfield), 24:192
Samuel, 21:27, 92; 25:30, 182
Sarah, 21:43; 22:58
Sarah (___), 23:225; 24:192
Sarah (Bill), 23:117
Sarah Sophia, 22:238
GARDOQUI
Joseph, 22:140
GARFIELD
Edward, 22:109
GARGAN
Thomas J., 23:16
GARLAND, 22:25
Judith, 24:218
Judy, 25:108
Mary (McAteer), 25:68
Nathaniel, 22:27
Richard, 25:68
GARNER
James, 22:52
GARRATY
John, 23:137
GARRETT
Nancy, 23:212
GARY
Hannah, 21:40
GASKILL/GASKILL
Provided (Southwick), 22:23, 217
Samuel, 21:27, 217; 22:23
GASTON
Count, 24:68
GASTON IV
Count, 24:68
GATCHEL
Joseph, 21:149
GATES, 22:160
Bill, 21:79
Lemuel, 23:145
Martha, 25:196, 200
GATOR
Judith, 25:201
GAUTIER
Marguerite, 25:106
GAVETT
Joseph, 23:145
GAVOT
Joseph, 22:223, 227
GAWENS
Samuel, 23:145
GAY
Ebenezer, 21:66
Jerusha (___), 21:66
Martin, 21:66
GAYLORD
Effie Matilda, 24:70
Emma Armina (Tripp), 24:70
Nelson Jones, 24:70
GEARE
Debora, 22:39
GEARHART
Marla, 24:119, 125

GEDDINGS
George, 22:151
GEDNEY
Bartholomew, 21:153
Hannah (Gardner), 25:182
Marget Davie, 25:182
Susanah, 25:182
William, 25:182
GEE
Elizabeth, 22:223, 231, 232
Nancy, 22:223, 232, 233
William, 22:223, 227-231
GEERE
___, Sister, 24:105
William, 24:107
GEERISH
Wm., 25:103
GEES
___, Capt., 23:152
GENN
Will, 23:145
GEORGE
___, Mr., 25:196
Alden, 24:22
Austin, 25:192
Betsey, 25:192, 198
Count, 24:68
Francis D., 22:77, 79
Henry, 21:20, 22
John, 24:68; 25:197
John Swadock, 25:188
King, 22:123
Magdalen (___), 24:68
Martha, 25:5
Mary, 25:188, 189
Nathaniel Ash, 25:197
Sally (Bradbury), 25:192
Sarah (___), 25:188, 197
Sarah (Ash), 25:188, 197
GEORGE II
King, 23:7
GEORGIEV
O., 24:70
GEROLD
Bobby, 24:223
GERRISH
___, Col., 25:188
Benjamin, 21:92, 192
Jacob, 22:48
Jane, 24:41, 87
Joseph, 22:37, 101, 102, 104; 24:87, 107
Rebecca, 25:164
GERRY, 22:135
Catharine, 22:140
Elbridge, 21:194; 22:140
Samuel Russell, 22:140
Thomas, 22:140
GEYER
Henry Christian, 25:167
GIBB
Margaret, 22:120
GIBBS
Daniel, 23:15; 24:217
GIBSON
Benjamin, 21:219
Mehittable, 21:219, 220
Rebecca (Errington), 23:175
GIDDINGS
Aaron, 22:220, 223, 231-234
George, 24:140
Sarah (___), 21:155
William, 21:155
GIDDONS
Lydia, 23:107
Martha, 23:104, 105, 107

GIDNEY
　　___ Mr., 22:218
GIFFORD, 25:9
　　John, 23:110
　　Lydia, 24:200
GILBERT
　　Humphrey, 22:40
　　Samuel, 22:220, 223, 228-234
　　Thomas, 23:236, 237
GILBERTSON
　　Phyllis Adele, 22:162
GILBORTH
　　Dan'll, 23:141
GILD see GUILD
GILES/GILLES
　　___, Dr., 23:189
　　Anna, 21:53
　　Chas., 21:207
　　Mary, 22:223, 227-229
　　Philip, 21:88
　　Returne (Ellinwood), 21:88
　　Thomas, 22:223, 230-233; 23:145
　　William, 22:223, 233
GILL
　　P., 24:69
　　Rachel, 23:211
GILLES see GILES
GILLESPIE
　　Paul J., 23:18
GILLETTE
　　Harvey, 23:130
GILLOW, 21:34
GILMAN
　　Frederick, 23:145
　　Martha (Nichols), 25:189, 190
　　Sally, 22:119
　　Sally/Sarah (Heard), 22:119
　　Samuel, 25:190
　　Samuel Thing, 22:119
GILMORE
　　John F., 23:17
GILPATRICK
　　Charles, 23:119
　　Elizabeth, 23:119; 24:116
GILSY
　　Rosanna, 23:94
GIN
　　William, 23:145
GIRDLER
　　Polly (Skidmore), 23:91
　　William, 23:91
GLEASON
　　Agnes, 23:130
　　Beulah (Haven), 21:157
　　Frank, 24:102
　　Moses, 21:157
　　Ruth, 21:156
　　Susanna (Haven), 21:157
　　Thomas, 21:157
GLEN
　　George, 23:15
GLIDDEN
　　Charles W., 21:232
　　Joseph, 22:77
GLOVER
　　James Gould, 22:236
　　John, 23:209, 211; 24:79
　　Jonathan, 22:236, 237; 25:53
　　Joseph, 22:236; 23:184
　　Mary (___), 25:53
　　Nanny (___), 22:236, 237
　　Samuel Newhall, 22:237
　　William Cook, 25:53
GOADE
　　Abigail, 22:58

GODDARD
　　Annah (Haven), 21:155
　　Edward, 21:158
　　Elisha, 21:155
　　Susanna, 21:158, 160
　　Susannah (___), 21:158
GODDAY
　　Alfred, 21:207
GODFREY
　　Elizabeth, 24:232
　　Mary, 22:239; 23:130
　　Mary (Brown), 22:239; 24:232
　　Peter, 22:239; 24:232
　　Rosalie, 22:195
GODKIN
　　Charlesetta L., 25:195
GOEN
　　Andrew Jackson, 21:102
　　Betsey, 21:100
　　Charles, 21:102
　　Deborah, 21:99
　　Elizabeth, 21:101, 105
　　Hale, 21:102
　　John, 21:99, 102
　　Lydia, 21:100
　　Lydia (Briant), 21:99
　　Mary, 21:100, 102
　　Noah, 21:100, 101
　　Sarah, 21:102
GOETZ
　　Edith (Mayer), 25:81
　　William, 25:81
GOLDSBURY
　　Ann T., 21:103
GOLDSMITH, 22:36
　　Elizabeth, 22:41
　　Hannah (Dodge), 22:41
　　Hutton, 22:37, 41
　　John, 22:41
　　Margaret (Cogswell), 24:31
　　Martha, 22:41
　　Martha (Hutton), 22:40, 41
　　Mary, 22:41
　　Mehitable (Kimball), 22:41
　　Mercy (Young), 22:41
　　Miriam (Kimball), 22:41
　　Richard, 22:41, 42; 24:106, 107
　　Tabitha, 24:31
　　Tabitha (Dodge), 22:41
　　William, 24:31
　　Zaccheus, 22:40, 41
GOLDTHWAIT/GOLDTHWAITE,
　　22:24
　　Ebenezer, 22:25, 27
　　Elizabeth, 22:23
　　Mehitable, 25:5
　　Thomas, 22:23
GOLDWIRE
　　Martha (Moyce), 23:54
GOOD see also GOODE
　　Sarah, 21:36, 37
GOODALE
　　Abigail, 21:36
　　Abigail (Eliot), 21:40
　　Abigail (Tarrot), 21:36
　　Abraham, 21:36, 40
　　Amos, 21:43
　　Ann, 25:203
　　Anna, 22:171
　　Benjamin, 21:40
　　Catherine (Kilham), 21:36, 39
　　David, 21:40
　　Eliza Ann, 25:152
　　Elizabeth, 21:39, 40
　　Elizabeth (___), 25:53
　　Elizabeth (Beauchamp), 21:39, 43

　　Elizabeth (Cousins), 21:36
　　Elizabeth (Witt), 21:40
　　Hannah, 22:175
　　Hannah (Colburn), 21:36
　　Hannah (Gary), 21:40
　　Hannah (Rhodes), 21:40
　　Hannah (Upton), 21:36, 43
　　Hester, 21:36
　　Isaac, 21:36
　　John, 21:36, 40, 43
　　Joseph, 21:39
　　Joshua, 22:171-176; 25:52, 53,
　　　　151, 152
　　Joshua Safford, 25:52
　　Lydia, 22:172
　　Lydia (Titus), 21:36
　　Mary, 21:39, 43; 22:173
　　Mary (___), 22:171-176
　　Mary (Abbe), 21:36
　　Mary (Buxton), 21:39, 40, 43
　　Mary (Hutchinson), 21:39
　　Mary (Small), 21:43
　　Mary (Tarbell), 21:40
　　Mary Henfield, 25:53
　　Mehitable (Burnap), 21:156
　　Nathan, 22:176
　　Nehemiah, 21:151
　　Patience (Cook), 21:36
　　Phebe, 21:43
　　Polly, 22:171
　　Rachel, 21:42, 43
　　Rebecca (___), 25:52, 53, 151, 152
　　Rebekah Putnam, 25:53
　　Robert, 21:36, 39
　　Ruth (Bound), 21:43
　　Samuel, 21:39, 40, 42
　　Samuel Page, 25:52, 151
　　Sarah, 21:40
　　Sarah (Horrell), 21:40
　　Sarah (Russell), 21:43
　　Sarah (Whipple), 21:39
　　Solomon, 21:156
　　Thankful, 22:174
　　Thomas, 21:40; 25:53
　　Zachariah, 21:36, 39, 42
GOODE see also GOOD
　　Hannah, 24:55
GOODELL
　　Catherine (___), 21:151
　　Hannah, 21:150, 151
　　Hannah (Haven), 21:150, 151
　　Jacob, 22:46
　　Joseph, 21:151
　　Margaret/Peggy (Atwell), 22:46
　　Martha, 21:150, 151
　　Mary, 21:151
　　Nehemiah, 21:151
　　Robert, 21:151
GOODENOW
　　___, Mrs., 25:162
　　___, Rev., 25:162
　　Hannah, 21:176
　　Mary, 25:6
　　Thomas, 25:6
GOODHUE
　　Abigail, 22:176, 236
　　Abigail (___), 22:236, 237
　　Beria, 22:176
　　Bethia, 25:202
　　Elizabeth, 24:74
　　Hannah (Dane), 25:202
　　Jane (___), 25:202
　　Marjory (Watson), 25:202
　　Mercy (___), 24:74
　　Moses, 22:175
　　Nancy, 22:235

Nicholas, 25:202
Sally, 22:175
Sally (___), 22:175, 176, 235
Samuel, 22:175, 176, 235, 237
Sarah, 23:145
William, 22:175, 236, 237; 24:74, 192; 25:202
GOODING see GOODWIN
GOODRICH/GOODRIDGE, 22:20
Abby, 23:201
Abby K. (___), 23:201
Charles F., 23:201
Daniel, 23:145
Elizabeth, 23:114
Elizabeth (Pillsbury), 24:232
Elizabeth Page, 25:151
James, 25:90
Jeremiah, 24:232
Joanna, 24:55
Joseph, 24:55, 164
Lizzie, 23:113
Marcy/Mercy (March), 24:164
Mary (Adams), 24:232
Mary (Bayley), 24:164
Mary (Lavenuke), 24:55
Mary (Rowe), 24:232
Priscilla (___), 25:151
Ruth, 24:232
Saml, 25:151
Saml Norris, 25:151
William, 23:145, 150; 24:232
William Lang, 25:151
GOODWIN/GOODING
Elizabeth, 21:215
John, 21:214, 216, 217, 219
Martha, 21:172
Mary, 21:180, 213, 214
Nat C., 23:56
Nathaniel, 21:211, 216
Patience, 21:177
Timothy, 21:217
GOOKINS
Daniel, 21:153
GOOLD see also GOULD
Ebenezer, 24:163
Olive (Parker), 24:163
Thomas, 23:52
GORDEN/GORDON see also
JOURDAN, 25:8
___, Mr., 25:108
George W., 23:42, 43
James, 23:39, 40
Nat, 25:82
Sarah Elizabeth, 22:120
Virgil, 24:173
GORE, 22:162
Benjamin, 22:237
Desire, 23:39
Francis, 22:237
Samuel, 23:39
Sarah, 22:237
Sarah (___), 22:237
GORGES, 23:231, 232
Ferdinando, 23:233
GORING
John, 22:74
GORMAN
Dennis J., 23:17
GORRY
Paul, 25:122
GORTON
G., 24:34
GOSS
Charles Carpenter, Mrs., 22:177
GOTT, 22:113
Benjamin, 23:26

Charles, 22:37-39, 103; 24:107
Chester, 21:208
Daniel, 21:149; 23:150
Edgar, 21:208
Jabez R., 23:165
John, 22:223, 230-233
Lemuel, 23:165
GOULD see also GOOLD, 23:87, 237
Abigail, 23:174
Abner, 21:45
Adam, 23:87, 88
Amos, 21:45
Anne (Haskell), 22:180
Eliezer, 21:45
Elizabeth (Towne), 21:45
Esther, 21:45
Hannah, 21:45
Hannah (Curtis), 21:45
Hannah (Perkins), 21:45
Huldah (Foster), 21:45
Jane, 21:157
Jeacob, 21:45
Jemima, 23:87, 88, 90
John, 21:45, 52; 23:236-238
Judith (___), 21:211, 222
Kezia, 21:45
Lydia, 23:102, 103, 106, 107
Marcy (Yeats), 21:52
Martha, 21:45; 22:58
Mary, 21:45; 23:238
Mary (Gould), 21:45
Mehitable (Barrett), 23:87
Mercy, 21:52
Nathaniel, 22:180
Olive (Parker), 24:162
Phebe, 21:45; 23:237
Phebe (French), 21:45
Phebe (Gould), 21:45
Phebe (Towne), 21:45
Priscilla, 23:238
Rebecca, 22:180
Richard, 21:45
Robert, 21:211, 222
Roxana (Burnham), 21:45
Ruth, 21:45
Samuel, 23:87
Sarah, 21:157, 160; 23:127
Sarah (___), 23:237
Sarah (Baker), 21:52
Silas, 23:145
Stephen, 21:45
Thomas, 21:45, 52
Zaccheus, 23:236-238
GOULDA
Joseph, 22:213
GOULDING
C. H., 23:113
GOULDWIRE
George, 25:96
GOVE
J. Sherman, 22:79
GOWDEY
Betsey (Robinson), 22:53
John, 22:53
Lydia Robinson, 22:53
GOWING
___, Mr., 23:114
Elizabeth, 23:174
GRAFFAM
Olive Blair, 25:149
GRAFTON, 23:234
Elizabeth, 23:230, 231
Joseph, 23:230, 231
Mary (Moore), 23:231
GRAHAM see also GRIMES, 25:10
John, 23:56; 24:103

Rhoda (Stevens), 24:103
GRAINGER
John D., 25:6
GRANES
Sarah (Cook), 23:223
GRANT, 24:32, 148
___, Pres., 22:70
Betsey, 23:208
Ebenezer, 23:145
Francis, 21:38
Jane, 22:167
John, 23:208; 25:8, 9
Lydia (___), 23:214
Margaret, 23:214
Margaret (Bessom), 23:207, 208
Mary, 25:25
Mathew, 22:192
Nath'el, 23:145
Peter, 25:8
Priscilla (Hawkins), 21:38
Ruth, 21:159
Thomas, 23:209, 214; 24:79, 80
GRANTHAM
Alice, 21:171
GRANTON
Cora B., 25:195
GRAVELY, 24:25
GRAVES, 23:212
Abigail (Williams), 21:33
Ann, 21:31; 22:210
Betsy, 22:141
Crispus, 21:31
Eleazer, 23:210
Elizabeth (Burrill), 21:33
Elizabeth (Lewis), 21:33
Hannah (Rand), 21:33
Jane (Verin), 21:33
John, 21:51
Mark, 21:199; 22:240
Martha (Kneeland), 21:51
Mary (Williams), 21:33
Meriam (Bessom), 23:210
Ran/Rand, 21:33
Samuel, 21:33
Sarah, 21:51
Sarah (Bessom), 23:210
Thomas, 21:35
GRAY
Benjamin, 21:154
Caroline, 24:192
Charlotte, 21:54; 24:19
David, 24:97
Dorothy (___), 21:50
Elizabeth (___), 21:151; 24:192
James O., 23:56
John, 21:151; 24:192
Lydia, 24:40, 84
Mary, 21:33
Mary N., 25:29
Robert, 21:34, 50
Sarah, 21:50; 24:43, 90, 192
Sarah (Hawkes), 21:154
William, 23:207
GREANEY
Daniel J., 23:18
GRECO
Charles R., 22:17
GREELAND
Henry, 25:96
**GREELE/GREELEE/GREELEY/
GREELY**, 25:187
Andrew, 23:54, 233
Clement, 25:189
Joseph, 25:187, 191
Reuben, 25:188

GREEN see also GREENE, 23:212
    "Babe", 25:160
    Abigall (Clark), 23:222
    Amy, 23:44
    Annie/Amy, 23:45
    Elizabeth, 22:74
    Elizabeth W., 22:79
    Esther, 21:219
    Henry, 21:222
    Henry S., 22:78
    James, 23:45, 145
    Joseph, 21:42
    Martha (___), 25:160
    Mary (Cooper), 23:45
    Nehemiah, 22:47
    Phebe, 24:160, 211
    Rebecca Hammon, 22:150
    Sam, 21:64, 65
    Samuel, 23:222; 24:160
    Solomon, 21:149
    Suzanne Revaleon, 21:139
    Thomas M., 23:17
    Unice/Eunice, 21:216
    William, 22:36
GREENAWAY
    Mary, 25:203
GREENE see also GREEN, 22:135
    Francis B., 24:78
    Jacob, 21:152, 153
    John, 25:3
    John Rose, 22:140
    Nehemiah, 22:48
    Susan Emerson (Thompson), 21:104
GREENELAND/GREENLAND/
    GRENLAND, 25:97- 99
    ___, Mr., 25:96, 100-103
    Henry, 25:95, 103, 104
    John, 24:156
GREENLAW
    William Prescott, 21:222
GREENLEAF
    E., 21:114
    Judith, 25:56
GREENOUGH
    Abigail (Parker), 25:141
    Anne, 25:90
    Betsy (Parker), 25:90
    Nathan, 25:141
    Susanna, 25:45, 138, 140
    Walter, 25:141
    William, 25:141
GREENWOOD
    Irving, 24:182, 188
    Susan M., 21:108
GREGG
    Daniel, 22:235-237
    Daniel Hopkins, 22:235
    Mary, 22:236
    Mary (___), 22:235-237
    Thomas, 22:237
GREGORY
    Joseph, 23:145, 150
    Pope, 22:108
GRENDELL
    Effie Blanche, 24:20
GRENHAM
    John, 25:65, 121
GRENLAND see GREENLAND
GRENLEFF
    Steven, 25:102
GRESLON
    Genevieve, 22:200
GREY
    Benjamin, 21:153
    Charlotte, 24:20
    Sarah (___), 21:153

GRICE
    Martha (Nazro), 21:33
    Samuel, 21:33
GRIEBEL
    Dorothea R., 21:175
GRIFFEN/GRIFFIN
    ___, Dr., 25:60a
    ___, Mrs., 24:196
    Gustavus, 22:223, 233
    Humphrey, 22:36
    Lucy W., 25:195
    Mary, 21:238
    Patrick F., 23:16
    T. McLean, 24:196
GRIFFITH/GRIFFITHS, 25:65, 67, 68
GRIMES
    A., 21:208
    Alden, 21:208
    Mark, 23:145
    William, 25:170
GRIMES see also GRAHAM
    Alexander, 25:8, 10
    Sara (Lambert), 25:10
GRIMM, 22:80
GRIMSHAW
    William H., 23:137
GRISWOLD
    ___, Bishop, 23:32
GROSE
    Elizabeth, 24:210
GROSS
    Abigail (Young), 21:237
    Laurania, 21:239
    Thomas, 21:237
GROTTEN
    Thomas, 23:145
GROVE
    Edward, 25:29
    Mary (___), 25:29
GROVER
    Abigaill, 23:145
    Ebenezer, 22:223, 229
    Edmund, 22:112
    Nehemiah, 22:112
GUALTER
    Thomas, 25:8
GUILD/GUILE/GILD
    Curtis, 21:209
    Ephraim, 22:162
    Martha (Bradley), 22:162
    Mehitabel, 22:162
    Samuel, 22:162
GUILFORD
    Joan S., 25:7
GUINIVAN
    ___, Miss, 21:21, 228
GUINN
    Abigail, 22:176
    Clarissa, 22:176
    Edward, 22:235, 236
    Hannah, 22:176
    James, 22:176
    Josiah, 22:176
    Marcy (___), 22:235
    Mercy (___), 22:176, 235, 236
    Rachel, 22:176
    Thaddeus, 22:176, 235, 236
    William, 22:235
GULLISON
    Henry, 23:145
GULLIVER
    Sophia, 21:53
GUN/GUNN
    Daniel, 25:9
    W.T.J., 24:67

GUNNISON
    John, 22:236
GURDEAN see JOURDAN, 25:8
GURNEY
    Samuel, 25:19
    Sarah (Atkins), 25:19
GUSCIORA
    Diane, 25:108
GUSTAVUS
    Duke, 24:68
GUTENBERG, 25:63
GUTHERIE/GUTHRIE
    Walter, 23:200
    Woodie, 24:60
GUTTERSON
    Lydia, 21:59
    Lydia (Stevens), 24:44
    Samuel, 24:44

HACKER
    Sallie, 25:148
HADDOCK
    Benjamin, 25:83
    Phebe (___), 25:83
HADLEY
    George, 25:8, 9
HADLOCK
    Samuell, 23:145
HAFFIELD, 24:141
    ___, Goodwife, 24:140
HAGATTE
    James, 23:145
HAGE
    James, 25:8, 10
HAGELBERT
    E., 24:69
HAGGETT/HAGGET
    Deborah (Stevens), 24:84
    Jacob, 24:84
    John, 24:104
    Sarah (___), 24:104
HALE, 22:20
    ___, Justice, 21:145
    Anne, 22:96
    Bradford, 23:145
    Catherine (Boutel), 21:215
    Charles, 21:208
    Edward Everett, 24:41
    Eunice, 22:97
    Hepzibah, 22:96
    Jacob, 22:96, 172
    Jane, 22:97
    John, 22:96
    Martha, 24:96
    Mary, 22:96, 165, 167
    Mary (___), 22:172
    Mary (Silver), 22:96
    Oliver, 21:215
    Rebecca, 22:96
    Richard, 22:96
    Robert, 23:118
    Samuel, 22:96
    Sarah, 22:96
    Sarah (Jaques), 22:96
    Stephen, 22:96, 172
    Thos., 21:114
HALIBURTON
    Thomas, 22:70
HALL
    Aaron, 22:223, 227; 23:146
    Deliverance, 22:190
    Dixon, 23:42
    Edward, 21:30, 210
    Elizabeth, 21:30
    Elizabeth (Rand), 21:30
    Ephraim, 21:30

Gordon, 25:60a
Henry, 22:206
Isaac, 21:30
Jacob, 22:172
Joseph, 21:30
Mary (___), 22:172
Mehitable, 22:218
Moses, 22:163
Nathaniel, 21:30
Polly, 22:172
Prince, 25:175, 176
Richard, 21:30
Samuel, 21:30; 23:54
Sarah, 21:30
Sarah (___), 21:30
Sarah (Johnson), 22:162, 163
Sarah (Rand), 21:30
Thomas, 23:146
William, 23:7, 8, 16
Zechariah, 21:30
HALLER
James, 24:186
HALLOWELL
Benjamin, 21:71
Mary, 21:71
Theophilus, 22:49
William, 21:71
HALLY
Shiply, 23:146
HAMILTON, 21:136
Alexander, 21:180a
Ludovine, 22:48, 50
HAMILTON-EDWARDS
Gerald, 23:85
HAMLIN
Africa, 25:195
Alfred, 25:199
America, 25:199
Asia, 25:199
Europe, 25:199
Hannibal, 25:199
John Chase, 25:195
Lydia (Chase), 25:195
Marie Antoinette, 25:199
Martha, 25:200
Martha D. (Nichols), 25:195
Nancy (Smith), 25:195
HAMMATT, 22:159; 23:163
Abraham, 22:161; 23:163
HAMMOND
Bethia (Blaney), 23:208
Richard, 23:208
HAMPSON
John W., 21:180
Olive (Clough), 21:180
HAMSON
John, 23:146
HANAFORD
___, Rev., 25:13
HANCHET
John, 22:151
HANCOCK
John, 21:60a; 23:11; 24:79
Mary, 24:157
Nathaniel, 24:157
Prudence (___), 24:157
HANDT
O., 24:70
HANKEY
John, 25:58
Mary, 24:55
HANNA
Charles A., 23:85
HANNIBAL
Isaac, 23:146

HANNISON
Catharine Elizabeth, 25:153
Eunice (___), 25:153
John Saunders, 25:153
Sarah, 25:153
HANSEN
Chadwick, 21:88
HANSON
Arletta (Davenport), 24:19, 20
Hannah, 21:54
James, 23:188
John, 24:19-21
HAPGOOD
Mary, 21:151
HARADEN/HARRADEN/HARIDON/
HAREDEN/HARADIN see also
HARRADEN, 24:112
Andrew, 25:151
Edward, 22:153
John, 22:223, 230, 232
Jonathan, 25:151
Lydia Ann, 25:151
Martha, 21:238
Mary, 25:151
Sarah (___), 25:151
Sarah Hardy, 25:151
HARDEN
Ebenezer, 24:209
HARDIES, 25:44
HARDING
Ann Borden, 25:23
Hannah, 21:237
John, 24:102
Mehitable, 21:156
Warren, 22:198
HARDY, 25:38
___, Capt., 23:41
Alice Augusta, 21:107
Daniel, 25:37; 25:191
Dorkes (___), 21:59
Ednah, 25:139, 142
Elizabeth, 22:223, 230; 23:239
Enoch, 24:92
Hannah, 25:139
Nathan, 21:59
Phineas, 22:45
Prudence, 24:44, 92
Ruth, 21:59
Sally, 24:220
Sandra, 22:168
Sarah, 24:92
Susanna, 25:140
William, 22:223, 227-230
HAREDEN, HARIDON see
HARADEN
HARKINS
Patrick, 23:16
Thomas M., 23:18
HARLOW, 24:146, 147, 149
Jean, 25:108
HARMON
Lydia, 21:36
HARNDEN/HARNDEL
Esther (Parker), 24:157, 160, 161
John, 24:161
HARNEY
John M., 23:17
HARPER
Martha, 23:58, 105, 107
HARRADEN/HARRIDAN/HARRIDE/
HARRIDIN/HARRIDINE/
HARRIDON see also HARADEN,
22:118; 24:33, 109, 111, 151;
25:136
John, 22:232, 233
Mary, 23:164

Edward, 24:109, 147; 25:134
HARRIGAN, 21:18
HARRIMAN
Hannah, 22:178
Jonathan, 25:195
Sarah (___), 25:195
HARRINGTON
Lucy J., 24:174
Nancy, 21:141
Silas, 25:161
HARRIS/HARRISE, 23:212
Anna/Nancy M., 23:209, 211
Bethia, 21:44
Deborah, 23:165, 179
Elizabeth (Hazen), 21:44
Elizabeth (Rundle), 22:179
Frankie Warren, 21:107
James, 21:179; 22:179; 23:146
John, 22:167; 23:146, 187, 188
Louise Mary, 21:179
Mary, 22:179
Mary (Roach), 21:179
Mary (Russels), 22:179
Mary Widger (Tucker), 23:187
Mehitable, 24:92, 101
Nathaniel, 21:44
Robert, 22:179; 23:211
Sarah, 21:44
Sarah (Martin), 23:211
Sarah Frances (Bryant), 21:107
Sydney Bryant, 21:107
Thomas, 22:167; 23:146, 165
Warren A., 21:107
Warren Bertram, 21:107
William, 22:167
HARRISON, 23:185
Eugene Myers, 25:60a
Eunice, 25:153
HARROD
Benjamin, 24:43
Phebe (Stevens), 24:42, 43
HARRY
Robert, 22:30
HART
Adam, 21:216
Isaac, 21:212, 216
John, 23:59, 119
Lydia (Curtis), 23:59, 119
Mary (Whitrige), 22:158
Mary/Molly, 23:59, 119
Phebe, 21:31
Samuel, 22:47, 158
HARTLEY
E. N., 23:116; 24:26
John, 23:146
Samuel, 23:146
HARTOPP
Joan, 22:165
HARTSHORN
Benjamin, 21:219, 221
Elizabeth (Boutall), 21:221
HARTWELL, 24:48
Jasan/Jezan (___), 24:47, 48
Sarah, 24:47
Sarah (Parker), 24:48
William, 24:47, 48
HARVARD
John, 24:25
HARVEY, 25:23
"Infant", 25:160
David, 22:178
Dorothy (Barnard), 22:178
George, 24:16, 175, 231
Isaac, 22:223, 233
Joan, 24:36
Joseph, 22:178

Judith (Chase), 22:178
Martha, 21:161
Mary (___), 25:160
Sarah, 24:16, 175, 178, 231
Sarah (Howard), 24:16, 175, 231
HARWOOD
Jonathan, 24:163
Mary (Parker), 24:162, 163
HASCALL see also HASKALL, 22:159
HASELTINE
John, 22:167
Robert, 22:167
HASEY
___, Lt., 21:211
Judith (___), 21:211, 222
Judith (Jacobs), 21:222
William, 21:211, 222
HASKALL/HASKELL/HASCALL,
22:78, 113; 24:33, 141, 146; 25:12
Abigail, 24:16, 175, 231
Anna, 21:238
Anna (___), 22:176
Anna (Haskell), 21:238
Anna (Millett), 21:238
Anne, 22:180
B., 24:34
Benjamin, 22:223, 231, 232
Caleb, 25:136
Cato, 23:146
D. L., 24:34
Elizabeth (Goldsmith), 22:41
Elizabeth (Hardy), 23:239
Enoch, 25:136
G., 24:34
Hubbard, 21:238; 22:176
Ira J., 21:238
Isaac, 21:225; 22:220, 227
Jos, 23:150
Josiah, 22:220, 223, 232-234
Louisa, 21:224-226
Lydia H. (Foster), 21:225
Mary, 23:57, 239; 24:16, 89, 175, 231
Mary (Brown), 24:16, 231
Mary (Leach), 23:239
Mary (Trask), 23:239
Mary (Tybbott), 24:16, 175, 231
Noah Davis, 22:176
Philemon, 22:220, 227
R., 24:34
Robert, 22:41; 23:239
Roger, 23:239
Ruth (West), 23:239
Sally, 25:13
Sally R., 25:13
Sarah Ring, 21:238; 25:11
Stephen, 21:238
William, 23:239; 24:16, 147-149, 175,
231
HASKINS, 23:212
___, Wid., 23:112
Agnes (Stilson), 21:37
Bros., 21:208
John, 22:223, 227-230
L. M., 21:208
Leander, 21:207
Roger, 23:112, 118
Thomas, 21:37
HASSAM
John T., 24:208
HASSE
Sarah, 24:41
HASSELTINE see HAZELTINE, 25:60a
HASSEY/HASEY, 21:222
HASTINGS
Daniel, 25:167
Elizabeth (Edwards), 21:211

James, 21:59
Joseph, 21:211
Mary (Foster), 21:59
HASZARD see also HAZARD,
HAZZARD, 21:230
Anna Mary (Compton), 21:16
Annie Sophia, 21:16
Annie Wilson (Campbell), 21:16
Arlene Ryder, 21:18
Carol Nancy, 21:18
Dian, 21:21, 22
Dian Jeannette, 21:18
Edith Stowe (Moore), 21:16
Elizabeth Viola, 21:18
Eunice, 22:218
Evelyn Virginia (Foster), 21:18
Florence Ellen (Lefavour), 21:18, 21,
110, 223, 225, 227-220; 22:238
George Ashley, 21:16
George Herbert Owen, 21:16
George Thomas, 21:16; 22:238
H. W., 21:230
Harry W., 21:110
Harry William, 21:18, 20, 227, 230
Helen Marilyn (White), 21:18
Henry William, 21:15, 16, 228, 238
Jane (Bagnall), 22:218
Judith Marilyn, 21:18
Kenneth Foster, 21:18
Louis Albert, 21:16
Louise, 21:16
Margaret (Owen), 21:16; 22:238
Nelda Virginia, 21:18
Owen Ingersoll, 21:18, 19, 21, 22, 110,
227, 228
Roger Bennett, 21:18, 21, 110, 227,
228, 235
Ruth Lucretia (Currier), 21:18
Sarah (Bears), 21:16
Sarah Sophia (Gardiner), 22:238
Thomas Rhodes, 22:218
Thomas Walter Douglas, 21:16
Viola LeFavour, 21:17-19, 21-23, 110,
223-225, 227-229; 22:238
Wallace Currier, 21:18
HATCH
Nattie E., 21:106
Orrin G., 21:192
HATCHARD
Harriet Victoria, 21:53
HATCHER
Patricia Law, 22:197; 23:171
HATHERN
Hannah, 25:45, 138, 139
HATHORN/HATHORNE, 22:120a,
218
___, Wid., 22:205
Daniel, 24:190; 25:29
Elizabeth (___), 25:29
Eunice, 25:29
John, 22:217; 25:29, 103
Joseph, 25:29
Mary (___), 25:126
Polly, 22:174
Rachel (___), 24:190; 25:29
Sarah, 24:190
William, 21:85, 92, 113; 22:120a, 208,
209, 217; 23:240a; 25:96, 126
HAUGH
Samuel, 21:210, 222
HAVEN
___ (___), 21:156
Abiel, 21:159
Abigail, 21:159
Abigail (Barber), 21:155
Abigail (Barde), 21:160

Abigail (Child), 21:157
Abigail (Clark), 21:157, 160
Abigail (Mellen), 21:158
Abigail (Prentiss), 21:157
Abraham, 21:157
Amariah, 21:157
Anna (Stowe), 21:159, 160
Annah, 21:155
Anne, 21:155
Asa, 21:158, 160
Benjamin, 21:156, 157
Betsey (Ellis), 21:160
Beulah, 21:155, 157
Catherine (Dexter), 21:159
Clarke, 21:157
Comfort (Pike), 21:156
Daniel, 21:155, 158-160
David, 21:157, 159
Deborah, 21:156
Ebenezer, 21:157, 160
Elias, 21:158, 159
Elizabeth, 21:151, 153, 155-157, 159
Elizabeth (___), 21:152, 155, 158
Elizabeth (Bridges), 21:160
Elizabeth (Haven), 21:157
Elizabeth (Hitchings/Hitchins), 21:151
Elizabeth (Travis), 21:152, 156, 160
Elkanah, 21:155, 159, 160
Esther (Streeter), 21:158
Eunice (Aldis), 21:160
Experience, 21:157
Gideon, 21:156
Hannah, 21:150, 151, 153, 155-159
Hannah (Baldwin), 21:159
Hannah (Bixby), 21:157
Hannah (Hichens/Hitchins), 21:152,
154, 160
Hannah (Walker), 21:159, 160
Hannah (Ware), 21:157, 160
Hannah (Wood), 21:159
Hannan, 21:158
Hepsibah, 21:155, 157
Hepsibah (___), 21:157
Hepsibah (Haven), 21:155
Hepsibah (Rugg), 21:157, 160
Hezekiah, 21:157
Isaac, 21:159
James, 21:157, 158, 160
Jane (Gould), 21:157
Jason, 21:159
Jedediah, 21:154, 157, 160
Jemima (Foster), 21:156
Jerusha (Whipple), 21:159
Jesse, 21:156
Joanna, 21:157
John, 21:149-152, 154-156, 158-160
Jonathan, 21:152, 157, 159
Joseph, 21:150, 151, 153, 155, 158-160
Josiah, 21:158
Lois, 21:155, 156, 158
Lois/Louisa, 21:158
Lydia, 21:159
Lydia (___), 21:155
Lydia (Whitney), 21:152, 158, 160
Margaret (Marshall), 21:156
Martha, 21:152, 156-158
Martha (___), 21:159
Martha (Walker), 21:158, 160
Mary, 21:149, 151, 155-159
Mary (Ballard/Bullard), 21:152, 155,
157, 158-160
Mary (Eames), 21:155
Mary (Flagg), 21:157
Mary (Messenger), 21:158
Mary (Walker), 21:155, 160
Mary Jones (Jeronel), 21:159

Mehitable, 21:155, 158-160
Mehitable (Appleton), 21:156
Mehitable (Bixby), 21:157
Mehitable (Harding), 21:156
Mehitable (Haven), 21:155, 159, 160
Mercy/Marcy, 21:157
Micah, 21:155
Miriam, 21:157
Miriam (___), 21:157, 160
Miriam (Bayley), 21:158
Moriah, 21:157
Moses, 21:150, 152, 154-160
Nathan, 21:155, 157, 160
Nathaniel, 21:150, 152, 154-157, 160
Patience, 21:155
Patience (Leland), 21:155, 159, 160
Phineas, 21:155
Rebecca, 21:157, 159
Rebecca (___), 21:158
Relief (Child), 21:157
Richard, 21:148-154, 156-160; 22:212
Ruth (Baldwin), 21:159
Ruth (Gleason), 21:156
Ruth (Grant), 21:159
Samuel, 21:152, 155
Sarah, 21:149-153, 156-159
Sarah (___), 21:157, 158, 160
Sarah (Bridges), 21:156, 160
Sarah (Gould), 21:157, 160
Sarah/Sally, 21:157
Sarah/Sally (Haven), 21:157
Silas, 21:158
Silence (Winch), 21:155, 160
Simon, 21:159
Squire, 21:157
Susanna, 21:149, 151, 154, 156-158
Susanna (Carroll), 21:156, 160
Susanna (Drury), 21:159
Susanna (Newhall), 21:148, 160
Susanna (Towne), 21:155, 158
Susanna (Vail), 21:157
Susanna (Westol), 21:151, 152, 160
Susannah (Goddard), 21:158, 160
Sybillah, 21:155, 156
Thomas, 21:148
Zedekiah, 21:156
Zerviah, 21:156
HAVENS
William, 21:148
HAWARD see also HAYWARD,
   HOWARD
Nathaniel, 24:158
Sarah, 24:155, 158, 159
Sarah (Parker), 24:158
Sarah (Willard), 24:158
HAWKES/HAWKS/HEWES
___, Mr., 23:28
Abigail, 21:155; 25:147
Abigail (Farrington), 21:154
Abijah, 25:147
Adam, 21:88, 93, 153, 214; 22:21, 53;
   23:27, 109
Alice Augusta, 21:104
Anna, 22:53
Anna/Nancy (Atwell), 22:52, 53
Charles, 22:53
Daty (Pratt), 25:147
Eliza, 22:53
Elkanah, 21:153, 154
Eunice (Newhall), 21:154
Eva, 21:99
George W., 22:53
James, 22:53
James Russel, 22:177
Jerusha (Merriam), 22:53
John, 21:93, 95, 104, 153; 22:53

Jonathan, 21:153-155
Joseph, 22:53
Lydia (Wiley), 21:214
Lydia Robinson (Gowdey), 22:53
Marie Anne, 22:177
Marie Catherine (Dench), 22:177
Mary, 22:53
Mary Ann (McGarvey), 22:53
Rachel, 22:53
Sarah, 21:85, 86, 88, 154; 23:109
Sarah (Cushman), 21:153
Sarah (Haven), 21:153
Sarah (Hooper), 21:85, 87, 88
Sarah (McLaughlin), 22:53
Sarah (Newhall), 21:154
Thomas, 21:151, 153
HAWKINS/HOAKINS
Abigail (___), 22:44, 45
Abigail (Shore), 21:38
Agnes (Stilson), 21:38
Elizabeth, 25:201
Elizabeth (Humphreys), 21:38
James, 21:37, 38
Joanna, 21:38
John, 21:38; 22:44
Mary, 21:38; 23:40, 42, 43
Mary (Mills), 21:38
Priscilla, 21:38
Robert, 21:38
Thomas, 21:38
HAWKS see HAWKES
HAWLEY
Margaret, 23:213
Peter, 21:208
HAWTHORN/HAWTHORNE, 22:33
___, Maj., 21:211
Elizabeth C. (___), 24:121
Elizabeth M., 24:121
Nathaniel, 21:82, 93; 22:120a,
   215, 217; 24:121, 232a
Ruth, 24:121
HAYCOCK
Joseph, 23:146
HAYDEN
Charles, 24:224
Geo. E., 23:56
Granville, 24:19
Michael R., 24:61
HAYES
Ann (___), 23:146
Edmund, 23:146
James, 22:223, 227
HAYNES
Hannah (Harriman), 22:178
Mary, 23:146
Mehitable, 22:178
Thomas, 22:178
HAYWARD/HAYWARY see also
   HAWARD, HOWARD, 23:212
Elizabeth, 24:51
Henry E., 23:56
Jonathan, 23:91
Lizzie (Stevens), 23:212
Margaret, 23:177
Nancy, 21:134; 23:34
Nancy C., 21:206
HAZARD/HAZZARD see also
   HASZARD
Barbara, 24:197
Eunice (Rhodes), 23:117
Jonathan, 21:15
Robert, 21:15
Thomas, 21:15; 23:117
HAZELTINE see also HASSELTINE
Ann, 25:60a

HAZEN, 22:167
Elizabeth, 21:44
Henry A., 23:218; 24:46
HAZLETON
Thomas, 23:146
HAZZARD see HAZARD
HAZZEN, 22:135
Richard, 22:140
HEAD
Samuel, 24:171
HEADEN/HIDDEN
Andrew, 24:168
Sarah (Houstin), 24:168
HEAL
Edward, 21:44
Elizabeth (Pritchet), 21:44
HEALEY
Joanna, 22:177
Mary (Sanborn), 22:177
Mary Ella, 21:108
William, 22:177
HEARD
Augustine, 25:60a
Sarah/Sally, 22:119
HEARN
Chester G., 24:79
Susannah, 21:151
HEATH, 23:212
Asa, 21:77, 188, 189, 191
David, 21:77, 188, 191
Dina (___), 21:77, 191
Dinah (___), 21:188, 189
Enoch, 21:77, 188, 191
James, 21:77, 188, 189, 191
John, 22:26
Joshua, 21:77, 188, 189, 191
Judeth, 21:77, 188, 191
Mary, 21:77, 188, 189, 191
Miriam, 21:77, 188, 189, 191
Stanley W., 22:77
Susanna, 21:77, 188, 189, 191
HEBERT see also HERBERT
___, Mrs., 23:49
James, 23:49
Sarah (___), 23:49
HEDDEN/HIDDEN
John, 24:196
Mary, 24:166, 168, 196
HEDGES
R., 24:70
HEFFERNAN
Richard, 24:224
HELLIWELL
Ernest Hyde, 23:51
HELM, 21:9
HEMENWAY
Abigail (___), 21:157
Benjamin, 21:159
Elizabeth (Haven), 21:157
Ichabod, 21:35
Isaac, 21:157
Jacob, 21:157
John, 21:35, 159
Jonathan, 21:159
Joshua, 21:157, 159
Lucy (Stone), 21:159
Lydia (Trowbridge), 21:159
Mary (Rand), 21:35
Moses, 21:159
Ralph, 21:159
Rebecca, 21:159
Rebecca (___), 21:159
Sarah, 21:159
Sarah (Haven), 21:157-159
Silas, 21:159
Solomon, 21:159

HENCHEY
William H., 23:17
HENCHMAN
___, Mr., 24:158
Nathaniel, 21:95
HENDERSON
Joseph, 22:223, 230
Robert F., 21:52, 116
Thomas, 23:146
HENEREY see also HENRY
Sarah (Bishop), 22:109
HENFIELD
Anna (___), 22:172, 174, 175
John, 22:175
Joseph, 22:172, 174, 175
Joseph Hardy, 22:174
Lydia, 22:172
Sarah, 22:172
HENRY see also HENERY
Count, 24:68
John, 21:166
Roderick, 25:136
HENRY II
King, 24:68
HERBER/HERBERD/HERBERT see
also HEBERT, 23:49
___, Capt., 21:217
___, Mrs., 23:48
Mark D., 25:122
HERBORN
Michael L., 22:220, 234
HERRICK, 24:92; 25:182
Abigail, 24:136
Ebenezer, 21:180
Edith (Laskin), 22:58
H., 24:120
Henry, 22:57, 58; 24:120
John, 22:78
Jonathan, 22:174, 175
Linda M., 25:124
Lydia, 21:102, 165, 167; 22:57, 175
Lydia (___), 22:57
Mary, 21:103, 167, 168
Peter, 23:146
Polly (___), 23:146
Rebecca (Stevens), 24:92, 101
Sally, 22:174
Susan J., 21:107
Temperance (Slade), 21:180
Theophilus, 22:220, 223, 232-234
HEUSSLER
Abigail (___), 25:29, 30
Elizabeth (___), 25:29
Elizabeth C., 25:30
George, 25:29, 30
HEWES
Bell, 22:78
John H., 22:78
HIBBARDS
Jacob, 23:143
HICHENS/HICHINS see also
HITCHINS, HITCHINGS
Hannah, 21:160
Daniel, 21:152
Ellinor (___), 21:152
HICKEE/HICKEY
Patrick, 23:146
Nora M., 25:122
Walter, 21:123; 25:117
William F., 23:17
HICKOK see also HITCHCOCK
Betsey (Fletcher), 21:179
Durlin, 21:179
Maria Elizabeth, 21:179
HICKS
Lydia (Daggett/Doggett), 22:47, 48, 54

Zachariah, 22:48
HIDDEN, 22:135, 136
___ (Crockett), 24:166
Andrew, 24:165-167
Ebenezer, 24:165
Eliazabeth (Story), 24:165
Elizabeth (___), 22:136
Elizabeth (Jewett), 24:166, 167
John, 24:165-168
Joseph, 22:136; 24:165-168
Mary, 24:166
Mary (Chandler), 22:136
Mary (Cressey), 24:166
Mary (Hale), 24:165, 167
Samuel, 24:165, 166
Sarah (Houstin), 24:166
HIGGINS, 25:67-69
Edward, 23:146
Eleazer, 21:239
Enoch, 21:237
Hannah, 21:239
Laurania (Gross), 21:239
Mary (Atkins), 21:237
HIGGINSON
___, Rev., 22:216
Francis, 23:180a; 24:176a, 232a;
25:30, 156a
Hannah (___), 25:30
Hannah (Gardner), 25:30
Henry, 25:30
John, 23:240a; 25:30
Margaret, 25:30
Margaret (___), 25:30
Mehetabel, 25:30
Sarah (___), 25:30
Thomas, 25:30
HILDRETH
Abigail, 25:35, 39
Abigail (Parker), 25:144
Jeremiah, 25:144
Joseph, 25:83
Lydia M., 21:105
Mary (Herrick), 21:103, 167, 168
Phebe, 25:83
Richard, 25:39
HILL see also HILLS, 22:135
___ (Hartwell), 24:48
Abiah, 24:93, 102
Abigail, 22:55; 25:92
Abraham, 24:156
Anna, 21:105
Anne, 25:92
Catherine/Katurah, 23:146
David, 21:105; 22:178
Deborah, 23:224
Deborah (___), 23:224
Dolly R., 22:50
Ebenezer, 22:161
Elizabeth (Dike), 22:55
Elizabeth (Goen), 21:105
Elizabeth Greenough, 25:92
Frances, 21:41
Hannah (Ware), 21:157
Huldah, 22:178
Isaac, 21:159; 24:158
Jacob, 24:158
James L., 22:147
John, 21:159; 24:158
John Parker, 25:92
Jonathan, 24:48
Joseph, 24:52
Josiah, 22:78
Lydia, 24:210; 25:41
Lydia (Fletcher), 25:42
Mary (Haven), 21:159
Mary (White), 22:161

Moses, 24:158
Nathaniel, 21:157; 24:52; 25:42
Olive, 23:146
Phippen, 25:126
Ralph, 24:52; 25:42
Robin, 24:154
Samuel, 23:224; 25:92
Sarah, 24:158; 25:92
Sarah (___), 25:126
Sarah (Haven), 21:159
Sarah (Parker), 24:158
Sarah (Thayer), 22:178
Stephen, 25:126
Tabitha, 24:158
Will, 21:19
William Carroll, 23:91
Zebulon, 22:55; 25:135
HILLER
Joseph, 22:49
HILLS see also HILL
___, Mr., 23:115
C. C., 23:113
Charles C., 23:114
Deliverance, 22:191
Deliverance (Cook), 22:191
Joseph, 21:189
Mary, 24:156
HILTON
Mary (Moulton), 21:88
HILTZ
Benjamin Thompson, 25:152
Hannah (___), 25:53, 151
Jacob, 25:53, 151
Jacob Carter, 25:53
Joseph, 25:152
Mary Elizabeth, 25:53
William Searls, 25:151
HINCHMAN
Thomas, 24:153, 154
HINCKLEY/HINCKLY/HINKLEY
Elvira (Stevens), 24:97
Isaac, 21:229
Joseph, 24:97
Kathleen W., 25:122
Mabel Demers, 21:44
HINES
Henrietta (___), 23:126
Simian, 23:126
HINKLEY see HINCKLEY
HIRST
John, 25:30
Mary (___), 25:30
William, 25:30
HITCHCOCK see also HICKOK
___, Col., 23:210
HITCHEN/HITCHENS/HITCHINGS/
HITCHINS see also HUCHENS
___, Dea., 21:217
Daniel, 21:151, 153-155
Elinor (___), 21:151, 153, 154
Elizabeth, 21:151
Hannah, 21:152, 154
Joseph, 22:173
Mary, 22:155
Nanny, 22:172
Polly, 22:172
Samuel, 21:155
William, 22:172, 173
HITLER
Adolf, 21:138
HOAG, 21:173
Ebenezer (Emery), 21:172
John, 21:172
Jonathan, 21:172
Martha, 21:172
Martha (Goodwin), 21:172

HOAR
   ___, Sen, 23:114
HOBART
   ___, Mr., 23:237
   Benjamin, 21:179
   Dorithy, 23:220
   Elizabeth, 23:220
   Elizabeth (Ibrook), 23:220
   Elizabeth (Whiting), 23:220
   Jeremiah, 23:220
   Lydia, 21:179
   Margrett, 23:220
   Mary (Wheeler), 21:179
   Peter, 23:220
HOBBS/HOBS
   Abigail, 23:238
   Delivrance, 23:238
   Jeremiah Smith, 25:153
   Jery, 25:153
   Jevy B., 25:153
   Jonathan, 23:146
   Robert, 25:153
   Sally (___), 25:153
   Thomas, 22:38
   William, 23:238
HODGE/HODGES
   Benj., 25:31
   Chauncy, 22:189
   Daniel, 22:189
   Gamaliel L., 25:127
   Hannah (___), 25:31
   John, 25:31
   Joseph, 25:127
   Lucy (___), 22:189
   Mary (___), 25:31
   Philo, 22:189, 190, 193
   Priscilla (___), 25:127
   Ruth Ann (Bunnell), 22:189
   William, 22:189, 190
HODGKINS
   ___ (Winthrop), 25:156
   Abigail (Hovey), 25:156
   Elizabeth (Hovey), 25:156
   Eunice, 23:57; 25:156
   Grace (Dutch), 25:156
   Jacob, 22:223, 227-229
   John, 23:146; 25:156
   Thomas, 25:156
   William, 25:156
HODGMAN
   Edwin R., 22:78, 124
HOFF
   Henry, 24:176
HOFFMAN
   William F., 25:122
HOGAN
   Patrick, 23:146
HOGG/HOOG
   John, 25:9
   Mary, 23:74
HOLBROOK
   Hannah (Harding), 21:237
   Hulda, 21:239
   Lydia, 21:175
   Mary (___), 21:176
   Thomas, 21:176, 237
HOLDEN, 22:51
   Annie K. (___), 23:201
   Barbara, 22:22, 215, 164; 24:27, 105, 176
   Barbara A., 21:111
   Barbara R., 21:171, 195; 22:111; 23:53, 109, 167, 236
   Bridget (Atwell), 22:52
   Charles, 23:201
   David, 22:52

Elias Upton, 22:22
Rebecca (Upton), 22:22
Richard, 22:22
HOLDER
   ___, Mrs., 25:106
   Luther Moffet, 25:106
HOLDRIDGE
   Deborah (Elliott), 22:179
   Hopestill, 22:179
   Tabitha, 22:179
   William, 22:179
HOLLAND
   James, 23:146
   Polly (___), 23:146
HOLLARD
   Henry, 24:170
HOLLEY
   Elizabeth (___), 24:70
   Samuel, 24:70
HOLLINGWORTH
   Elianor, 25:182
   William, 25:182
HOLLORAN
   Peter C., 23:135
HOLLOWAY
   Hopestill, 21:176
HOLLOWELL
   Benjamin N., 22:223, 230
HOLMAN, 22:46
   Lydia, 22:174
   Mary Lovering, 23:51; 25:89
   Rachel (Skidmore), 23:92
   Robert, 23:92
   Seeth, 25:6
   Winifred Lovering, 23:169
HOLMES
   Ann, 23:235
   Elizabeth, 24:39, 41, 116
   Frank, 21:89
   Lydia (Parker), 24:210
   Obadiah, 23:168
   Richard, 22:167; 24:170
HOLT
   Anna (Stevens), 24:94
   Asa, 24:91
   Betty (Stevens), 24:89
   Caleb, 24:84
   Chloe, 24:44
   Chloe (Holt), 24:44
   David, 24:97
   Deborah (Stevens), 24:43, 90
   Ebenezer, 24:37
   Ede (McIntinre), 24:94
   Eliza/Elizabeth (Stevens), 24:43, 97
   Elizabeth, 24:84
   Hannah (Farnum), 24:37
   Hannah (Stevens), 24:93
   Hephzibah (Stevens), 24:90
   Isaac, 24:93
   Jacob, 24:94
   James, 24:38
   Jedediah, 24:97
   John, 24:43, 44, 90
   Joseph, 24:97
   Levi, 24:89
   Loammi, 23:146
   Lydia (Stevens), 24:91
   Lydia Farnum, 24:103
   Margaret (Dolliver), 24:94
   Mary (Merrick), 24:84
   Mehitable (Foster), 24:98
   Mehitable (Stevens), 24:37
   Nancy, 22:223, 232, 233
   Nathan, 22:26
   Nathaniel, 24:43, 98
   Nich., 21:114

Nicholas, 21:195, 199; 24:89
O., 24:43
Oliver, 24:43
Peter, 24:90, 94
Phebe (Bachelder), 24:89
Rebecca, 24:98
Samuel, 24:37
Sara (___), 24:97
Sarah (Thorndyke), 24:97
Stephen, 24:86
Susan (Wright), 24:43
Tabitha, 24:84, 94
Thomas, 24:91
Timothy, 24:94
Timothy Abbott, 24:94
Timothy Parker, 24:44
HOLTON
   Beatrix, 21:43
   Joseph, 22:57
   Sarah (Ingersol), 22:57
HOLUBAR
   Allen, 23:228
   Mary (Strible), 23:228
HOLYOKE
   ___ (Pinchard), 22:204
   ___, Mr., 21:29
   Edmund, 22:204
   Edward, 22:204
   Eliyesus, 22:204
   Sarah, 22:204
HOMAN, 23:212
HONEY
   Mary, 23:146
HOOD
   ___, Mrs., 22:77
   Jacob, 22:77
HOOG see HOGG
HOOKER
   Thomas, 22:184
HOOKS
   Abigail, 22:236
HOOPER
   Robert, 23:10, 11
   Sarah, 21:85-88
   William, 21:86
HOPKINS
   Daniel, 22:171-174
   G. M., 22:149
   Mary, 22:174
   Nathaniel, 22:171
   Stephen, 25:21
   Susanna, 22:172
   Susanna (___), 22:171-174
HOPKINSON
   Judith, 25:139
   Michael, 22:167
HORNE
   ___, Dea., 21:92
   Hope Braley, 24:108
HORRELL
   Sarah, 21:40
HORTON
   Benjamin, 22:235
   Hannah, 22:235, 237
   Hannah (___), 22:235-237
   Hariot, 22:235
   Lemuel, 22:235-237
   Mary L., 22:236
   Nathaniel, 22:235
   Rufus, 22:235
   Sarah, 22:58
   Sukey, 22:235
   William, 22:235
HOSKINS, 23:212
   Bennett, 23:146
   Catherine, 22:150

Christopher, 22:150
Henry Box, 22:150
Mary Green (Jewett), 22:150
HOTTON
See Hutton, 22:39
HOUDLETTE
Louis, 24:81
HOUGH
Benjamin, 23:146
Benjamin K., 22:223, 227-229
HOULTON
Abigail (Flint), 22:57
Elizabeth, 22:57
Henry, 22:57
HOURDEN see JOURDAN
HOUSTIN/HOUSTON/HUSTINGS/
HUSTON see also HUSTIN
Samuel, 22:220, 223, 228, 229
Sarah, 24:166, 168
HOVEY
Abigail, 25:156
Abigail (Andrews), 25:156
Benjamin West, 22:236
Daniel, 25:156
Ebenezer, 25:156
Elizabeth, 25:156
Elizabeth (Dennis), 25:156
Esther (Treadwell), 25:156
John, 22:236; 25:52, 53, 151
Mary West, 25:52
Melvil, 25:53
Samuel, 25:53
Susan, 25:151
Tabitha (___), 22:236; 25:52,
53, 151
William Caswell, 25:151
HOW see also HOWE
Abigail, 23:163, 164, 179
Elizabeth, 23:238
Ephraim, 23:237
Hannah (Haven), 21:155
Israel, 24:38
John, 23:237
Joseph, 21:210
HOWARD see also HAWARD,
HAYWARD 23:212; 24:155
Augustus, 21:101
Bengamin, 24:155
Betsey (Young), 24:116
Cecil Hampden Cutts, 23:226
Easter, 23:146
Edward, 22:47
Elizabeth (Gilpatrick), 23:119; 24:116
Elizabeth/Betsy (Young), 23:119
Ezra, 24:116
George, 21:101; 23:180a
Jacob, 24:155
Jason, 21:101
John, 24:116
Jonathan, 23:119; 24:116, 155
Loea Parker, 21:209
Lydia (___), 24:116
Lyman, 21:101
Marie, 24:155
Mary (Colby), 24:116
Micah, 23:119; 24:116
Molly/Mary (Tyler), 21:101
Nathaniel, 24:155
Rachel, 24:155
Rebeca, 24:155
Sameuell, 24:155
Sarah, 24:16, 175, 231
Sarah (Parker), 24:154, 155
HOWCHIN/HOUCHENS/HOUCHIN,
21:48

HOWE see also HOW
Elizabeth (Woolson), 21:154
Hannah (Hichins), 21:154
John, 21:154
Mark, 24:40
Martha, 21:155
Martha (Bent), 21:154
Mary (Stevens), 24:40
Samuel, 21:154
HOWELL/HOWELLS, 21:9; 22:135
___, Mr., 22:204
George Rogers, 23:226
Joshua, 22:140
William, 23:146
HOWLAND
Alice, 24:183, 185
W. R., 22:149
HOWLET/HOWLETT
___, Ens., 21:211
Susannah, 21:97
Thomas, 24:140
HOYT, 23:234
D. W., 22:177
David W., 25:197
Dorothy (Colby), 21:177
Elizabeth, 21:177
Jacob, 24:40
Sarah, 21:103
Susanna (Stevens), 24:40
William, 21:177
HUBBARD
___ (Whiting), 23:219
Hannah, 24:92, 100
Henry, 23:146
James E., 22:127
Jeremiah, 23:219
Persis, 21:215
Samuel, 23:219
William T., 24:19
HUBBELL
Carol, 25:106
HUBER
Joseph C., 25:124
HUBLEY
Claire, 24:223; 25:81, 108
Claire Marjorie (Wardwell), 24:226
Dale Lynne, 24:226; 25:108
Richard Elmer, 24:226
HUCHINSON
Hananiah, 22:45
Thomas, 21:216
HUDSEN/HUDSON
J. W., Mrs., 23:114
Elizabeth, 24:183-185
Ethel, 24:182-186, 188
Rebecca, 21:158
William, 21:148
HULL
Isaac, 22:140
John, 23:54
HUMFREY/HUMPHREY/
HUMPHEREY/HUMPHREY/
HUMPHRIES, 23:167, 169
___, Mr., 23:168
Dorcas, 23:167
Elizabeth, 21:38
John, 21:29; 23:120a, 168
Susan (Fiennes), 23:167
William, 23:146
HUMPHERY-SMITH
Cecil, 23:67
Cecil R., 23:86
HUNCKINS/HUNCHIAN see
HUNKINS
HUNGER
Elizabeth, 23:239

HUNKINS/HUNCKINS
John, 23:119
Lydia, 22:51
HUNN
Priscilly, 21:91
HUNNAWELL
Mary, 24:210
HUNT, 23:35
___, Mr., 21:48
Ann (___), 25:91
Ann (Weed), 21:177
Asa, 24:70
David, 25:91
Edward, 21:177
Elinor, 24:103
Eliza (Dennett), 24:103
Elizabeth, 25:182
Elizabeth (___), 24:222
Elizabeth (Hoyt), 21:177
Elizabeth (Redding), 24:222
Ephraim, 21:177; 22:91
Esther (Searle), 24:70
Eunice (___), 25:31, 182
Eunice (Stone), 21:177
Eunice S., 21:177
George, 24:103
Hannah, 22:92; 25:182
Horace, 22:177
Ichabod, 21:177
Jeremiah, 24:52
John, 21:71
John G., 21:46
Joseph, 23:92; 24:70; 25:182
Katherine (Acres), 22:91
Lewis, 25:182-184
Lydia, 22:173
Marie Antoinette, 22:177
Marie Antoinette (Towle), 22:177
Mary, 21:71
Mary (___), 24:222; 25:16, 183
Mary (Hunt), 21:71
Phebe (Skidmore), 23:92
Raymond, 24:103
Rebecca, 24:70, 83, 92; 25:146
Rebecca (Hunt), 24:70
Richard, 24:196
Richard M., 24:165
Ruth, 25:93, 183
Ruth (Todd), 24:222
Samuel, 24:222; 25:16, 91
Sarah, 21:71; 23:224; 25:31, 91, 184
Sarah (___), 25:183
Sarah (Crosby), 23:224
Stephen, 21:177
Susan (Mitchell), 21:177
Susanna, 24:70
Susanna (Frink), 21:177
Thomas, 23:224
Thos. D., 21:167
Vilma, 25:11
William, 22:173; 24:222; 25:31, 182,
183
HUNTER
Christian, 22:36
Elizabeth, 22:55, 56; 23:176; 24:136
Robert, 22:167
HUNTRESS
Robert, 23:146
HURBERDING
Michael, 23:146
HURD
D. Hamilton, 21:232
Hamilton, 23:159
Jacob, 23:7
HURLEY
Bernadette, 23:200

HUSE
Lydia, 24:83, 93
HUSSEY
Betsey (King), 23:200
Betsey K. (___), 23:201, 202
Christopher, 23:54
John, 23:202
Joseph, 23:200, 202
Nathan K., 23:202
HUSTIN/HUSTINGS/HUSTON see
also HOUSTON
Almira (Curtis), 24:72
David Thomas, 24:72
Effie Matilda (Gaylord), 24:70
Harrison Valeau, 24:70, 72
Louise Almira, 24:70
Samuel, 22:228-233; 23:146
HUTCHARD
Hannah (South), 21:53
Henry, 21:53
HUTCHINGS see HUTCHINS
HUTCHINGSON see HUTCHINSON
HUTCHINS/HUTCHINGS/
HUCHENS see also HITCHINS
Benjamin, 21:46, 48
Daniel, 21:152, 154
Elinor (___), 21:152, 154
Elizabeth, 21:46-48
Elizabeth (Farr), 23:168
Frances (___), 21:46, 48
Francis A., 22:223, 233
Hugh, 21:49
Ida Florence, 21:53
Isaac, 21:54
Jack Randolph, 21:49
John, 21:46-49
Joseph, 21:46, 49
Love, 21:46, 48
Nicholas, 23:168
Olive A. (Ward), 21:54
Samuel, 21:48
William, 21:46-48
HUTCHINSON/ HUTCHINGSON
___, Lt. Gov., 23:11
Anne, 22:240a
Benjamin, 21:214; 25:27
Elizabeth, 21:41
Israel, 23:89
John, 21:46; 25:188
June, 22:170
Mary, 21:39
Mary (Nichols), 25:188
Nathan, 21:214
Phebe, 24:96
Rebecca K. (___), 23:202
Ruth, 21:42
Samuel, 23:200, 202
Thomas, 22:69
HUTTEN/HUTTON, 22:104
Elizabeth, 22:37, 38, 40
Elizabeth (Kilham), 22:36, 37
Isabel (Story), 22:40
John, 22:37, 40
Margaret, 22:40
Martha, 22:37, 40, 41
Richard, 22:36-42, 103
Samuel, 22:40
Susanna (More), 22:36, 37
HYDE
Elliot J., 21:234
John, 24:94
Nancy (Stevens), 24:94

IANNIZZI
Marcia, 25:111

IBROOK
Elizabeth, 23:220
ILSLY
Wiliam, 25:98
INGALLS
___, Mrs., 21:29
Anna (Telbe), 23:51, 59
Anne (Tripp), 25:202
Deborah (Stevens), 24:41
Dolly, 24:88, 95
Edmund, 23:51, 59, 167; 25:202
Edward, 21:29; 23:169
Elizabeth, 25:202
Elizabeth (Stevens), 24:86
Francis, 21:148; 23:51, 167, 169;
24:39, 40
Henry, 21:29; 24:37
Hephziba, 24:40, 83
Jacob, 22:51
James, 24:37
John, 23:168; 24:41
Joseph, 23:146
Lydia (Stevens), 24:39, 40
Lydia Hicks (Atwell), 22:50
Martha, 22:51
Martha (___), 22:51
Mary, 24:35, 37, 38
Mary (Osgood), 24:37
Mary (Stevens), 24:37
Nathaniel, 22:47
Phineas, 24:86
Robert, 21:29
Sarah, 23:51, 52; 24:90, 99
William, 22:50
INGERSOL/INGERSOLL
Alice, 23:239
Ann (Langley), 22:58
David, 22:236
Elianor (___), 22:172, 173
Elizabeth (Bray), 25:127
Elizabeth (Gardner), 24:218
George, 23:162
Hannah (___), 22:173, 176, 235, 236
John, 22:173, 176, 235, 236; 25:127
Judith, 22:176
Mary, 22:235
Nanny, 22:173
Nathaniel, 22:235; 25:27
Phillip, 25:127
Richard, 22:58; 25:108a
Sally, 22:172
Samuel, 22:172, 173; 24:218; 25:127
Samuel Bridge, 22:173
Sarah, 22:57; 24:218, 219
Susanna (___), 25:127
INGHAM
Norman, 22:240
INGRAHAM
Margaret, 23:218
Sarah (___), 23:147
INNES, 23:86
IRESON
Sarah, 25:35
IRISH
John, 21:145
IRVINE
Sherry, 23:85; 25:122, 124
ISHERWOOD, 23:48
Hiram, 23:46, 50
Mary Catherine (Rhodes), 23:46, 50
IVANOV
P.L., 24:69
IVORY
Ann, 21:30
Ann/Hannah/Anna, 21:31
Benjamin, 21:31

Mary (Davis), 21:30, 31
Sarah, 21:31
Silas, 21:31
Tabitha, 21:30, 31
Theophilus, 21:31
Thomas, 21:30, 31
William, 21:30

JACKSON, 23:185
___, Miss, 23:8
Andrew, 23:13
Charles, 23:8
Christopher, 23:240
Deborah (Fifield), 23:240
Elizabeth, 23:239
Hannah (Tracy), 23:8
James, 23:8
John, 23:11, 240
Jonathan, 23:8
Joseph, 24:85
Margaret (Taft), 23:240
Martha, 25:25
Nathaniel, 23:11
Nicholas, 22:167
Patrick Tracy, 23:8
Susan (Johnson), 23:240
William, 22:167
Xena Christina, 23:240
JACOB/JACOBS
Benjamin, 22:27; 23:147
Daniel, 22:25
George, 22:20
Joseph, 21:31, 32
Judith, 21:222
Martha (Appleton), 21:222
Richard, 21:222
JACOBUS
Donald Lines, 22:188; 23:219; 24:61
JACQUES
Henry, 21:172, 195
JAMES, 23:85
Alwyn, 23:85
Ebenezer, 22:223, 231, 232
Edward T., 23:137
Frances, 23:146, 150, 151
Janet Wilson, 23:137
Sarah, 21:30
JAMESON/JAMIESON/JAMISON
see also TOMPSON, 25:9
Andrew, 25:8
Eliza T., 21:106
Ephraim Orcutt, 24:33
Susan B., 23:126
Thamezin, 21:156
JANSEN
Marie, 23:56
JAQUES
Betsy (George), 25:199
Henry, 25:102, 103
Sarah, 22:96
Theodore, 25:199
JASON, 25:120
JASONOWICZ, 25:120
JAYNE
John, 25:127
Priscilla (___), 25:127
Susanna, 25:167
JEFERRY/JEFFORDS/JEOFREYS/
JEFFREY, 24:25
Elizabeth (Cole), 21:92
James, 25:171
Simon, 21:92
JEFFERSON, 23:185
Thomas, 23:3, 11, 126
JEFTS
Elizabeth (Hayward), 24:51

Hannah, 21:117
Henry, 24:51
Mary (Parker), 24:51
Simeon, 24:51
JEMMERSON
William, 23:147
JENKIN/JENKINS, 24:217
Betty (Tyler), 21:99
Hannah (Curtis), 21:177
Jabez, 21:177
Joel, 21:187
Joseph, 21:237
Nancy, 21:239
Nanna/Nancy (Tyler), 21:99
Obadiah, 21:216
Phebe (Featherstone), 21:237
Sarah, 21:177, 178
JENKS
Abel, 22:176
Andrew, 22:176
Annis (___), 22:235-237
Annis Rilling, 22:235
Elizabeth (Darling), 25:155
George Washington, 22:236
Hannah, 22:176
Hannah (___), 22:174
Horace Howard, 22:237
John, 22:174, 176, 213, 235-237
Joseph, 23:109, 110, 155
Martha, 22:176
Martha (___), 22:176
Mary Orne, 22:235
Priscilla, 22:176
Richard Pulling, 22:237
Sally, 22:174
Samuel, 21:35
Sarah (Tyler), 21:99
JENNESS
Kelley, 21:229
JENNINGS
Benjamin, 24:84
Elizabeth (Stevens), 24:84
JERONEL
Mary Jones, 21:159
JEWETT/JEWITT
Amos Everett, 24:222
Elizabeth, 23:100; 24:166, 167
Elizabeth (___), 24:166
Frederic Clarke, 24:168
Isaiah, 22:220, 234
Jesse, 22:150
John, 24:166
Jonathan, 23:119
Joseph, 21:148; 22:167; 24:166
Margaret/Peggy (Richards), 23:119
Mary Green, 22:150
Maximilian, 22:165-167
Rebecca Hammon (Green), 22:150
Elizabeth (Parker), 25:93
Jedidiah, 25:93
JOANNA
Queen, 24:68
JOHN II
King, 24:68
JOHNS/JOHNSON, 21:32; 22:135, 236;
24:223
___, Capt., 22:37, 38; 23:26
Abel, 22:162
Abigail (Bessom), 23:210
Allen, 23:137
Andrew, 21:31; 22:236
Arabella, 24:176a
Bethia, 22:236
Betsy (Graves), 22:141
Caroline, 21:102
Charles, 22:236

Daniel, 21:29
Daniel A., 22:141
Ebenezer, 23:117
Edward, 21:33; 22:236
Edward K., 22:141
Eleanor (Edwards), 23:117
Eleanor Edwards, 21:120; 22:238
Elias, 25:91
Eliza Ann, 25:147
Elizabeth, 22:163; 25:5
Elizabeth (Dane), 21:88
Ephraim, 22:162
Esther (Stevens), 24:41
Francis, 21:88
Franklin E., 22:141
George, 23:210, 147
Hannah, 22:162, 163
Hannah (Clarke), 21:88
Hannah (Eaton), 22:162
Henry, 25:52
Isaac, 23:180a; 24:176a
John, 22:162, 223, 228-230, 236;
23:147; 24:41, 42
John Barry, 22:237
Joseph, 21:156; 22:141
Josiah, 24:36, 38
Lucy, 22:236
Lydia, 22:162, 163
Martha, 22:236
Mary, 22:162, 163
Mary (___), 22:236
Mary (Collins), 21:33
Mary (Cozzens), 21:156
Mary (Haven), 21:155
Mehetabel, 22:162
Mehitabel (Guile), 22:162
Miraiah, 22:236, 237
Misaiah, 25:52
Nabby, 22:236; 24:84, 94
Nathaniel, 21:155; 22:162, 163
Phebe (Robinson), 24:41
Polly, 21:120; 22:120, 25:155
Rachel, 22:236
Rebekah, 22:236
Richard, 21:31; 22:44
Richard B., 23:167
Sally, 22:236
Samuel, 21:214; 22:209
Sarah, 22:162, 163, 236
Sarah (___), 25:52, 236, 237
Sarah (Basto), 22:162
Sarah (Hawkes), 21:88
Sarah/Sally (Foster), 21:120; 22:218
Seth, 22:162
Stephen, 21:88, 120; 22:218
Susan, 23:240
Susanna, 21:87
Timothy, 22:169
William, 22:206, 209, 212
JOHNSTON, 22:81
Elizabeth (___), 22:80
John, 22:223, 233, 234
Moses, 22:80
JONAS
Linda, 25:121
JONES, 24:126
Daniel, 25:192
Elizabeth, 21:203; 22:179
Jennie, 23:172
John, 22:223, 233, 234; 23:147, 172
Judith (Elliott), 25:192
L. L., 23:56
Lydia, 21:151; 22:223, 232
Mary Elizabeth, 22:180
Peter, 25:31
Robert B., 23:56

Samuel, 21:64; 23:147
Thomas W., 22:200
JORDAIN/JORDAN see also
JOURDAN, 23:162
Alice M., 23:127
Ann, 24:55
James, 23:147
Lewis, 23:48
Mary, 24:161
Michael J., 23:17
William B., 23:161
JOSEPH
Peter, 23:147
JOSLEN/JOSLYN
R. D., 24:61
Roger D., 23:59
Sarah, 22:46, 54
JOURDAN/HOURDEN/GURDEN see
also GORDEN/GORDON,
JOURDAIN
James, 25:8
William, 25:8
JOURNEY
Thomas, 23:147
JOWDERS
Ruth Archie, 21:18
JOY
___, Mrs., 23:180
Mary (___), 21:240
Matthey (___), 21:240
JUAN II
Rey, 24:68
JUDD
David, 21:41
Martha (Preston), 21:41
JUDSON
Adoniram, 25:60a
Andrew T., 23:44
Ann (Hazeltine), 25:60a
JULIAN-JAMES
Carrie Mason, 25:14

KAHN
Bonheim, 23:126
KANADA, 23:150
John, 23:147
KANEB
Ginny, 22:169
KARLBERG
Britta, 22:17, 111
KARLSEN, 25:135
KAROLIK
Martha, 25:14
Maxim, 25:14
KARR
Nole M., 23:86
KAUFFMAN
Christopher J., 23:137
KEARNS
Doris, 22:169
KEASER
George, 22:204, 209
KEATING
Patrick M., 23:17
KEATON
Charles, 22:120
Levina/Lovina, 22:120
Sally, 22:120
Sarah Elizabeth (Gordon), 22:120
KEAYNE see also KEENE
Robert, 21:28
KEDDER see KIDDER
KEEF, 23:150
Constant, 23:147
KEENAN
John J., 23:17

KEENE see also KEAYNE, 22:135
  William Gerry, 22:140
KEHEW/KEHOE
  Annie M. (___), 23:180
  Bethiah (___), 25:127
  John, 23:180
  Lydia, 25:127
  Mary, 23:180
  Paul, 25:127
KEITH
  Huldah, 24:98
KELLAM
  Daniell, 22:36
KELLCHER
  J., 24:34
KELLEY see KELLY
KELLOCH
  Margaret, 23:119
KELLY/KELLEY, 25:73
  Abigail (___), 25:31
  Annis O., 23:211
  Edward, 23:126
  Hannah (Upton), 21:36
  John, 23:16
  Margaret, 21:179
  Mary, 23:180
  Oliver H., 23:170
  Sue, 25:204
  Wilfred F., 23:17
  William, 23:49
KELSAY
  Isabel Thompson, 24:71
KELTON
  Thomas, 25:8
KEMBAL/KEMBLE see KIMBALL
KEMP, 21:9
  Edward, 24:106
  Susanna, 25:85, 145
KENDAL/KENDALL/KENDLE
  Abigail/Nabby, 21:213; 23:147
  Augustus, 22:26
  Elizabeth, 24:70
  Elizabeth (___), 24:70
  Francis, 25:5
  Jabez, 25:35
  John, 24:70
  Jon'a, 23:147
  Rebecca, 21:221
  Rebecca (Parker), 25:35
  Ruth, 21:213
  Thomas, 21:210, 214; 25:164
KENDER
  Nancy, 25:153
KENDLE see KENDAL
KENDRICK
  Deborah, 21:52
KENISTON
  Allen, 21:90
KENNEDY
  Ruth, 24:19, 21
  Thomas R., 23:17
  William D., 23:138
KENNEY
  Ann (Putnam), 21:44
  Anne, 21:44
  Dinah, 21:43, 44
  Donald S., 22:100
  Esther, 21:44
  Henry, 21:43, 44
  Jemima, 21:44
  Jemima (Pond), 21:44
  John, 23:147
  Mary, 21:44
  Mehitable, 21:44
  Priscilla, 21:44

Priscilla (Lewis), 21:44
Theophilus, 21:44
KENT, 24:148
  Hannah, 24:115
  R., 21:114
  Rebecca, 24:83, 92; 25:95
  Richard, 21:111-113; 25:103
  Steph., 21:114
KENTON
  Eliza A., 24:221
  Mary Ann (Lufkin), 24:221
  Thomas, 24:221
KENWORTH
  Edward, 23:25
  James, 23:25
  John, 23:25
KEOHANE
  John S., 23:17
KEOUGH
  ___, Miss, 23:180
  Ann, 21:240; 23:180
  James, 23:180
  Mary (Kelly), 23:180
KERRIGAN
  John, 23:130
KETTEL/KETTLE
  James, 21:159
  Sarah (Haven), 21:159
  Jonathan, 23:59
KEVILLE
  William J., 23:17
KEY
  Francis Scott, 21:81
KEYES
  John, 21:33
  Mary, 21:32-34
  Mary (Eames), 21:33
KEYSAR/KEYSER/KEZER
  George, 21:209; 22:204, 208
  Hannah (Davis), 22:93
  John, 22:93
  Leon, 22:99
  Sarah, 22:93, 94
  Judeth (Heath), 21:77, 191
KIBEL
  Edward, 23:168
KIDDER/KEDDER
  Abigail, 25:43, 86, 91
  Alice, 24:43, 88
  Amos, 24:53
  Anna, 25:35
  Benjamin, 25:35, 91
  David, 25:35
  Elisibeth, 25:35
  Enoch, 25:91
  James, 25:35
  John, 25:33, 34
  Jonathan, 25:35
  Josaph, 25:35
  Lydia (Parker), 25:33-35
  Mary, 25:35
  Nathanill, 25:35
  Rachel (Danforth), 24:88
  Samuel, 25:91
  Sarah, 23:223
  Sarah (Hunt), 25:91
  Sary, 25:35
  Solomon, 25:91
  Thomas, 24:88, 104; 25:35
KIGGEN
  John A., 23:17
KILBORN/KILBOURN
  ___, Dr., 21:226
  George, 22:167
KILGER/KILGORE
  C., 24:70

Benjamin, 21:53
Drusilla Chandler, 21:53
Emma (Kimball), 21:53
KILHAM/KILLAM/KILLUM, 22:41
  Abigail, 22:88
  Alice (___), 22:36
  Andrew, 24:107
  Asa, 22:173-175, 235
  Austin, 22:36; 24:106
  Catherine, 21:36
  Catherine, 21:39
  Daniel, 22:37, 174
  Daniel Abraham, 21:224
  David, 22:173
  Elizabeth, 22:36, 37
  Elizabeth Gallop (Lefavour), 21:224
  Grace, 21:224
  George Washington, 22:235
  John, 22:173
  Mary, 22:173
  Mary (___), 22:173-175, 235
  Robert Leach, 22:175
  Ruth, 22:174
KIMBALL/KEMBAL/KEMBLE/
  KINBALL, 22:75; 24:172
  ___, Capt., 22:38; 23:89
  Abigail Tyler, 22:238
  Abraham, 22:57
  Augusta, 25:54
  Benjamin, 25:139
  Caleb, 22:57
  Catherine, 25:153
  Charles, 24:170
  David, 22:223, 227-230, 232; 23:147;
    24:36
  Dorothy, 24:92
  Ebenezer, 22:97
  Edith, 21:120
  Eliphalet, 25:54, 151-153
  Elizabeth, 22:57, 60a
  Elizabeth (Black), 23:179
  Elizabeth (Fowler), 22:40
  Elizabeth (Houlton), 22:57
  Emma, 21:53
  Eunice, 23:117
  Hannah (Parker), 25:138, 139
  Henry, 23:179
  Henry Thornton, 25:54
  Huldah (Cue), 22:57
  Huldah P., 22:57
  James William, 25:54
  Jemima, 22:97, 98
  John, 21:96, 120; 22:218, 236; 24:170
  Jonathan, 22:223, 227-233; 23:147
  Joshua, 22:236
  Lydia, 25:152
  Lydia (___), 25:54, 151-153
  Martha, 21:51
  Mary, 24:102
  Mary (___), 22:57
  Mehitable, 22:41
  Mercy (Dodge), 22:57
  Miriam, 22:41
  Moses, 23:117
  Moses W., 24:171
  Peter, 24:74
  Rebecca (Poor), 23:117
  Richard, 21:49; 22:37, 57, 58,
    153; 25:8, 10
  Ruth (Eaton), 22:98
  Sally Hasseltine, 25:151
  Samuel, 22:40, 223, 233
  Sarah, 22:236
  Sarah (___), 21:120; 22:57, 236
  Sarah (Eastman), 21:120; 22:218
  Stephen, 24:104

Thomas, 21:96; 23:147
Turner, 24:74
Ursula (Scott), 22:58
KIMPTON
C., 24:69
KINBALL see KIMBALL
KINCAID
Patrick, 24:81
KING
___, Mr., 21:30
Abagail, 23:203
Allen, 23:147
Amos, 23:200, 203-205
Andrew, 23:147, 154
Betsey, 23:200
Daniel, 23:167-169, 204
Elizabeth, 23:168
Elizabeth (___), 23:168
Elizabeth (Goldthwaite), 22:23
Elizabeth (Marsh), 22:23
Elizabeth (Walker), 23:169
Geo., 21:114
Hannah, 23:169
Hannah (Southwick), 22:23
John, 22:23
Katherine (___), 25:183
Lucy (___), 23:204
M.C., 24:72
Mary (___), 23:204
Mary (Marsh), 23:200
Mary-Claire, 24:72
Nathan H., 23:205
Patrick J., 22:135; 23:3, 18
Ralph, 23:168, 169
Rebecca, 23:200, 205
Rebecca (___), 23:205
Samuel, 22:23
Sarah, 23:169
Tabitha (Walker), 23:169
William, 22:23, 216; 25:183
Zachariah, 22:23; 23:205
KINGSBERRY/KINGSBURY
Aaron, 23:147
Felicia Doughty, 24:140
J. D., 21:95
KINNEY
Joan, 22:240
KINSMAN
___, Mrs., 24:196
John, 23:185
Robert, 24:150
William L., 24:196
KIPPEN
Priscilla, 25:11
KIRBY
Edward L., 23:18
KIRTLAND
Elizabeth, 21:30
John, 21:30, 149, 152
Mary, 21:30
Mary (Rand), 21:30
Nathaniel, 21:30, 152
Philip, 21:149, 210
Priscilla, 21:30
Rose (___), 21:149
Susanna, 21:149
KITCHEN
Elizabeth (Grafton), 23:231
John, 23:231
KITTREDGE, 24:102
___, Dr., 22:83; 24:98
Martha, 24:102
Myra, 24:101
Rebecca Adams, 21:105
KLAPES
Jeff, 22:170

KNAPP
___, Capt., 21:166
Maria Louise, 21:106
Samuel L., 23:16
Samuel Lorenzo, 23:13
KNEELAND see also NEALAND, 21:51
Abigail, 24:98
Edward, 21:51
John, 24:96
Martha, 21:51
Martha (Fowler), 21:51
KNIGHT, 23:152, 212
Alexander, 23:58
Ann, 23:168
Charles, 22:176
Ebenezer, 24:136
Elizabeth (___), 21:92
Elizabeth (Boynton), 24:136
Elizabeth (Pitman), 21:30
Esther, 25:25, 28, 58
Francis, 23:147
Hannah, 21:30; 23:58
Hannah (Rand), 21:30
Hannah (Tutty), 23:58
Jacob, 21:30; 25:25
John, 21:114; 22:187; 25:96
Joseph, 23:147
Mary, 21:92-94
Mary (Chin/Chinn), 23:209
Rebecca (Stevens), 21:30; 25:25
Reuben, 22:176
Richard, 21:114; 25:103
Sally (___), 22:176
Samuel, 23:147
Sara, 25:98
Sarah (Burt), 21:30
William, 21:30, 92, 210; 23:209, 236;
25:25
KNIGHTS
George, 22:223, 227
Joseph, 23:147
Parker, 23:147
Peter R., 23:135
Thomas, 22:223, 229-231
KNOGHT, 23:147
KNOULTON
Moses, 23:147
KNOWLES
___, Mr., 21:29; 22:208, 209
KNOWLTON
___, Deac., 24:111
A., 24:34
Abraham, 23:147
Azor, 23:163
Bethia (Edwards), 22:105, 107
Charles, 22:223, 233, 234
Churchill, 23:119
Elizabeth (___), 21:36
Hannah (___), 24:74
Jane (Rogers), 23:119
John, 22:36, 105
M., 24:34
Mary, 21:36, 37
Mary (Dodge), 23:119
Moses, 23:147
Nathan, 23:147
Nathaniel, 23:147; 24:74
Rice, 23:119
Susanna (More), 22:36
Susanna (Whitrige), 22:158
Thomas, 22:37, 40; 24:109, 112
William, 21:36; 22:158, 220, 223, 230,
231; 23:147; 24:109, 111, 142, 151
KNOX see also BROCK
___, Gen., 21:136
Andrew, 23:15

Elizabeth, 25:197
Henry, 23:10, 12
Lucy (___), 23:49
Thomas, 24:170
William, 23:49
KNUTTSFORD
Stephen, 23:147
KORONOWSKI
Sue, 22:195
KUNSTLER
James Howard, 22:159, 161
KURZWEIL
Arthur, 25:123
KYLE
Francis, 21:140

LaFAVRE, 23:189
LaMOY
William, 21:82; 22:116
LABANNAR
Louis, 23:147
LACAILLADES, 25:155
LACKEY
Richard S., 22:200
LACY
Maurice J., 23:17
LADD
Annie Rachel (Bessom), 23:211
Daniel, 21:144
E. T., 23:211
Lydia (Singletary), 21:144
LADISLAUS II
King, 24:68
LADLE see LUDDLE
LADY
Manfelda (Perez), 24:67
LAFAVOR/LEFAVOUR/LEFEVOR,
21:223
Betsy, 22:172
Edward, 22:237; 25:53
Elizabeth, 22:236
Elizabeth (___), 22:172, 173, 237;
25:53
Florence Ellen, 21:17
Grace, 21:17
Israel, 21:17
Lydia, 22:172
Nathaniel, 22:172
Owen, 21:18
Paul H., 21:223
Polly, 22:172
Robert, 22:172, 173
Sally, 22:172
Sarah Strickland (Benett), 21:17
Thomas, 22:237; 25:53
Thomas Hovey, 22:237
Viola, 21:18
LAHA
James, 23:148
William, 23:148
LAINHART
Ann, 24:228
Ann S., 23:123, 134; 24:161
Ann Smith, 21:63; 22:46; 25:137
LAKE
Mary, 23:227
Veronica, 24:224
LAMBERT
Benjamin, 21:12
Christopher, 22:175
David, 22:9; 23:77, 132
David Allen, 23:135
Francis, 22:167
Jennie, 24:77, 78, 81
John, 21:12, 13
Jonathan, 22:175, 176

Joseph, 24:74
Lydia, 22:176
Mary (___), 22:175, 176
Nathaniel, 22:175
Richard, 22:102
Sara, 25:10
LAMPSON/LAMSON see also
SAMPS0N, 23:151
Caleb, 23:148
Elizabeth (Bancroft), 21:212, 213
Joanna, 21:213
John, 21:213; 23:148
Joseph, 21:212; 25:166
Sarah, 21:213
William, 21:187
LANCASTER
T. Sewall, 25:13
LANDER, 21:10
Benjamin, 21:13
LANE, 23:161; 25:65
"Daughter", 25:11
Anna (Haskell), 21:238
Catharine, 23:221
Edward, 25:11, 14
Epes, 22:223
Eunice (Norwood), 25:14
Fitz H., 25:13
Fitz Henry, 25:11-17
Fitz Hugh, 21:238; 25:11, 12, 14, 15
Franklin S., 25:11
George, 22:223, 234
Gideon/Gidion, 22:223, 232, 233
Gustavus A., 22:224, 234
James, 23:148
Job, 24:52
John, 23:221, 222, 224; 24:171, 172
Jonathan, 25:11, 13
Jonathan Dennison, 25:11, 13, 238
Katharine (Whiting), 23:222
Margaret, 25:66
Michael, 25:66
Nancy (___), 25:31
Nathaniel Rogers, 25:11-13, 15, 16
Nicholas, 25:31
Oliver G., 22:224, 234
Richard J., 23:17
Sally (Haskell), 25:13
Sally R. (Haskell), 25:13
Samuel, 22:224, 231-233
Sarah (Haskell), 25:11
Sarah Ann, 25:12
Sarah Ring (Haskell), 21:238
Stephen, 21:238; 25:11
Steven, 25:11
LANG
Betsy, 22:175
Bridget (___), 22:171-176
David, 22:171
Deborah, 22:173
Edward, 22:173
Elizabeth (___), 25:192
Elizabeth P. (Elliot), 25:193, 199
Esther, 22:171
Hannah, 22:173; 25:152
Hannah (___), 25:127
Harriet, 22:176
Hasket Derby, 22:174
James, 23:148
Jeffery, 25:127
John, 25:193
Katharine (___), 22:171
Lowell Y., 25:192, 193
Lucy, 22:172
Patty, 22:175
Priscilla, 22:173
Rachel (___), 22:173

Richard, 22:171
Sally, 22:176
Samuel, 22:171
Sarah Drummond, 24:82
Thomas E., 25:199
William, 22:171-176
LANGLEY see LONGLEY
LANGLOIS
Pilippe, 23:215
LANGSFORD
Eunice, 21:161
LANMAN
Joanna, 21:237
LAPHAM, 25:198
Content, 25:188, 191
King, 25:191
Lucy (Barker), 25:191
LAPRIERE
Robert, 21:144
LARCOM
Anna (___), 21:98
Lucy, 21:82, 233
Modicai, 25:132
LARKIN
David, 24:186
Edward, 22:56
Joanna (___), 22:56
Sarah, 22:55; 23:176
LARNARD/LARNED see also
LEARNED, 22:45
Ellen D., 22:162
LARRABEE, 21:50; 23:35
___ (Mains), 22:43
Benjamin, 21:93
Elizabeth (Felt), 22:43
Joanna, 21:31
John, 22:43, 44
Priscilla (Townsend), 22:43, 44
Stephen, 22:43
William, 22:43
LARRANCE see LAWRANCE
LARSEN/LARSON
Rebecca, 21:79
Daniel, 23:148
LASKEY/LASKY
Elizabeth, 23:213
Hannah, 23:213
James, 23:213
Jesse, 25:82
Margaret (Hawley), 23:213
LASKIN
Edith, 22:58
LASKY see LASKEY
LASSONDE
Francois Bordua, 21:54
Maryann (Desranleau), 21:54
LASZIO II
Mag Kir, 24:68
LATHROP
George Parsons, 22:120a
LAUD
William, 23:180a
LAUGHERTY
Caroline Elizabeth (Rhodes), 23:46, 50
William, 23:46, 50
LAUGHTON
Thomas, 21:29
Thomas, 22:208
LAVENUKE
Mary, 24:55
LAWRANCE/LAWRENCE/
LARRANCE
Abel, 25:31
Abigail (___), 25:31
Amos, 25:84
Dianne, 23:148

Henry, 25:31
Joan (Antrobus), 25:201
Margaret, 25:202
Marie, 25:201
Mary, 22:47, 48; 25:31
Mary E., 23:96
Nathaniel, 21:52
Nicholas, 25:166
Polly, 25:31
Rebecca, 22:51
Robert, 23:162
Roland, 23:148
Sarah (Morse), 21:52
Sarah/Sally, 21:52; 22:52
Thomas, 25:201
William, 23:144, 148
LAWSON
Elmire Lasonde, 21:53
LAWTON
Heugh, 23:26
John, 23:23
Martha, 23:23, 28
LAYMAN
George S., 22:72
LEACH see also LEECH, 22:135
Alice (Ingersoll), 23:239
Anna, 21:41
Ezekiel Walter, 22:141
Hannah (___), 23:239
John, 21:59; 22:105
Lawrence, 23:240a
Mary, 21:42, 59; 23:239
Mary (Edwards), 22:105
Mary (Partridge), 21:59
Mary Hardy, 25:152
Robert, 23:239
Ruth Ropes, 25:152
Samuel, 23:148
Sarah (___), 21:59
LEADBETTER
Elizabeth (Haven), 21:157
Israel, 21:157
Martha (___), 21:157
LEADER
Richard, 23:110
LEADY
John P., 23:17
LEARNED see also LARNED
___, Mr., 21:158
Isaac, 21:188
Mary, 21:188
Mehitable (Towne), 21:158
LEATHE
Sarah, 21:213
LEATHERLAND
Elizabeth (Perkins), 21:59, 240; 23:58
Margaret (___), 21:240; 23:58
Rachel (___), 21:240; 23:58
Sarah, 21:120; 23:58
William, 21:59, 240; 23:58
Zebulon, 21:240; 23:58
LEAVER
Thomas, 22:87
LEAVITT
John, 25:154
Thomas, 25:154
LeBARON
Dian (Haszard), 21:21, 22
Dian Jeannette (Haszard), 21:18
Thomas Sullivan, 21:18
LeBLANK, 23:215
LeBOUTILLIER, 23:215
LeBRUN, 23:215
LeCLAIR
Cherie (Linane), 24:108

LeCRAS
Jeanne, 23:213
LEE
___ (Jackson), 23:8
___, Capt., 23:212
Abigail (Herrick), 24:136
Ann, 24:179, 187
Elizabeth, 22:218
Henry, 23:8, 17
Jacob, 24:136
John, 23:148; 24:140
Joseph, 21:135, 136; 24:86
Lillian, 23:56
Richard, 22:105, 107
Robert, 23:148
Sarah (Edwards), 22:105, 107
Seward, 21:165
William, 23:148
LEECH see also LEACH
John, 21:92; 22:58
Mary, 22:57
Sarah (Conant), 22:58
LeFAVOUR/ LeFEVOR/LEFAVOUR,
LEFAVOURS see also LaFAVOR,
FAVOR, 21:17
Abigail (Dodge), 22:218
Abigail Grace Elkins (Trefethen),
21:224
Alice, 21:224
Amos, 21:223; 22:218; 23:117
Anna (Delaware), 23:117
Blanche Bennett, 21:109, 227, 229
Charles Porter, 21:224, 225
Effie, 21:236
Effie Fettyplace, 21:109, 110, 223,
226, 227, 229, 230, 234, 236
Elizabeth (___), 25:53, 54, 153
Elizabeth Gallop, 21:224
Elizabeth Jane, 25:153
Florence, 21:20, 236
Florence Ellen, 21:18, 19, 21, 108,
110, 223, 225, 226, 228-232, 238
Frances (Simmons), 21:224
Frances R. (Simmons), 21:229, 230
Francis Hovey, 25:53
Grace, 21:19, 236, 237
Grace Strictland, 21:108, 110, 223,
227-231
Howard Richards, 21:224
Israel, 21:15, 18, 19, 108, 223-226,
229-238
John, 21:223, 224, 231, 238
John Henry, 21:224
Louise (Haskell), 21: 224-226, 228
Louise Haskell, 21:108
Lucy Ellen (Eaton), 21:224
Mary Ann (Richards), 21:224
Mary Ober, 21:224
Nancy (Woodbury), 21:223; 22:238
Nancy Augusta, 21:19, 21, 225, 228
Richard Merrit, 25:54
Roger, 21:19
Sarah Ellen (Bennett), 21:229, 235
Sarah Strickland (Bennett), 21:18, 108,
224, 226, 230, 234, 236-238
Thomas, 21:223; 25:53, 54, 153
Viola, 21:22
Woodbury P., 21:234
Woodbury Prince, 21:224
LEGGATT
Mary (___), 25:160
LEGRO
John, 22:213
LEIGHTON
Richard, 22:167
Rufus, 22:224, 234

Tobias, 23:148
LEITCH
Jannet, 21:52
LeJEUNE, 23:215
LELAND
Ebenezer, 21:155
Patience, 21:155, 159, 160
Patience (___), 21:155
LeLOURTE
___, Father, 22:67
LEMPESIS
Theresa, 25:148
LENDALL
D. H., 24:34
LENNON
Henry, 21:205
LENOR
Reyna, 24:68
LEONARD, 25:9
Henry, 23:110
Jack, 22:170
James, 23:110
Rachel (___), 24:220
Solomon, 24:119
William, 23:148; 24:220
LEONOR I
Reine, 24:68
LERVER
Thos., 22:167
LeSEELEUR
Jeanne, 23:213
LESENBE/LESENBY/LESSONBY
Henerie, 25:97, 98, 104
LESLIE
___, Col., 23:89
Alexander, 21:60a; 24:56a
LESSONBY see LESENBE
LEUKHART
Cora S., 21:89
LeVALLIER
Margaret, 23:207
LEVESQUE
George A., 23:135
J. L. R., 21:205
LEVINE, 21:9
LEWIS/LUIS, 22:204
Alice, 22:43
Alonzo, 21:89, 148; 22:44
Benjamin, 23:209
Eben, 22:175
Edmund, 23:210
Elizabeth/Betsy, 21:33; 22:175;
23:209, 210
Emma (___), 22:175
George, 22:43
John, 22:209
Mary (Cass), 21:44
Mary (Cram), 21:44
Mary (Cross), 21:44
Mercy, 21:37, 42, 44
Philip, 21:44
Priscilla, 21:44
Richard Alan, 24:62
Samuel, 23:86
Sarah (Errington), 23:175
Tabitha (Russell), 23:210
William, 22:175
LIBBEY/LIBBY, 21:36; 24:168
Chalmers H., 21:106
Charles Thornton, 22:43; 23:160;
24:217; 25:22
Henry, 22:44
L. E., 21:18
Lydia Alice (English), 21:106
LIE
Jessie, 25:204

LILFORTH
Thos., 22:167
LILLIE
George, 21:94
LINANE
Cherie, 24:108
Judith, 24:108
Phyllis Southard, 24:108
LINCOLN, 23:185; 24:148, 149
(Earl Of), 21:209
Alice/Allis, 22:224, 228-231
Ebed, 23:148
Mehitable (Frost), 21:71
Rachel, 21:215
Richard, 22:224, 227
Thomas, 21:71
LIND
Edmund G., 21:81
Edward, 21:71
LINDALL
Timothy, 25:18
LINDBERG
Marcia, 21:33, 63, 134, 209; 22:24, 81;
23:66, 109
Marcia W., 21:28; 22:43; 23:51, 169;
24:45
Marcia W., C.G., 21:148
Marcia Wiswall, 22:3, 134, 149, 168,
195, 204, 206; 23:115, 214, 215;
24:35, 83; 25:94
LINDSAY/LINDSEY
Bertha, 24:186
Eleazer, 22:48
LINNEHAN
Richard 'Skinny', 24:224
LIPSON
Dorothy Ann, 23:138
LISCOMB
Mary, 22:96
LISTER
Nick, 25:108a
LISTERNICK
Roselyn (Ratcliff), 22:195
LITCH
Caleb, 21:52
James, 21:52
Jannet (Leitch), 21:52
Jennet (Wingate), 21:52
John, 21:52
Marcy, 21:52
Marcy (Deane), 21:52
Rebecca (Upton), 21:52
LITCHMAN
Charles II., 23:138
LITTLE
Abiah (Clement), 25:56
Adaline A., 23:114
Alice (Poor), 25:56
Daniel, 25:56
Dody, 21:66
George, 25:56
George Thomas, 25:23
John, 23:15, 148
Joseph, 25:56
Mary (Coffin), 25:56
Otis, 21:66
Ruth, 21:180; 25:56
Thomas, 21:66
LITTLEHALE
Sybil, 21:59
LITTLETON
Elmer F., 24:123
Mary B. (___), 24:123
LIVERMORE
Betsy (Parker), 24:207
John, 25:37

Martha, 25:34, 37, 38
Mary A., 23:114
LOBEL
Bob, 22:169
LOCK/LOCKE
Jonathan, 21:156
Joseph, 21:156; 23:148
Lydia, 21:158
Martha (___), 21:156
Mary (Haven), 21:156
LOCKER
Lydia, 21:27
LOCKWOOD, 24:33
Mary, 21:229
LOGAN
John, 22:224, 227, 228; 23:148
Peggy, 23:148
LOMBARD
Bathsheba, 21:178
Rebecca, 21:178
LONG
Zechariah, 25:166
LONGFELLOW
Henry Wadsworth, 23:11
LONGLEY/LONGLY/LANGLEY
Ann, 22:58
John, 21:148
Mary, 21:149
William, 21:29, 149, 210
LONGWORTH, 24:120
LOOKE
Mary, 21:45
LORD
___, Goodman, 24:110
___, Mrs., 24:195
Abigail, 23:148
Alice (Rand), 21:28
Benjamin, 21:32
Elizabeth, 25:54
Margery, 22:36
Mary (___), 25:31
Mary (Ward), 21:28
Nathaniel, 24:170
Otis P., 24:195
Robert, 21:28; 22:40; 25:103-105
Thomas, 21:28
William, 21:92; 25:31
LORING
George B., 24:232a
Hannah (___), 25:53, 54
Mary, 21:36, 37
Mercy Gwinn, 25:54
Samuel, 25:53, 54
LOTHROP
Gilbert M., 23:17
LOVAN see LOUVAN
LOUD
Halah H., 22:76, 78, 79
LOUIS
Count, 24:68
Prince, 24:69
LOUIS IV
Alice, 24:69
LOUIS 16
King, 23:24
LOUISE
Nancy, 25:151
LOUVAN/LOVAN
Francis, 23:148
LOVEJOY, 23:212; 24:98
Asa, 21:116
Christopher, 21:116
Ebenezer, 24:98
Elizabeth, 24:93
Elizabeth (Phelps), 21:116
Hanna/Hannah (Stevens), 24:38

Hannah, 24:38
Harriet, 25:147
John, 21:195, 199
Jonathan, 21:116
Lydia (Nevins), 21:116
Mary (Austin), 21:116
Nathaniel, 24:96
Samuel, 24:38
Sarah (Russ), 21:116
Suanna (Rideout), 21:116
William, 21:116
William Nevins, 21:116
LOVELL
Mary, 21:120; 23:180
Thomas, 22:117
LOVETT
Bethiah, 22:55
J., 21:164
J. B., 21:167
John, 22:56
Mary (___), 22:56
S. P., 21:167
S. S., 21:167
LOW/LOWE, 22:135
___, Maj., 24:102
Caleb, 22:27
Daniel, 22:229-233; 23:240a
Daniel W., 22:224, 234
David, 23:148
Edward, 22:224, 230-233
Francis, 22:220, 227
Ivory N., 23:36
J. O., 24:34
Jeremiah, 23:148
Jno, 24:34
John, 22:220, 224, 227-233; 24:217
Jonathan, 22:220, 224, 227-231; 23:148
Jos, 24:34
Louise (___), 23:36
Patricia, 25:123
Polly, 23:148
R. S., 24:34
Sarah Jane, 24:97, 102
Seth, 22:137
Symonds, 23:140, 147, 154
Thomas, 24:28
William, 22:224, 231; 23:36
LOWELL/LOWLE
___ (Jackson), 23:8
Benjamin, 22:91
Eliza (Nichols), 25:189, 196
Elizabeth, 22:91
Francis, 23:8
Hannah, 25:191
Harrison G., 25:200
Jacob Washington, 25:196
Maria, 24:103
LUCAS
Deborah (Tyler), 21:99
James, 21:99
LUDDLE/LADLE
James, 25:8
LUEBKING
Sandra Hargreaves, 24:228
LUES
Isaiah, 25:21
LUFKIN/LUFKINS, 22:115, 118; 24:109, 110, 112, 146, 149, 151; 25:135
Aaron, 23:148
David, 22:224, 234
Lydia (Story), 23:57
Martha, 22:240; 23:57
Mary (___), 25:203
Mary Ann, 24:221

Moses, 23:148
Nathaniel, 23:57; 25:203
Rachel (Riggs), 25:203
S., 24:34
Sarah (Downing), 25:203
Stephen, 23:148
Thomas, 23:148; 25:203
William, 23:148
LUIS see LEWIS
LULL
Joanna, 25:155
LUNDIE
Alexander, 23:148
LUNT
Alice Francis, 21:108
Daniel, 21:112
Ella N. (Bryant), 21:107
H., 21:114
Jane, 24:89, 97, 98
Micajah, 21:107
Thomas Bryant, 21:107
Thomas Simpson, 21:107
LURVEY
Eleazer, 22:112
Peter, 23:148
LUSCOMB
Elizabeth Mansfield, 22:235
Hannah, 23:91
Henry, 25:153
Henry William, 25:153
Israel, 25:153
Lucy, 22:237
Martha, 22:236
Mary, 22:236
Mary Mugford, 25:153
Mehitabel (___), 22:237
Mehitable, 22:235
Mehitable (___), 22:235-237
Polly (___), 25:153
Thomas Balch, 25:153
William, 22:235-237
LUTHER
Nathan, 23:148
William, 23:148
LUTI
Vincent, 25:204
LUTTRETT
Sam'l, 23:148
LUTZ
Melinda, 23:164
LYNCH
Daniel J., 23:17
Francis J., 21:26
LYNDE
Amos Porter, 21:239
Esther, 24:160
Jabez, 24:161
Joanna, 24:160
John, 21:239
Joseph, 21:237; 24:42
Louisa Jane, 21:239
Mary (Porter), 21:237
Nancy (Jenkins), 21:239
Rachel (Parker), 24:157, 160, 161
Sarah, 24:38, 42
Sarah (Belcher), 24:42
Sarah Ann (Sprague), 21:239
Thomas, 24:160
LYNN
Ellen, 22:55
Priscilla, 21:40
LYON, 23:212
Hannah (Bessom), 23:210
Thomas, 23:210
LYTTON
Genevieve, 23:56

MABER
Dorcas, 21:39
John, 21:39
Mary, 21:39, 52
Mary (Allen), 21:39, 52
Richard, 21:39, 52
MACALL
Duncan, 25:10
James, 25:8
MACAULEY
Cornelius, 23:130
MacCALLUM
John, 25:8
Malcolm, 25:8
MACCARTY
Thaddeus, 25:167
MacCONGHAIL
Mire, 25:122
MacDONALD
Marion, 22:196
Marion A., 23:169
MACEY
Thomas, 23:231
MacINTIRE/MacINTYRE/
MACKINTIRE/McATEER see also
MACKENTIRE, 22:25, 30; 25:68
MACK
Harriet O., 24:195
MACKALINSTEN
Almister, 25:3
MACKANNELL
Daniell, 25:4
MacKAY
Donald, 22:71
Ed, 22:73
William, 23:9, 12, 16
MACKAY
Harvey C., 22:224, 231, 232
MACKCLAFLIN, 25:10
Robert, 25:10
MACKDONNELL
Daniel, 25:4, 5
MACKENNELL
Dan., 25:4
MACKENTIRE see also MacIntire
Phillip, 21:214
Robert, 25:8
MACKFARSON
Origlais, 25:3
MACKFASHION/MACKFASSE
Ambrose/Anguish/Angus, 25:8, 9
MACKHOME
David, 25:4
MACKILUDE
Murtle, 25:5
MACKINTIRE see MacINTIRE
MACKINTOSH see also TOISH, 25:9
MACKJLUDE
Murtle, 25:3
MACKWATER
William, 25:9
MacLEOD
Earle II., 24:224
MACMALLEN
Alexander, 25:10
John, 25:8
MacMILLAN
Alexander Stirling, 22:73
MACSHANE
John, 25:10
MACSHANE/MASKAM, see also
MASON
John, 25:9
MACY, 22:20
Thomas, 23:53

MADISON, 23:185
___, Pres., 21:194
MADOX/MEDOX
Judith, 22:224, 228
MAGDALEN
Duchess, 24:68
MAGEE
Bernard, 23:12, 13
James, 23:12, 13, 16
Pat, 21:130
MAGINNIS
Charles D., 23:17
MAGNER
James, 23:12
MAGOON
Benjamin, 24:98
Rebecca (Holt), 24:98
MAGRATH
John, 23:16
MAGUIRE
John M., 23:16
MAHER
Joseph C., 23:17
MAHEW
Eunice, 22:224, 227
Thomas, 21:169
MAHONEY
Carol, 22:170
MAIN
Abigail (Worden), 21:175
Ezekiel, 21:175
Henry, 23:148
Jeremiah, 21:175
Mary (___), 21:176
Ruth, 21:175
Ruth (___), 21:175
MAINE/MAINS
Elizabeth, 22:44, 54
Elizabeth (___), 22:44
Hannah, 22:43
Henry, 23:148
John, 22:43-45
Lydia, 22:46
MAINWARING see also
MANWARRING
Charles William, 23:220
MALCOLM
Daniel, 23:8, 9
John, 23:9
MALLEN
Alice (Carney), 21:53
Annie (McLaughlin), 21:53
Annie Theresa, 21:53
Owen, 21:53
Patrick, 21:53
MALONE
Robert P., 23:17
MALOON
Daniel, 22:171
Eunice (___), 22:171
William, 22:171
MANCHESTER
Daniel, 21:35
MANEY
H. Joseph, 22:195
MANN
Thomas, 23:149
MANNING, 25:168
Anstis (___), 25:31
Betsy, 22:175
Harriet, 22:175
Jacob, 22:176
John, 22:224, 227-230, 235; 23:149
Lucy, 22:172
Lydia, 22:174
Mary, 23:130

Nabby, 22:172
Rebeckah (___), 22:172-176, 235
Robert, 24:121
Samuel, 23:189
Susanna, 24:93, 102
Thomas, 22:172-176, 235; 25:31
William Tufts, 22:176
MANSFIELD, 21:34
___, Capt., 21:165
___, Goody, 21:92
Abigail, 21:32
Amos, 22:171
Andrew, 21:29; 22:204; 23:180
Anna, 21:32
Anna (___), 22:171
Bethiah, 21:100, 219
Betsey, 25:147
Daniel, 21:31, 214, 219
Ebenezer, 22:49, 50
Eliza, 25:54
Elizabeth, 21:32
Elizabeth (___), 22:206
Elizabeth (Whittemore), 21:32
Freelove, 25:152
Hannah, 23:180
Hannah (___), 21:219
Henry, 22:49, 50
James, 22:224, 227-234; 23:149
James S., 21:32
Joanna, 22:50
John, 22:50
Jonathan, 22:171
Joseph, 21:32; 22:50
Martha, 21:32
Mary, 21:32; 22:49, 50
Mary (___), 22:49, 50, 171
Mary (Newhall), 23:180
Mary (Norwood), 22:50
Mary (Rand), 21:32
Michael, 22:171
Patty, 22:171
Rebecca, 22:49
Rebecca (___), 22:49
Richard, 21:32
Robert, 21:32, 33, 209; 22:206
Rufus, 22:49, 52
Samuel, 21:29, 30; 22:49, 50
Sarah, 21:32
Susannah, 21:32
MANSUR
John, 24:102
Martha (Kittredge), 24:102
Rebecca, 24:102
MANUEL
Blanca (De La Cerda), 24:68
Blanche (___), 24:68
John, 24:68
Juan, 24:68
Juana, 24:68
MANWARRING see also
MAINWARING, 23:144
Edward, 23:149
MARBLE
Hannah, 24:89
Job, 24:86
Mary (Dow), 21:59
Nathaniel, 21:59
Nicholas, 22:157; 25:135
Ruth (Hardy), 21:59
MARCH
Anna, 24:164
Anna (___), 23:52
Anna (Telbe), 23:59
Frances, 23:52
Hannah (___), 25:192
Hugh, 25:103, 104

Isaac, 23:146
Jacob, 24:204
John, 23:52, 59
Marcy/Mercy, 24:164
Ruth, 24:164
Ruth (Bradshaw), 24:164, 204; 25:44
Samuel, 24:164
Stephen, 25:192
Theophilus, 23:52, 59
MARCHANT see also MERCHANT
Epes, 22:224, 231, 234
Henry, 22:220
Nathaniel, 24:220
MARGARET
Princess, 22:66
MARGERSON
Tucker, 21:208
MARGUERITE
Navarra, 24:67
MARIA
Duchess, 24:68
MARKELL
Myron, 23:139
MARLAND
Abraham, 23:23-33, 115
Harriet, 23:25
John, 23:23, 30
Jonathan, 23:23
Martha (Lawton), 23:23, 28
Martha Lawton, 23:28
Mary (Sykes), 23:26-28, 31-33
Thomas, 23:115
W. S., 23:31
William, 23:30
MARQUAND
John, 21:173
MARSH
Elizabeth, 22:23
John, 22:23
Mary, 23:200
Ruth, 21:39
Stephen, 22:224, 227; 23:149
Susannah (Skelton), 22:23
William, 23:38; 25:19
Zachary, 22:23
MARSHALL/MARSHEL
___, Capt., 21:210; 22:209, 212
Abigail (Cogswell), 24:31
Abigail (Parker), 24:49, 50
Benjamin, 23:149; 24:30; 25:135, 202
Bethia (Goodhue), 25:202
Ebenezer, 21:155, 159
Edmond, 25:135, 202
Edward, 21:214
Elizabeth, 21:59, 180; 23:57; 25:202
Eunice (Rogers), 24:50
George, 21:156
Isaac, 24:31; 25:89
John, 22:224, 228-230; 24:49-51, 112
John White, 23:159
Margaret, 21:156
Margaret (Marshall), 21:156
Mary Jones (Jeronel), 21:159
Mehitable (Haven), 21:155
Millicent (Blinman), 25:202
Prudence (Woodward), 25:202
Sargent, 21:209
Thankful (___), 21:156
Thomas, 21:29, 149, 152, 210; 22:211
Thomas O., 22:224, 234
William, 21:156
MARSTON
Elizabeth (Poore), 22:92
Hannah (Gould), 21:45
Jacob, 22:92
Mary, 22:92

Robt., 23:231
Samuel, 21:45, 199
MARTIN
Abigail, 24:40, 85
Bertha, 21:240
Betsy, 23:211
Charles, Mrs., 23:130
Dorothy, 24:40, 84
Dorothy (___), 22:43
Ebenezer, 22:97, 160
Elisabeth Puckett, 22:160
Elizabeth (___), 22:97
Ephraim, 22:97
George, 23:54
John, 22:97; 24:36
Jonathan, 22:97; 24:42
Joseph, 23:214
Joshua, 22:97
Mary (Bessom), 23:214
Nathaniel, 22:97
Richard, 22:43
Ruth (Silver), 22:97
Samuel, 22:97; 24:170
Sarah, 23:211
Solomon, 21:199
Susannah, 23:54
MARTINO
Carolyn, 21:33
MARTON
Nancy, 23:209
MARY
Duchess, 24:68
MASHOONE see MASON
MASKAM see MACSHANE, 25:9
MASON/MASHOONE/SHENN see
also MACSHANE, 25:10
___, Capt., 21:24; 24:56a
Alphonso, 22:224, 234
David, 23:149
John, 22:221, 224, 228, 230-234;
25:9, 10
Joseph, 23:149
Lowell, 22:60a
Sidney, 25:14
Thomas, 23:149
MASSASOIT
___, Chief, 22:204
MASSEY, 23:111
Jeffrey, 23:149
John, 23:112, 118
Martha (___), 23:149
Nathaniel, 23:118
MASURY
Mary (___), 25:32
William, 25:32
MATHER, 24:126
Cotton, 21:195, 203; 22:165; 24:25
Nathanael, 25:32
MATHEWS, 22:140
___ (Bown), 22:185
___, Mr., 22:185
Adelaide, 22:184
Barbara J., 22:183, 200
Betsy, 22:186
Carol Nancy (Haszard), 21:18
Daniel, 21:149
Emily (Warden), 22:185, 186, 193
Irene, 22:186
William Charles, 21:18
MATIGNON/MATIGON
___, Fr., 21:204; 23:12
MATTHEOU
Antonia S., 25:123
MAUGER
Catherine (___), 22:119
Elizabeth/Eliza, 22:119

Philip, 22:119
MAULE
Thomas, 22:215-217
MAUMENEE
I. H., 24:62
MAXCY/MAXE/MAXEY, 25:169
Alexander, 25:8, 10
Margaret, 22:44, 45, 54
MAXWELL, 23:212
MAY
Anne (Errington), 23:175
John, 23:175
John Joseph, 23:223
Samuel Pearce, 25:22
MAYER
___, Mr., 25:108
Edith, 25:81
Irene Gladys, 25:81
Lance, 25:204
Louis B., 25:82, 108, 202
Louis Burt, 25:81
Margaret (Shenberg), 25:81
MAYES
James, 23:15
MAYHEW, 25:19
___, Mrs., 23:149
MAYNARD
Mehetable, 21:155
Susan, 24:179
Susan, 24:187
MAYNES
Thomas, 22:44
McALLISTER
Jim, 21:60a
McATEER see **MacINTIRE**
Annie (Quinn), 25:68
Elizabeth, 25:70
Hughie, 25:70
James, 25:68
Mary, 25:68
Michael, 25:68
McCALLION
Donald J., 23:18
McCALLUM
Alexander, 23:64
Black Duncan, 23:64
Duncan, 23:64
Red Alex, 23:64
McCARTHY, 25:74
Richard, 21:81
McCLEARY
Daniel, 24:38, 39
Ruth (Stevens), 24:38
McCLURE, 21:9
Rhonda, 21:7
McCOBB
David P., 21:154
McCUE
John, 23:149
McDANELS/McDANIEL, 23:144
Paul, 23:149
William, 23:149
McDERMOTT
James F., 23:17
McDONOUGH
Daniel, 22:187
John L., 23:17
McEACHERN/McEARCHERN
Grace Carolyn, 23:101, 106
McFALL
Daniel, 23:15
McFARLAND
___, Capt., 24:95
Susanna (Stevens), 24:95
McGARVEY
Mary Ann, 22:53

- 49 -

McGLENEN
 Edward W., 23:226; 24:161; 25:92
McGOWAN
 Hannah, 24:116
McGREGOR, 23:70
McGUINNESS
 Marilyn B. (___), 25:149
McHONEY
 Mary, 23:146, 149, 153
McHUGH
 Terrence, 23:16
McINTINRE/McINTIRE/McINTYRE
 see also MacINTIRE, 22:30, 31, 33,
  34
 Ede, 24:94
 Elizabeth (___), 25:127
 Hannah, 25:127
 Joseph, 25:127
 Micum, 22:31
 Philip, 22:30-32
 Samuel, 21:180a; 22:32, 33; 24:232a;
  25:127, 128
 Stuart A., 22:29
McINTOSH
 ___, Maj., 22:130
McINTYRE see McINTINRE
McISSAC
 Daniel V., 23:17
McKAY
 T. A., 25:17, 23. 24
 William P., 23:16
McKEENE
 John, 21:69
McKENNA see also MICKENNA
 Francis, 23:16
McKEOWIN
 Wilson, 22:126
McKINSTRY
 Mary (Towne), 21:158
 Theodore, 21:158
McKUSICK
 Victor A., 24:59, 61
McLANE
 Jas. A., 23:56
 M., 21:208
McLAUGHLIN
 Annie, 21:53
 Edward A., 23:17
 Margaret (Whitney), 21:54
 Patrick, 21:53
 Sarah, 22:53
McLEAN
 Calvin B., 22:79
McLENNAN, 23:70
McLEOD
 Mordecai, 25:5
McLOLIN
 Abigail (___), 23:149
 Lorance, 23:149
McMAHON
 Patrick, 25:67
McNAMARON
 Hugh, 23:149
McPHERSON, 23:68
 Alexander, 23:69, 70, 72
 Ann McCallum, 23:68, 71, 72
 Annie, 23:69
 Robina (Ross), 23:68, 69, 72
McQUSTON
 Anna (Osgood), 24:215
 William, 24:215
McRAY
 Nancy, 24:96
McVANN
 Hannah (Riley), 22:120
 James Edward, 22:120

 John, 22:120
MEACHUM
 Jeremiah, 22:24
 Sarah, 22:24
MEAGHER
 Timothy J., 25:122
MEARS
 D., 24:34
 John, 23:149; 24:215
 S., 24:34
 Sarah (Parker), 24:215
 W. H., 24:34
MEDCALF, 23:164
 Abigail, 23:163, 179
 Abigail (___), 23:163
 Joseph, 23:163
 Lydia (Black), 23:163, 179
 Rebecca (___), 23:163
 Thomas, 23:163, 179
MEDOX
 Judith, 22:228, 229
MEEK
 Henry M., 24:122, 123
MEEME/MEENY see MINNS
MEIER/MEIR
 Frederick A., 21:140
 Eliezer, 25:81
MEKAS, 21:230
MELLEN/MELLON
 Abigail, 21:158
 Mary B. (___), 25:13
 Elizabeth (Fisk), 21:154
 Esther (Towne), 21:154
 Simon, 21:154
 Susanna (Haven), 21:149, 154
MELNYK
 Marcia, 21:3, 78; 22:3, 9
 Marcia (Iannizzi), 25:111
MELOIN
 Samuel, 24:171
MELVILL/MELVILLE
 Hannah, 25:52
 John, 21:13
MEMORS
 Thomas, 21:213
MENDELSSOHN, 23:56
MENDON
 George, 25:18
MENSEY
 John, 23:149
MERCHANT see also MARCHANT
 E. W., 21:207
 Henry, 22:331, 233, 234
MERIEL
 ___, Fr., 22:95
MERRIAM
 Ebenezer, 22:213
 Jerusha, 22:53
MERRICK/MERRICKE
 ___, Mrs., 25:102
 James, 25:102
 Mary, 24:84
MERRILL, 21:19
 ___, Mrs., 21:20
 Amos, 23:113, 114
 Anne Maria, 23:211
 Fred W., 23:53
 Jane, 24:100
 Joan (Kinney/Ninny), 22:240
 John, 24:43
 Louis E., 21:18
 Mary (Stevens), 24:43
 Mehitable, 23:117
 Nathaniel, 22:240
MERRIMAN
 Brenda McDougall, 25:121

 Nathaniel, 22:191
 Sarah (Bartholomew), 22:191
MERROW
 Daniel, 21:214
 Henry, 21:212
MERRY
 Ralph, 22:49
 Robert, 22:166
MESSENGER
 Lydia (Rhodes), 23:43
 Mary, 21:158
MESSER
 Nellie Stearns, 25:60a
MESSINGER
 Lydia (Rhodes), 23:42
METACOMET
 ___, Chief, 22:204
METCALF
 Abiel (___), 21:159
 Abiel (Haven), 21:159
 Elizabeth, 21:212
 Hannah (Haven), 21:159
 James, 21:159
 John D., 25:18
 Joseph, 21:159
 Martha, 23:52, 59
 Michael, 21:159
MEYER/MEYERS
 August, 24:110
 Martha Pamelia, 22:161
MICKENNA see also McKENNA
 Daniell, 25:5
MIGHILL
 Ezekiel, 22:87
 Thomas, 22:165, 167
MILBAREY
 William, 23:143
MILES
 Esther, 23:180
MILL
 Thomas, 23:149
MILLER, 22:135; 23:212
 Alexander, 23:38, 39
 Arthur, 21:41
 Benjamin, 21:100
 Daniel, 23:38
 Eliza (Colton), 21:103
 Elizabeth (Murray), 22:80
 Esther, 21:100, 101; 23:38
 Hannah (Tyler), 21:100
 Hannah T., 21:100
 Jacob, 22:80
 James Lucas, 21:100, 103
 John, 22:137, 165, 167
 June, 23:136
 Lizzie N., 21:103
 Marinda, 21:100
 Mary, 21:100
 Newton C., 21:103
 Orra E., 21:103
 Peter, 23:149
 Prosper, 21:100
 Thos., 22:167
 Viola Smalley, 25:21
MILLET/MILLETT/MILLIT
 Andrew Stephens, 22:171
 Anna, 21:238
 Benjamin, 23:149
 Charles, 21:165
 Elizabeth (___), 22:171; 24:137
 John, 24:137
 Jonathan, 21:13; 24:137
 Joseph, 22:171
 Mary, 24:232; 25:203
 Mary (Greenaway), 25:203
 Nathan, 21:238; 23:140; 24:137

Rebecca (___), 24:137
Sally (___), 25:128
Sally Leonard, 25:128
Sarah (___), 24:137
Sarah (Babson), 21:238
Thomas, 22:224, 227-231; 23:149; 25:203
William, 25:128

MILLIKEN
Benjamin, 24:85

MILLIT see MILLET

MILLS, 22:135
Clarissa (Stevens), 24:100
Elizabeth Shown, 22:3, 200
Genevieve, 22:147
Hazen, 24:100
James, 21:191
Mary, 21:38
Richard, 22:183, 200
William Stowell, 22:41, 105

MILNER
Margaret, 23:240
Paul, 25:121

MINER see also MINOR
Ephraim, 21:176
Hannah (Avery), 21:176

MINNS/MEENY/MEEME
Robert, 25:9

MINOR see also MINER
Grace, 21:175

MINOT
___, Mr., 23:149
Christopher, 23:149
James, 25:92
Jonathan, 24:159
Susanna/Sukey, 25:92
Timothy, 25:92

MIRECK
Mary, 22:120

MISSERVY
Jane, 23:209

MISSUD
J., 23:56

MITCHEL/MITCHELL
"Child", 25:140
Abigail, 25:140
Abraham, 21:37
Alice (Parker), 25:140
Bathsheba (Lombard), 21:178
Ellis, 25:138
Frederick, 24:169-173
Hannah, 21:177; 24:170, 171
Hannah (Mitchell), 21:177
Hannah (Vickery), 21:177
Hannah L., 24:169, 172
Isaac, 21:177
Jacob, 21:178
John, 21:177
Joseph, 21:178; 25:140
Juda, 25:140
Louisa (___), 24:169
Mary, 23:66; 24:226
Mary (Knowlton), 21:37
Mary (Vickery), 21:177
Nathaniel, 24:169; 25:140
Noah, 21:177
Rachel (Parker), 25:138
Rebecca, 25:140
Rebecca (Cushman), 21:178
Rebekah/Rebecca (Parker), 25:140
Sukey, 25:138
Susan, 21:177

MOKOTOFF
Gary, 25:123

MOLLO
Denise Kovalchik, 25:186

MOLYNEUX
Nellie Z. R., 21:214

MONNETTE
Orra Eugene, 21:144

MONTANA see also COLMAN
Donald, 24:224
Helen (Wherett), 24:224
Lynn, 24:224
Paige, 24:224
Raymond, 24:224
Robert, 24:223-225
Roberta (Pandolfini), 24:223
Roy, 24:223
Ruth, 24:223

MONTANARI
Albert, 25:116
John, 25:116
Saturno, 25:116

MONTGOMERY
Robert H., 23:17

MOOAR/MOOARS see also MOORE, MORSE
Abiah (Hill), 24:93, 102
Abraham, 24:90, 95, 103
Annis (Stevens), 24:83
Benjamin, 24:93, 102
Daniel, 24:83
Hannah (Stevens), 24:103
Joseph, 24:100
Lydia (Abbott), 24:90
Maria, 24:43
Martha, 24:95, 103
Martha (Allen), 24:95, 103
Mary, 24:93, 97, 101, 102
Sarah (Stevens), 24:100
Sarah F. (Poor), 24:103
Stephen, 24:103
Susannah (Stevens), 24:90
Abraham, 24:44
Sarah (Stevens), 24:44

MOODY, 24:85
David, 23:85
Deborah, 23:167, 240a
Deborah (Dunch), 23:168
Engram, 25:9
George, 21:137
Robert E., 21:49
W., 21:114
William, 21:111

MOONEY
Thomas, 23:16

MOORE/DUNSMOORE see also MOOAR
___, Master, 25:11
Abraham, 23:16
Catherine (___), 25:55
Edith Stowe, 21:16
Enoch, 25:55
Eugene, 23:56
James, 25:9
John, 23:49
Lydia, 21:213
Mary, 23:231
Matthew, 21:145, 146; 25:9
Ruth (Pinion), 25:9
Samuel, 23:15
Sarah, 25:55-57
Sarah (___), 23:49

MOOREHEAD
John, 23:4

MOORES/MOORS see also MORCE, MORSE, 25:23
Thomas, 23:149
Zachariah, 23:149
Esther (___), 25:83
Joseph, 25:83

MORAN
John B., 23:16
Joseph, 22:170

MORCE see also MORCE, MORSE
Humphry, 23:149

MORE
___, Dr., 25:60a
Caleb, 25:32
Christian (___), 25:32
Christian (Hunter), 22:36
Jane (___), 25:32
Richard, 21:149; 22:36; 24:190; 25:32
Susanna, 22:36, 37

MORENCY, 22:33

MORGAN, 21:79
G., 21:9
George C., 23:19, 197; 24:75
George G., 21:191; 25:49, 106
Milton W., 21:206
Rainey B., 25:106

MORGRAGE
Hannah, 21:177

MORISON see also MORRISON, 24:54
Samuel Eliot, 23:8; 24:26

MORLAND/MURLEY, 22:167

MORRE
Thomas, 25:141

MORRILL
Abraham, 25:43
Alice (Parker), 25:138
Ara, 25:138
Hannah, 22:51

MORRIS
W. T., 24:61

MORRISEY/MORRISIE
Cornelius, 24:230
Denis H., 23:16
Hannah (___), 24:230
Thomas, 24:230

MORRISON see also MORISON
George F., 24:20, 21
Leonard Allison, 25:198
Villa (Davenport), 24:20, 21

MORRISSEY
Ann, 23:228
Charlotte, 25:58
David, 23:228
Edward, 24:55
Mary (___), 23:228
Mary (Ayres), 24:55
William P., 23:17

MORS/MORSE see also MORCE, MORSE
___, Dr., 21:18, 228
___, Goody, 22:21
Abel, 25:38
Abner, 22:76
Ann/Sarah, 25:38
Anth'y, 21:114
Benjamin, 23:120
Edward Sylvester, 24:232a
Ezekial, 21:156
Ezra, 23:149
Frances (Stevens), 24:100
Grace (Parker), 25:38
Hannah, 24:169
Isaac, 24:100
Joseph, 25:163
Mercy (Bell), 23:120
Minot Cobb, 25:23
Rebecca (Cozzens), 21:156
Sarah, 21:52; 25:89
Sarah/Mary, 25:43
Susanna (___), 23:120
Wm., 21:114
Zebediah, 24:170

MORTIMER
Philip, 23:15
MORTON
Marcus, 22:113
MOSES
Hannah (___), 25:32
Joseph, 25:32
Mary, 25:32
MOTTEY
___, Rev. Mr., 22:75, 78
Joseph, 22:78; 25:128
Mehetable (___), 25:128
MOTYLEWSKI
Karen, 22:16
MOULD
Elizabeth, 25:32
Mary (___), 25:32
Thomas, 25:32
MOULTON/MOUTON
___, Mrs., 23:149
___, Sister, 24:105
Abigail (Goade), 22:58
Ebenezer, 21:35
Ezekiel, 22:52
Hannah, 22:57
Hannah (Goode), 24:55
J., 21:35
James, 24:107
John, 22:93
John T., 22:207
John, Mrs., 23:114
Lois, 24:55
Lydia (Taylor), 22:93
Mary, 21:88
Mary (Cooke), 24:116
Moses, 23:149
Nathan, 22:93
Robert, 21:26; 22:58; 24:55, 116
Ruth, 22:178
Ruth (Emery), 22:178
Samuel, 22:103
Sarah, 22:93
Sarah (Keyser), 22:93, 94
William, 22:178
MOWER
John, 21:35
MOYCE
Martha, 23:54
MUDDLE
Henry, 25:132
MUDG/MUDGE
Anna (Breed), 22:50
Charles O., Mrs., 23:224
Edwin, 21:104
Francis Brown, 21:104
H., 23:155
James, 22:49
Joseph, 25:32
Lydia Nichols (Briant), 21:104
Lydianna Bryant, 21:104
Nancy (___), 25:32
Ruthe/Ruthy (Atwell), 22:49
Samuel, 22:50
Sarah Wilson, 21:104
MUDGET/MUDGETT
Ebenezer, 21:77, 189, 191
MUESILWAIT, 21:114
MULLABY
William, 23:126
MULLICHERS
Robert, 25:38
MULLIGAN
Gerald T., 23:18
Joseph I., 23:18
MULLIN
Mary Ann, 21:54

MULLINER
Thomas, 23:168
MULLINS
Priscilla, 24:114
MUNCEY
E. B., 24:61
MUNJOY
Mary, 23:235
MUNN
Donald, 24:226
Lavina Jane, 24:226
Mary Jane (Smith), 24:226
MUNRO
Elizabeth (Johnson), 25:5
Martha, 25:4
Martha (George), 25:5
Mary (Ball), 25:5
R. S., 25:7
William, 25:4-6
MUNSON
John, 22:188
MURASKIN
William, 23:138
MURLEY see MORLAND
MURPHY
A. Maureen, 23:18
Russell, 23:17
Thomas, 23:16
William, 23:149
MURRAY
Catherine (___), 22:80
Elizabeth, 22:80
Elizabeth (___), 22:80
Eva (Schneider), 22:80
George, 22:81
Hannah, 22:80
Jacob, 22:80
John, 22:80
Samuel, 22:80, 81
MUZEY
Joseph, 25:102
MYCRIST
Benoni, 22:187
Daniel, 22:187
Mary, 22:187
MYERS
Carrie Mason, 25:14
John F., 22:63
MYLES
Leo T., 23:17

NANCE
Grace (Bessom), 23:207-209
Joseph, 23:209
Margaret Bubier, 23:209
NAPOLEON, 25:171
NASH
Mary, 25:160
NATHANIEL
John, 22:74
NATHANS
___, Dr., 24:63
J., 24:62, 63
NAZRO
Martha, 21:33
NEAFF
William, 25:96
NEAL, 25:160
___, Mr., 23:190
Daniel, 23:15
David A., 23:184
Eunice, 25:152
Eunice (___), 25:152, 153
Jonathan, 22:174; 25:152, 153
Julia, 24:186
Mary, 25:152

Mehitabel, 22:174
Mehitabel (___), 22:174
Sarah Ann, 25:153
NEALAND see also KNEELAND
Edward, 21:51
Philip, 21:51
NEALE
Joseph, 25:183
Judath, 25:183
Judath (___), 25:183
NEEDHAM
Anthony, 23:59
Edmund, 23:169
Ezekiel, 23:169
Safah (King), 23:169
NEFFE/NEAFE
William, 25:97, 101
NEGRO
Abraham, 21:197
Candace, 21:197
Cato, 21:197
Dinah, 21:197
Dodo, 21:197
Isaac, 23:140
Jack, 21:196
Lydia, 21:197
Nan, 21:197
Primas, 21:197
Reuben/Ruben, 23:140
Simon, 23:221
NELSON, 21:96
Cynthia A., 21:107
Emma, 21:184
John, 21:208
Lynn, 25:123
Philip, 24:166
Thomas, 22:167
NESBIT
Hannah (___), 22:59
NEVENS/NEVINS
Lydia, 21:116
Margaret (___), 21:116
Mary (Ulrich/Woolrich), 21:116
Thomas, 21:116
William, 21:116; 23:149
NEWBURY
Susan, 23:177
NEWCOMB
Caroline Elizabeth, 25:195
Elizabeth (Tilton), 25:193
Luther, 25:193
NEWELL see also NEWHALL
Abraham, 21:28
Harriet (___), 25:60a
Joseph, 23:149
Samuel, 25:60a
Susanna (Rand), 21:28
NEWGAR
Abigail (Rand), 21:33
Peter, 21:33
NEWGATE
Mary, 24:54
NEWHALL see also NEWELL, 21:50; 22:135
Benjamin, 21:31, 32
Daniel, 22:49
Elizabeth (Mansfield), 21:32
Eunice, 21:154
Ezra, 25:77
George J., 22:147
Gertrude C., 25:94
Isaiah, 22:49
Jacob, 21:31; 22:213
James R., 21:89; 22:44
Joel, 22:47, 48
John, 21:29, 35, 95; 22:204

Joseph, 21:214
Josiah, 22:79
Martha (Mansfield), 21:32
Mary, 21:148, 175, 176; 22:50; 23:180
Mary (___), 22:49
Mary (Woodland), 21:148
Nathaniel, 22:50
R., 22:49
Rebeka, 21:34
Ruth, 22:49
Salley (Alley), 22:50
Sally L., 22:50
Samuel, 21:94
Sarah, 21:154
Susanna, 21:148, 160
Sylvanus L., 23:114
Thomas, 21:148, 151, 210; 22:52, 209, 210
William, 21:32

NEWHAM
Darah (___), 22:174
Nathaniel, 22:174
Thomas, 22:174

NEWMAN, 23:147; 24:105
___ (Endicott), 24:107
Antipas, 24:107, 176
Henry, 21:35
John, 21:208; 22:153; 23:149
John J., 25:122
Patience, 23:226
Samuel, 24:107
Thomas, 23:149

NEWMARCH
John, 22:58, 167
Martha, 22:58
Martha (Gould), 22:58

NEWTON
Daniel, 24:169

NICHOLAS see also COLE, 21:89; 22:118

NICHOLAS II
Czar, 24:69

NICHOLES/NICHOLLS/NICHOLS/
NICHOLAS see also NICKOL
___, Dr., 22:84, 85, 108
___, Mrs., 22:83
Abigail, 25:189, 190
Abigail (Kendall), 21:213
Alpheus, 21:159
Amos, 22:120
Andrew, 22:83
Ann Elizabeth (Ayer), 25:194
Annas (___), 21:213
Benjamin, 22:235; 25:189
Benjamin L., 25:192
Benjamin Little, 25:196
Betsey (Burbank), 25:194
Betsey P., 25:195
Betsy, 22:173; 25:189, 193, 194
Betsy (Burbank), 25:190, 193
Christianna, 25:196
Clarissa (Fairbanks), 25:190, 196
Content, 25:192
Content (Lapham), 25:188, 191
David, 25:187-197
Doley (Chase), 25:191
Dolly, 25:187, 188, 191
Dorothy/Dolly (Chase), 25:187, 188
Dorian, 22:175
Ebenezer, 21:213
Eliabeth (Boutel), 21:213
Elisabeth, 22:235
Eliza, 25:189, 196
Elizabeth, 25:190, 193
Elizabeth/Betsy, 25:192
Eunice, 25:191

Frances P., 25:193, 195
Franklin R., 25:196
George, 25:189, 190, 194
Harriet, 25:189-191, 193, 194
Iona, 25:198
James, 21:213; 22:235-237
Jane, 22:180
Jane/Jenny (Burbank), 25:190, 195, 196, 200
Joanna (Lamson), 21:213
John, 21:156, 217; 22:236; 23:150; 25:189, 190, 195, 196
John B., 25:192-195
John Burbank, 25:194
Jonathan, 21:213; 25:187, 188, 191-193, 195, 196
Jond, 25:198
Joseph, 21:156; 22:188
Lavinia Brickett (Chase), 25:194
Levina/Lovina (Keaton), 22:120
Lucinda, 25:192
Lydia, 22:235
Lydia (___), 24:195
Lydia (Sargent), 25:190, 194
Lydia W. (Williams), 25:194
Marcy (___), 22:235
Maria Parker (Fairbanks), 25:196
Martha, 25:189, 190
Martha (___), 21:156
Martha D., 25:195
Mary, 21:213; 25:55, 57, 188-191
Mary (___),21:216; 22:235-237
Mary (Challis), 25:187
Mary (George), 25:188, 189
Mary (Haven), 21:156
Mary (Poole), 21:213
Mary E. (Bartlett), 25:197
Mary Eliot, 24:193, 195
Mary Louisa (Weeden), 25:196
Mercy (Parker), 24:210
Minerva, 25:195
Nancy, 22:51; 25:194, 195
Nancy (Nichols), 25:194, 195
Nancy M. (___), 25:196
Nathan, 25:195
Nathan B., 25:193, 194
Nathaniel, 21:216; 25:190, 195, 196; 25:189
Nathaniel B., 25:195
Otis, 25:196
Paulina (Staples), 25:190
Phebe, 22:173; 25:189, 196
Polly, 22:235; 25:191
Rebecca (Hemenway), 21:159
Richard, 21:213
Sally, 22:174, 235; 25:191, 198
Sally (Keaton), 22:120
Samuel, 22:173-175; 24:210
Samuel Barker, 22:237
Sarah, 21:213; 22:47; 25:188-190 195
Sarah (___), 22:173-175
Sarah Jane, 25:194, 195
Sophia Louisa (Shaw), 25:197
Thomas, 21:216, 219; 25:187-197
Wealthy, 25:192
William, 21:213

NICKERSON, 22:69

NICKOL/NICKOLS see also NICHOLS
David, 25:189
Sarah, 22:46, 54
Thomas, 25:189

NIELSON
Maude, 25:82

NIEPCE
Joseph Nicephore, 23:19

NIGH
David, 21:71

NINNY
Joan, 22:240

NISBET
Judith Marilyn (Haszard), 21:18
William Fairbanks, 21:18

NISSENBAUM
Stephen, 21:37, 88

NIXON
___, Pres., 23:8
John, 22:145

NOBEL/NOBLE
Desire King, 25:53
Elizabeth, 23:150
Francis, 23:150
James, 23:145, 150
John, 23:15
Joseph, 25:53
Mary (___), 24:220
Sarah (___), 25:53
William B., 24:220

NOIC/NOICE see also NOYES
Hana, 25:100
William, 23:150

NOLAN
William, 25:122

NORMAN
Elizabeth (Whitrige), 22:158
Richard, 22:158

NORRIS
Edward, 22:171, 172, 174, 176; 23:240a
George, 22:172
Henry Lee, 22:174
Jeremiah, 22:176
John, 22:171
Sarah (___), 22:171, 172, 174, 176

NORTHEND
Agnes, 21:171

NORTHY
Francis, 21:214

NORTON, 22:135
George, 24:106
John, 22:137
W.W., 24:71
Wm., 22:152

NORWARD/NORWOOD, 22:113
Adelaide/Adeline G., 21:161
Eunice, 25:14
Eunice (Langsford), 21:161
Eva (Hawkes), 21:99
Francis, 22:224, 230, 231; 23:146
John, 21:99
Mary, 21:33; 22:50, 224, 227
Nathan, 21:161
Sarah, 21:99
William, 22:224, 229-231

NOTT
Samuel, 25:60a

NOURSE, 23:35
Henry S., 23:223; 25:7

NOWELL
Increase, 23:180a
Lydia, 25:79
Mary (___), 25:79
Zachariah, 25:79

NOWERS
Deborah K., 22:55, 57

NOYES/NOYSE see also NOIC, 21:36; 22:135; 23:161-163; 24:168
___, Mr., 21:113, 172
Edmund, 22:138
Elizabeth (Bradford), 21:65, 66
Enoch, 25:91
Hanah, 25:104

- 53 -

Hannah (Faulkner), 24:102
J., 21:114
James, 21:111, 112, 114
John, 21:65, 66; 25:167
Joshua, 22:143
Mary, 24:98; 25:100
Mary Butler, 24:100
Nicholas, 21:112
Prudence (Stevens), 24:84
Samuel, 24:102
Sarah, 24:98
Susanna (Parker), 25:91
Susanne, 24:95, 102
Sybil, 22:43; 23:160; 24:217; 25:22
Timothy, 24:96
Ward, 24:84, 96, 98

NUNEZ
Isabel (___), 24:67
John, 24:67
Juan, 24:67
Juana, 24:67
Teresa (Alvarez), 24:67

NURSE
Benjamin, 21:156
Bethiah (Bridges), 21:156
Ebenezer, 21:157
Elizabeth (Haven), 21:156
Experience, 21:156
Francis, 21:40; 22:31, 33, 187
George, 21:35
Mercy, 21:157
Mercy/Marcy (Haven), 21:157
Moses, 21:157
Rebecca, 21:37, 40, 41, 42, 44
Rebecca (___), 22:31, 33
Rebecca (Towne), 21:40, 41; 22:22,
  23, 215; 23:238
Sarah (Tarbell), 22:187
Thamezin, 21:156
Thamezin (Jameson), 21:156

NUTTING/NUTTINGS, 22:25; 24:154
Wallace, 23:116

OAKES
Benjamin, 23:150
Ebenezer, 22:224, 229-231
John, 22:224, 227, 228
Jonathan, 24:209
Sarah (Parker), 24:209

OBEAR/OBER, 21:225
Elizabeth, 21:100, 163; 23:117
Evelyn, 21:103
Frederick A., 21:232, 236
Hannah (Burman), 23:117
Hepzibah, 22:218
James, 21:100
John, 22:224, 231, 232
Jonathan, 23:150
Josiah, 23:117
Lydia (Cleaves), 21:100

O'BRIEN
Barbara, 22:30
Denis W., 23:16
Hugh, 23:16
John, 21:205
Rosemary H., 22:82

O'CALLAHAN
Daniel, 23:16

O'CONNELL
Daniel, 25:67
Patrick A., 23:17

O'CONNOR
Charles S., 23:17
P. H., 23:113, 114
Thomas, 25:122
Thomas H., 23:135

ODEL/ODELL/OWDELL
Benjamin, 21:92
Sally, 22:236
Sarah (Cole), 21:92

O'DONOGHUE
John F., 23:17

O'DOUL
Eileen, 25:74

OESTRICH
Judith Ann (Southard), 21:53; 24:17
Judith Southard, 24:77

O'FLAHERTY
T. J., 23:16

OGDEN
John, 21:144

OGILVIE
Helen, 22:169

OLDFIELD, 21:9

OLIPHANT
D., 21:163
Robert W., 22:123

OLIVER
___, Dr., 22:83
Betsy (Parker), 24:210
Daniel, 22:60a, 235
Edward, 24:208
Elisabeth (___), 22:235
Elizabeth, 22:239
Elizabeth (Kemble), 22:60a
Henry K., 24:232a
Henry Kemble, 22:60a
Herny, 22:49
Mercy (Wendell), 22:60a
Nathaniel, 22:60a
Peter, 22:69
Sarah (Cook), 22:60a
Sarah (Parker), 24:208, 210
Thomas, 22:60a
Thomas Henry, 22:235

O'LOUGHLIN
Patrick, 23:17

OLSON/OLSSON, 24:223
Nils William, 23:135

O'MAHONIE
Tege, 21:209

O'MALLEY
Charles J., 23:17
John C., 23:18

O'NEAL/O'NEIL/O'NEILL, 23:147
John, 23:150
George E., 23:17
Joseph A. F., 23:17
Robert K., 25:121

ORDWAY
Aaron, 25:152, 153
Ann (Emery), 22:239
Benjamin Henry, 25:152
Caroline Pond, 25:153
Catherine (___), 25:152, 153
Edward, 21:113
Esther, 22:239
James, 21:172; 22:239; 25:98
John, 22:239
Martha, 22:119
Mary (Godfrey), 22:239
Samuel, 22:42
Sarah (Bailey), 22:120

ORENS
Martha, 21:3

O'RILEY
Cornelius, 25:73

ORMES
John, 21:41
Mary, 21:41
Mary (___), 21:41

ORMSBY
Abigail (Abbe), 21:37
Jonathan, 21:37
Joseph, 21:37
Mercy (Abbe), 21:37

ORR
Shirley, 22:195; 23:34

OSBORN, 22:25
___, Mrs., 23:114
Caroline, 25:151
Charles, 25:151
Edward Lang, 25:151
Esther, 25:151
John Norris, 25:151
L. P., Mrs., 23:115
Lyman P., 23:113-115
Lyman P., Mrs., 23:113
Martha Lang, 25:151
Mary A., 23:114
Mary Cook, 25:151
Nancy (___), 25:151
William, 25:151
William Kendall, 25:151

O'SELZNICK
David, 25:202

OSGOOD
Abigail, 24:176
Anna, 24:206, 215
Asa, 24:87
Benjamin, 24:176
Caroline, 25:153
Charles, 25:153
Christopher, 21:213; 24:89, 97, 176
Deborah (Poor), 21:213
Dorcas, 24:89, 97
Dorcas (Stevens), 24:87
Elizabeth, 25:153
Elizabeth (___), 25:153
Gayton, 21:199
Hannah (Stevens), 24:89
Herbert, 24:176a
Jacob, 24:98
John, 21:195-197, 199, 213; 24:36
Lucretia (___), 24:195
Lucy, 24:97
Lucy Ann, 25:153
Martha, 21:35
Martha (___), 25:128
Mary, 22:59; 24:37
Mary (Gooding/Goodwin), 21:213
Mehitabel, 24:43
Nathaniel Hopkins, 25:153
Nathl, 25:153
Peter, 24:96; 25:128
Priscilla, 24:43
Samuel, 24:89
Sarah, 24:42
Thomas, 24:89
Timothy, 21:197, 213
William, 21:213; 24:176

O'SHEA
John, 25:113

OTIS
James, 23:8, 11

OTTEN
Marjorie Wardwell, 21:85, 109, 177

OTZI, 24:70

OUTERSON
Christian, 22:119

OVERGAARD
John Eric, 24:115
Marion Lindsay (Cowley), 24:115

OWEN
Ann (Campbell), 22:238
Arthur, 22:218
Elizabeth (Lee), 22:218

Margaret, 21:16; 22:238
Thomas, 22:238
W. F., 23:56

PAABO
S., 24:70
PACKARD
Mary, 21:105
PACKER
Elizabeth, 24:136
PADDY
William, 25:163
PADISHALL
Martha (___), 22:44
PAGE/PAIGE, 22:135
___, Mr., 21:154
Charles Grafton, 25:151
Charlotte Elizabeth, 25:151
Daniel, 24:43
Elizabeth, 25:77
Faith (Dunster), 21:52
George William, 25:152
Hannah (Wilkins), 24:43
Harlan Winslow, 22:143
Harriet Lang, 25:151
Henry Lawrence, 25:151
Jeremiah, 23:89, 90, 92
Jery, 25:151, 152
Jevy Lee, 25:151
John, 21:52; 25:77
Jonathan, 21:149
Lois (___), 25:77
Lucius P., 21:150, 209; 25:7
Lucy (___), 25:151, 152
Lucy Ann Williams, 25:151
Martha Ellen, 25:151
Mercy (Gould), 21:52
Nathaniel, 21:52
Nicholas, 22:45
Prudence, 21:52
Samuel, 21:52; 24:39; 25:77
Sarah (___), 24:39; 25:77
Sarah (Lawrence), 21:52
Sarah (Stevens), 24:39
Susanna (Haven), 21:149, 154
William, 24:39
PAINE see also PAYNE
Amos Martin, 24:226
Elizabeth, 25:165
Lavina Jane (Munn), 24:226
Robert, 24:24-26; 25:104
William, 24:24-26
Zemira Aureta, 24:226
PALFRAY/PALFREY, 21:24
Benjn, 25:77
Hannah, 22:51
Hannah (___), 22:51
Warwick, 22:51; 25:77
PALMER, 22:120
Ann (Denison), 21:176
Betty/Betsy, 25:199
Comfort (Fairbanks), 21:175
Cornelius S., 22:119
Daniel, 23:37
Ebenezer, 21:175
Elenor (___), 22:119
Elizabeth/Betty, 25:56, 193, 195
Frances (Prentice), 21:176
Frank W., 22:50
George, 21:175
Gershom, 21:176
Gertrude May, 22:119
Grace (Minor), 21:175
Hannah, 21:175
Hannah (Palmer), 21:175
Hepsibah (Abbe), 21:37

J. B., Mrs., 23:113
Joseph, 21:176
Lucy, 21:175
Mary (Brooks), 22:119
Mary (Voden), 21:41
Mary Marion (Shaw), 22:119
Richard, 21:41
Samuel, 21:37
Stephan A., 22:119
Stephen, 22:119
Thomas, 22:119, 167
Wait, 21:175
William, 21:175
Zebulon, 21:175
PANDOLFINI
Roberta, 24:223
PANTON
___, Lt., 23:10, 11
PARDEE-KING
Marta, 24:129, 134
PARIS
Amos, 24:79
Susannah, 24:77, 79, 81, 82
PARISH
George, 24:81
John, 24:81
PARISI
Betty, 25:147
PARK/PARKE
'Children', 25:159
Elizabeth (Stevens), 24:39
John C., 23:16
Joseph, 23:38
Rebecca (___), 25:159
Thomas, 25:159, 168
Timothy, 24:39
William, 25:167
PARKER/PERKER see also BARKER,
21:10; 23:48; 25:160
___, Lt., 21:213
___, Mr., 21:113, 173
___, Rev., 21:172
"Child", 24:215, 216; 25:38, 89
"Twin", 25:86
Aaron/Arone, 24:162; 25:39, 45, 46,
84, 87, 139, 140-145
Abel, 25:143, 145
Abiel, 25:87
Abiel (Corey), 25:87
Abigail, 24:50, 162; 25:39, 45, 86, 90,
92, 138, 139, 141, 142, 144
Abigail/Nabby (___), 24:162; 25:34,
139, 146
Abigail (Bailey), 25:89
Abigail (French), 24:48, 50
Abigail (Hildreth), 25:35, 39
Abigail (Kidder), 25:43, 86, 91
Abigail (Osgood), 24:176
Abigail (Scripture), 25:35
Abigail (Whitaker), 24:48, 50, 51
Abigail (Winship), 25:39, 45
Abraham, 24:153, 206; 25:33-43, 45,
83-85, 87-91, 137, 138, 140, 142,
143, 145, 146
Alice, 25:137, 138, 140
Alice (Tompson), 25:43, 137, 138
Amos, 25:90
Anah/Hannah, 25:37
Andrew, 22:224, 231-233
Ann, 24:215
Ann (___), 24:153
Ann (Rendall), 24:161
Ann/Sarah (Mors), 25:38
Anna, 22:173, 174; 24:162, 216;
25:34-36, 42, 84, 85, 89, 90, 92, 139
Anna (___), 25:41, 144

Anna (Barrit), 25:45
Anna (Foster), 24:206, 216
Anna (Osgood), 24:206, 215
Anna (Parker), 25:90
Anna/Anne (___), 25:43
Anne, 25:44, 89, 91, 93
Anne (Errington), 23:175
Anne (Greenough), 25:90
Anne/Anna (Tarbell), 25:41, 52, 88
Augusta, 24:101
Augustus, 24:100
Benjamin, 21:178; 23:34; 24:46-52,
153-161, 205, 206, 211-216; 25:39,
40, 43, 90, 91, 140, 141, 145, 146
Benoni, 24:158
Bethiah, 24:50, 210
Bethiah (Parker), 24:210
Betsey (___), 25:140
Betsy/Bette/Betty, 24:207, 214; 25:44,
86, 87, 89, 90, 138, 141, 210
Bradstreet, 25:44, 45, 139-142
Bridget, 25:83, 84, 144
Bridget (Comings/Cummings), 25:45,
143, 146
Bridget (Fletcher), 25:144
Broadstreet, 25:139, 141
Charlotte Augusta, 25:94
Chase, 25:138
Clarissa, 25:93
D. F., 22:78
Danforth, 24:211
Daniel, 23:48; 24:176211, 212, 216;
25:38, 43, 44, 89-93, 137
David, 24:52, 53, 157, 160, 205, 206,
208-210, 214; 25:43, 85, 92, 137,
138, 142, 143
David/Daniel, 21:213
Dean, 25:90
Deborah, 21:217; 23:34; 24:51; 25:142
Dorcas, 24:215
Dorothy, 25:142
Dorothy (Fletcher), 25:45, 142
Dudley, 25:140
Easter, 24:157; 25:85
Easter (Parker), 25:85
Ebenezer, 21:34, 35, 94; 24:154, 158,
162, 163, 209, 211-214; 25:39, 41,
42, 88, 142
Edmund, 25:43, 90
Ednah, 25:139
Ednah (Hardy), 25:139, 142
Eleanor, 24:53
Eleanor (Robbins), 24:53
Eliab, 23:156
Eliphalet, 25:139
Eliphalet Hardy, 25:140
Elizabeth, 21:32, 34, 35; 24:54, 158,
162, 163, 205, 208, 209; 25:33-36,
39, 44, 46, 85, 86, 91-93, 138,
143-146
Elizabeth (___), 25:43
Elizabeth (Blodgett), 24:205, 213
Elizabeth (Bowers), 25:35
Elizabeth (Bradstreet), 25:38, 44
Elizabeth (Cheever), 24:160, 208, 209
Elizabeth (Fletcher), 25:91
Elizabeth (Gowing), 23:174
Elizabeth (Grose), 24:210
Elizabeth (Parker), 25:39, 158, 162
Elizabeth (Tufts), 25:137
Elizabeth (Walker), 25:86
Elizabeth (Warrin), 24:159, 205, 206
Ephraim, 24:53; 25:85, 86, 93
Esther (Pillsbury), 25:43, 89
Esther/Ester, 24:160, 161, 209, 211;
25:40, 42, 46, 83, 84

Esther/Ester (___), 25:36, 37, 41
Esther/Ester (Fletcher), 25:35, 40, 42
Eunice, 25:146, 212
Eunice (Twiss), 24:207
Franklin, 22:82, 108
Frederick Augustus, 25:92
Free, 25:140
Free Groves, 25:140
Gardner, 25:93
George, 25:93, 141
Grace, 25:38
Hananiah, 21:212, 213, 217
Hannah, 21:150, 153, 177; 24:50, 53, 92, 100, 206, 207; 25:42, 44, 45, 86, 87, 89, 138-142
Hannah/Anna, 25:34
Hannah (___), 25:41, 45, 85
Hannah (Brown), 24:41
Hannah (Chase), 25:45, 138
Hannah (Dutton), 24:212, 213
Hannah (Fletcher), 25:88, 143
Hannah (Hardy), 25:139
Hannah (Hathern), 25:45, 138, 139
Hannah (Haven), 21:153
Hannah (Parker), 25:139, 141
Hannah (Parkhurst), 25:42
Hannah (Stevens), 24:41, 176
Henry, 24:159; 25:92
Henry Bradstreet, 25:142
Henry Broadstreet, 25:141
Henry S., 25:87
Henry Spaulding, 25:87
Huldah, 24:209, 211
Isaac, 21:197; 24:91, 96, 209, 210; 25:33, 35, 40-42, 46, 84-86, 143-146
Isaiah, 24:216; 25:142, 143
Jacob, 24:153-162, 205-216; 25:35, 39, 41, 85, 87, 88, 145
James, 22:178; 23:227; 24:46, 153; 25:33, 35, 40, 84, 87
James Butler, 25:140
Jedduthan, 24:213, 214
Joanna, 24:157, 160; 25:83, 84, 87
Joanna (___), 24:153
Joanna (Butterfield), 25:41, 87
Joanna (Call), 24:155, 156
Joel, 24:207
John, 21:153, 211, 216, 217; 22:171; 23:150; 24:41, 46-53, 104, 153, 147, 147, 157, 160, 176, 207, 209-211; 25:33, 35-37, 40-43, 85-89, 91, 93, 137, 139, 144
John E., 25:141
John Eaton, 25:141
John Minot, 25:92
Jonah, 25:87
Jonas, 24:53; 25:87
Jonathan, 21:212, 213, 217; 24:159, 176, 206, 207, 214, 216; 25:35, 36, 41, 87, 143, 145
Joseph, 21:153, 195, 199; 24:35, 41, 46, 153, 159, 162, 176, 206, 207, 213; 25:34, 39, 83, 84, 143, 145
Joshua, 24:208, 209; 25:142
Josiah, 25:42
Judith, 25:139
Judith/Jude (___), 24:46
Judith (___), 25:45
Judith (Bancroft), 21:212, 213
Judith (Hopkinson), 25:139
Kendall, 21:216, 219
Leonard, 25:87, 143
Levi, 24:52; 25:145, 146

Lois (Blood), 25:85, 146
Love, 23:150
Lucretia, 25:86
Lucy, 24:53, 162, 163; 25:39, 46, 91, 144
Lucy (___), 25:91
Lucy (Barrat), 24:206, 214
Lucy (Dunbar), 24:207
Lydia, 22:171, 178; 23:227; 24:51-53, 210, 216; 25:33-38, 40, 42, 143
Lydia (___), 23:34
Lydia (Chamberlain), 24:49, 51, 52
Lydia (Hill), 24:210
Lydia (Patterson), 22:178
Lydia (Richardson), 23:227
Mara, 24:159
Marah (Barrot), 25:45, 142
Marah/Mary, 25:84
Marcy Nichols, 24:209
Mare, 25:35
Mare (Parker), 25:35
Margaret, 24:162
Margerit (___), 25:35, 39
Maria, 25:92
Martha, 25:44, 86, 90, 91, 93
Martha (Brown), 23:174
Martha (Foster), 24:213
Martha (Livermore), 25:34, 37, 38
Mary, 21:153, 213, 220; 23:150; 24:49, 51, 52, 92, 100, 153, 154, 156, 158, 162, 163, 206, 207, 209-211, 216; 25:33-37, 39, 45, 87, 90, 92, 93, 138, 141-143
Mary (___), 22:171-174; 24:154, 157, 160, 211; 25:45
Mary (Abbott), 24:176
Mary (Ayer), 21:85, 86, 93
Mary (Carder), 25:35
Mary (Chandler), 24:176
Mary (Corey), 24:51, 52
Mary (Crosbey), 24:50
Mary (Danforth), 25:34-36
Mary (Fletcher), 24:155, 157, 158; 25:39
Mary (Hancock), 24:157
Mary (Hunnawell), 24:210
Mary (Jordain), 24:161
Mary (Parker), 25:33, 34
Mary (Poodney), 24:48
Mary (Rhodes), 23:41, 43, 48
Mary (Robbins), 25:143
Mary (Shattuck), 25:92
Mary (Stevens), 24:44; 25:43, 90, 92
Mary (Trull), 24:48
Mary (Upham), 24:160, 207, 209, 211
Mary (Willis), 24:157
Mehitable, 25:140
Mehitable (Bancroft), 21:213
Mercy, 24:210
Molly, 24:53; 25:90
Molly Belknap, 24:53
Moses, 25:144
Moses, 24:154, 162, 206; 25:33-35, 37, 39, 45, 46, 83, 84, 141-145
Nancy, 25:91
Nanne, 25:90
Nathan, 21:85, 195; 24:176, 209, 211; 25:90
Nathaniel, 24:41, 47, 52, 53, 164, 176; 25:44, 45, 85, 138, 139
Nehemiah Abot, 25:84, 145
Olive, 24:162, 163; 25:39
Oliver, 25:85, 86
Paul, 25:45, 138, 139

Peleg, 25:138
Peter, 25:141
Phebe, 24:53, 89, 209, 211
Phebe (Green), 24:160, 211
Phebe (Swallow), 24:53
Philemon, 22:172-174; 24:211
Philip, 24:205, 206, 215
Phineas, 24:92; 25:35, 139, 140
Phoebe, 24:212
Polly, 24:207; 25:141
Polly/Mary (Duren), 25:93
Priscilla, 25:141
Rachel, 24:47, 153-155, 157, 160-163, 206, 216; 25:39, 41, 45, 87, 88, 138-140
Rachel (___), 25:41, 85, 88
Rachel (Buterfeild), 24:159, 206; 25:145
Rachel (Sargent), 25:44
Rebackah (Bach), 25:45, 139
Rebackah (Balch), 25:140, 141
Rebecca, 22:172; 23:174; 24:53, 153-155, 157, 159-163, 208-210, 215; 25:35, 41, 83, 86, 87, 89, 138, 140, 141
Rebecca (___), 24:210; 25:36, 40, 87
Rebecca (Danforth), 24:155, 157, 159, 160
Rebecca (Emerson), 24:160, 208
Rebecca (Fletcher), 24:206; 25:39, 83, 146
Rebecca (Hunt), 25:146
Rebecca (Lombard), 21:178
Rebecca (Proctor), 25:87
Rebeka (Newhall), 21:34
Rebekah (Roby), 25:88
Retire, 25:139, 140
Retire H. P., 25:138
Retire Hathorn, 25:142
Retire Hathorn/Retier Hathen, 25:139
Reuben, 24:53, 213, 216
Rhoda, 24:215
Richard, 24:210
Robert, 21:112; 22:169; 23:34; 24:46-48, 50-52, 210
Rose (Whitlock), 25:33, 34
Ruth, 24:52, 53, 206; 25:85, 145, 146
Ruth (___), 24:162
Ruth (Blood), 25:40, 84
Ruth (Bradshaw), 24:164; 25:44, 45
Ruth (Hunt), 25:93
Sally, 24:209, 210; 25:90
Sally (Parker), 25:90
Sampson Warren, 25:94
Samuel, 22:45; 23:41, 174; 24:44, 48, 52, 207; 25:35-38, 41, 43, 45, 46, 85, 88-90, 92, 94, 143, 145, 146
Samuel Abbot, 25:94
Sarah, 21:153; 24:47-49, 51, 53, 153-155, 158, 159, 162, 176, 208-213, 215; 25:33, 42, 84, 87, 89, 90, 92, 93, 138, 140-142, 145
Sarah (___), 24:51, 52, 153; 25:85, 145, 146
Sarah (Barrat), 25:86
Sarah (Briant), 21:99
Sarah (Dunbar), 24:207
Sarah (Eaton), 25:141
Sarah (Fletcher), 25:45, 143
Sarah (Foster), 24:163, 212, 213
Sarah (Hartwell), 24:47
Sarah (Haward/Hayward), 24:155, 158, 159
Sarah (Ireson), 25:35

Sarah (Parker), 24:176, 206; 25:84,
   145
Sarah (Richardson), 25:85
Sarah (Warren), 25:94
Sarah Bowers, 25:94
Sarah/Mary (Mors), 25:43
Sary, 24:163; 25:38, 143
Silas, 24:162, 209, 211-213; 25:143
Simeon/Simon, 24:52, 53, 213
Solomon, 24:216
Stephen/Steven, 25:43, 86, 89, 90,
   92, 93, 137
Susan, 24:210
Susanna, 25:91, 93, 139, 145, 146, 210
Susanna (Greenough), 25:45, 138, 140
Susanna (Hardy), 25:140
Susanna (Kemp), 25:85, 145
Susanna (Thompson), 24:160, 207
Susanna/Sukey (Minot), 25:92
Sybal (Parker), 25:86
Sybil, 25:85, 86, 93, 145
Sybil (___), 25:93
Sybil (Warren), 25:86
Sybil/Sibbel (Parker), 25:93
T., 21:114
Tabitha, 24:153-155, 159, 206
Tabitha (Wilson), 24:160, 211, 212
Thankful, 25:86
Theodore, 25:90
Thomas, 21:111, 112, 114,
   171, 216, 219; 23:174, 227;
   24:153-155, 157-160, 162,
   163, 176, 207-209, 211, 212;
   25:34-37, 39-42, 85, 141
Thomas Stone, 25:93
Three Groves, 25:138
Ursilla (Eaton), 24:157, 161
Ursula, 24:161, 162
Warren, 25:86
Willard, 24:206, 216
William, 24:52, 53, 158, 162, 163,
   209, 210, 212, 213; 25:39, 41,
   42, 84, 85, 87, 90, 138-141,
   · 145, 146
William Balch, 25:142
Woodbridge, 25:90
Zebulon, 24:213, 214

PARKHURST
Hannah, 25:42
Jonathan, 25:42
Martha, 21:104
Mary, 23:240

PARKMAN, 22:135
Abagail, 23:239
Bridget (___), 23:177
Deliverance, 23:177; 25:128, 183
Elias, 23:177
Margeret (___), 25:183
Mehitabel (___), 25:128
Samuel, 22:140; 25:183
Sarah, 23:177
Sarah (Veren), 23:177
Susannah (___), 25:184

PARMAL
Pamela, 25:149

PARRAT/PARRATT/PARRETT
Anna, 22:191
Francis, 22:167
John, 22:167
Martha, 22:90; 25:56

PARRIS
___, Rev., 21:37, 40, 41; 22:32

PARRISH
John, 22:45

PARSON/PARSONS, 22:113; 23:212
Aaron, 24:220

Abigail (Haskell), 24:16, 175, 231
Betty, 22:224, 227
Dorcas, 22:224, 227
Eben/Ebenezer, 22:224, 228-230;
   23:142
Elizabeth, 23:228
James, 22:112, 224, 227, 228
Jeffery, 23:174, 228; 24:16, 175, 231
Jonathan P., 22:224, 228-230
Judith, 24:16, 175, 231
Mark, 23:143
Moses, 23:165
Nathaniel, 22:224, 231, 233; 24:16,
   175, 231
P., 23:154
Polly, 23:150
Samuel, 23:143
Sarah (Vincent), 24:16, 175, 231
Sarah (Vinson), 23:228
William, 22:112; 23:150

PARTICULAR
Nothing, 23:128

PARTRIDGE
Abel, 21:157
Mary, 21:59
Miriam (Haven), 21:157
Ralph, 21:203

PATAS
William, 23:150

PATCH
Caroline, 22:161
Hannah, 21:51
John, 21:13
Martha (Goldsmith), 22:41
Simon, 22:41
Thomas, 22:105

PATEE see PATTEE
PATHE, 25:81

PATRICK/PETRICK
James, 22:224, 230, 231
Katy, 23:91
Mary, 22:224, 229, 230

PATTEE/PATEE, 24:108; 25:187, 189,
   193
Annie Theresa (Mallen), 21:53
Asa, 22:178
Cyrus Charles, 22:178
Drusilla Chandler (Kilgore), 21:53
Earnest Laforest, 21:53
Elizabeth (Scribner), 22:178
Eunice (Sargent), 22:178
Hannah (Dow), 22:178
Harrison Morrill, 22:161, 178
Huldah Aldrich (Dunn), 22:178
John, 22:178
Mary Alice, 21:53
Moses, 21:53
Peter, 22:178; 23:120
Richard, 22:178; 23:120
Stephen K., 21:53

PATTEN
Elijah, 24:91
Elizabeth (Read), 23:222
Lydia (Stevens), 24:91
Mary, 24:157
Mary (Potter), 24:91
Stephen, 24:91
Thomas, 24:157
William, 23:222

PATTERSON see also PATTISON
Joseph, 22:161
Lydia, 22:178
Mary (___), 22:161
Rebecca, 25:53
Rebecca (___), 25:53
William, 25:53, 128

PATTING
John, 23:150

PATTISON see also PATTERSON
James, 25:5
Rebecca (Stevenson), 25:5, 6

PAUL
Elizabeth, 22:46, 202, 203, 206, 214
Howard, 21:207
Howard H., 21:208
James Balfour, 23:86
John, 25:9

PAULLIN
Louise, 23:56

PAYNE see also PAINE
William, 25:131, 132

PAYSON
Edward, 21:167

PEABODY, 21:10; 22:25
Achsah, 22:82-85, 108
Anna, 24:90
Charles Henry, 25:53
Elisabeth (___), 22:237
Ephraim, 21:95
Francis, 23:99, 100; 24:232a
George, 21:79-81; 22:22, 27, 82-85,
   108; 23:35, 114
Hannah, 24:96
Harrie, 25:53
Jacob, 25:53, 54
Jacob Low, 25:53
Jeremiah, 22:85
John, 23:99
Judith, 22:82-85
Judith (___), 22:82-85
Lucy Manning, 25:53
Lydia (___), 25:53, 54
Mary, 25:153
Mary (Brown), 23:99, 100
Nathaniel, 22:237; 24:232a
Samuel, 22:27
Sarah, 24:43, 88
Selim Hobart, 23:99
Sophia, 22:237
Stephen, 23:99
Thomas, 21:96; 22:82
William, 23:99
William Augustus, 25:54

PEACH
Bethia (Blaney), 23:208
Ebenezer W., 23:208
John, 25:17
Lot, 23:208
Robert Westly, 25:17
Sarah (Blaney), 23:208

PEAK/PEAKE/PEEKE see also PIKE
Cyrus H., 25:23
Elias, 25:24, 25, 28, 58
Elizabeth, 25:26
Elizabeth (Taynour), 25:25, 58
Esther (Atkins), 25:58
Esther (Knight), 25:25, 28
George, 25:25, 26, 28, 58
Hannah, 25:26
Hannah (Trevett), 25:26, 58
Jacob, 25:26
John, 25:26
Mary (Grant), 25:25
Rebeckah, 25:26
Samuel, 25:26
Sarah, 25:26
Sarah (___), 25:58
See Pike, 25:17
Tabitha (___), 25:26. 58

PEAKE see PEEK

PEARCE see also PEARSE, PEIRCE,
   PIERCE
   Jane/Jean (Bessom), 23:208, 209
   John, 25:35
   Mary (Parker), 25:35
   Robert, 23:208, 209
   Samuel, 22:224, 234
   William, 22:224, 232
PEARL
   Abigail Tyler (Kimball), 22:238
   Elizabeth (Holmes), 24:39, 41, 116
   Elizabeth (Stevens), 24:39
   Eunice (Kimball), 23:117
   George, 22:238
   John, 23:117; 24:39, 41, 116, 218
   Mehitable (Hall), 22:218
   Richard, 24:41, 85, 86
   Ruth Mehitable, 22:238
   Sarah (Stevens), 24:41
   Timothy, 24:39
PEARSE see also PEARCE, PEIRCE,
   PIERCE
   Samuel, 22:87
PEARSON see also PIERSON
   Anna, 22:180
   John, 21:214; 22:167, 203, 214; 24:54
   Joseph, 22:180
   Joseph Gerrish, 25:196
   Leonard J., 22:224, 234
   Mary (Chase), 22:180
   Maudlin (Bullard), 24:54
   Phebe, 25:190
   Phebe (Nichols), 25:196
   Rebeckah, 21:220
   Sarah, 24:54
PEASE/PEEAS
   Daniel, 25:128
   Henry, 21:54
   Ida Florence (Hutchins), 21:53
   Josephine (Watson), 21:54
   Leola Maud, 21:53
   Obadias, 25:168
   Walter Scott, 21:53
PEASLEE
   Joseph, 21:172; 23:53
   Martha (Hoag), 21:172
PEBBLES
   Almana M. (Tyler), 21:103
PECK see also PIKE
   Henry, 24:61
   Ira B., 25:23
   Joseph, 25:23
   Mary, 25:21
   Priscilla (Rand), 21:30
   Samuel, 21:30
PECKER
   Ann (Davis), 22:94
   James, 22:94
   Mary, 22:94
PECKHAM
   Sarah, 23:94
PEDRICK
   John, 21:60a; 23:215
   Mary Elizabeth, 21:106
PEEAS see PEASE
PEEKE see PEAK
PEELE
   Elizabeth (___), 25:54
   Elizabeth Ropes, 25:54
   Mary (___), 22:172
   Robert, 22:172; 25:54
   William, 22:172
PEIRCE/PEIRS see also PEARCE,
   PEARSE, PIERCE
   Benjamin, 22:171; 24:155
   Betsy, 22:172-174

Bridget (Parker), 25:84
Catherine Cornelia (Cooke), 23:119
Elizabeth (Cole), 24:155
Elizabeth (Parker), 25:34
Ephraim, 25:84
Esther (___), 25:83
Henry, 22:175
Jacob, 24:155
James, 25:34
Jerathmeel, 22:171-175
Joseph Adams, 22:171
Marion Wentworth, 23:119
Sally, 22:172
Sally (___), 22:172
Sarah, 24:155
Sarah (___), 22:171-175
Stephen/Steven, 24:154, 155; 25:83
Tabartha, 24:155
Tabitha (Parker), 24:154
Thomas, 24:155
Thomas Wentworth, 23:119
PELHAM
   Henry, 23:7
   Mary (Singleton), 23:7
   Peter, 23:7, 15
PELL
   Joseph, 21:148
PENDER
   James, 23:68, 69
   Robina, 23:68, 60, 72, 77
PENDEXTER
   Arletta 'Letta' (Davenport), 24:20
   Charles F. 'Fred', 24:20
PENDLETON
   Ann, 21:175
   Hannah (Goodenow), 21:176
   James, 21:176
PENFIELD
   Hannah, 22:179
PENNY
   Joan (___), 24:147; 25:135
   Thomas, 24:147; 25:135
PENNYCOOK, 24:36
PENTECOST
   Ernest Harvey, 23:119
   Marion Wentworth (Peirce), 23:119
PEPPERELL
   William, 22:65
PEPYS
   Samuel, 25:107
PERADEAU
   Marie Ann, 21:50
PERCE/PEIRS see PEIRCE
PEREZ
   Manfelda, 24:67
PERHAM, 25:41
   Jonathan, 24:216
   Mary (Parker), 24:216
PERKER see PARKER
PERKINS , 22:153; 23:35, 237; 24:141,
   148, 150, 152
   ___, Goodman, 22:157
   Abraham, 22:156, 160; 24:150
   Elizabeth, 21:59, 240; 22:148; 23:58;
      25:201
   Elizabeth (___), 23:58
   Elizabeth (Sparks), 25:201
   Elizabeth (Whipple), 25:201
   Ezra, 24:33
   Hannah, 21:45; 22:93
   Hannah (Knight), 23:58
   Isaac, 23:58
   Jacob, 22:156; 23:58; 25:134, 201
   John, 22:56, 115, 152, 156, 157, 159;
      23:58, 231; 24:142, 151; 25:135,
      201

Judith (Gator), 25:201
Lydia, 21:85
Martha (Gould), 21:45
Mary, 22:55; 23:58, 240
Moses, 23:150
Phebe (Gould), 23:237
Samuel, 21:45
Sarah (Wainright), 23:58
Thomas, 23:237
Thomas H., 23:12
William, 23:236
PERLEY, 22:135, 234
   Hannah, 21:45
   M. V. B., 23:164
   Sidney, 21:27, 90, 240a; 22:27, 101,
      106, 137, 240a; 23:60a, 107,
      111, 118, 160, 174; 25:18, 20,
      25, 26, 28
PERRY
   Anna, 22:190
   Hannah, 24:99
   John, 23:150
PERSON
   ___, Lieut., 21:93
PERZEL
   Edward S., 24:26
PETER/PETERS
   Charlotte, 24:99
   Elizabeth, 21:88; 22:224, 229, 230
   Henry, 23:150
   Hugh, 22:21, 240a; 23:240a; 24:105,
      107, 232a
   John, 23:150; 24:88
   Richard, 23:150
   Sarah (Peabody), 24:88
PETERSON
   Jonathan, 24:116
   Lydia (Wadsworth), 24:116
   Sarah (Rhodes), 23:42, 43
PETRICK see PATRICK, 23:91
PETTENGILL/PETTINGILL
   Charles Henry, 25:151
   Elizabeth Melvill, 25:53
   Hannah (___), 25:53, 54, 151
   John, 25:53, 54, 151
   John Melvill, 25:53
   Josiah, 25:54
PETTY
   Joseph, 23:180
   Sarah (Edwards), 23:180
PEW
   Richard, 23:150
   William, 23:150
PFEIFER
   Lula (Bennett), 24:173
PHELAN
   William, 21:25
PHELPS
   Annis, 24:40, 43, 44, 83
   Elisa, 21:42
   Elizabeth, 21:116
   Elizabeth (Putnam), 21:42
   Henry, 22:224, 227, 228; 23:150;
      24:220
   John, 21:42, 214
   John Punchard, 22:176
   Jona., 25:77
   Lucy, 22:235
   Martha, 24:83
   Mary, 24:43, 89, 90
   Nicholas, 22:216, 217
   Rachel (___), 25:77
   Sally, 22:176
   Sally (___), 22:176, 235
   Sarah (Chandler), 21:116
   William, 22:172, 176, 235

PHILBRICK
Benjamin, 22:93
Hannah, 21:240; 22:93
Hannah (Perkins), 22:93
James, 22:93
Mary, 22:93
Rachel, 22:93
Sarah (Silver), 22:93
PHILIP/PHILLIP
King, 21:152-154; 22:86, 89, 123, 124,
204, 205; 24:107; 25:4
Prince, 24:67, 69
Samuel, 24:42
PHILIPS/PHILLIPS, 22:135
___ (Sergeant), 22:109
___, Mr., 25:150
___, Mrs., 24:196
Asa E., 23:18
Elizabeth, 22:109
Elizabeth (___), 24:195; 25:77
Elizabeth (Barnard), 24:96
George, 22:109
Henry, 25:77
James D., 21:25, 26
James Duncan, 22:240a; 23:118
John, 21:196; 23:29
Lois (Rand), 21:31
Mary, 24:43
Patrick, 23:16
Rebecca, 21:33
Samuel, 21:196, 197; 22:136; 24:43;
25:37
Stephen, 21:31
Stephen W., 24:196
PHIPPEN
George D., 21:24
Joseph, 25:128
Lois (___), 25:129
Wm., 25:129, 184
PHIPPS/PHIPS
___, Gov., 21:41, 87; 24:132
Elizabeth, 24:221
Elizabeth (Stevens), 24:37
Mary (Danforth), 24:37
Samuel, 24:37
Solomon, 24:37
William, 23:238
PICKE see PIKE
PICKERING
Benjamin, 22:236
John, 23:240a; 25:108a
Timothy, 21:180a; 24:56a
PICKETT, 21:232
Richard, 21:163
PICKMAN
Abigall (Willoughby), 25:78
Hannah, 23:231
Joshua, 25:78
Mary T., 24:195
PIEMONT/PIEMONTE
Catherine K., 21:11
John, 23:89
Kay, 25:60a, 150
PIERCE see also PEARCE, PEARSE,
PEIRCE
Benjamin, 24:56a
Elizabeth, 25:35
Elizabeth (Parker), 25:33, 35
Frederic Beech, 24:155
Hannah (___), 21:158
James, 25:35
James, 25:33, 35
Mary (Haven), 21:158
Mary/Molly (Underhill), 22:177
O., 24:34
Rebecca, 25:35

Richard D., 22:101, 106
Susan/Sukey, 22:177
Thomas, 21:158
PIERCY
Caroline, 24:186
R., 24:69
PIERPONT
___, Rev., 25:166
PIERRON
John, 21:204
PIERSON see also PEARSON
___, Mr., 24:39
George Noble, 22:180
Lydia (Stevens), 24:38, 39
Mary Elizabeth (Jones), 22:180
PIKE/PICKE see also PECK
A. R., 25:23
Allen Raymond, 25:17, 23, 24
Ann, 25:21
Ann (Snow), 25:21
August, 23:54
Comfort, 21:156
Deborah (Brown), 25:21
Elias, 25:19, 20, 23, 24, 26-28
Elisha, 25:21
Elizabeth, 23:54; 18, 19, 21, 22
Elizabeth (Taynor), 25:24, 27
Esther (Atkins), 25:19, 22
George, 25:17-25, 27
Hannah (Travett/Trevett/Trevitt),
25:19, 24, 25
Hester (Atkins), 25:18
J., 21:114
James, 25:23, 187
John, 21:172; 23:55; 25:17, 21, 23, 24
Leonard, 25:21
Martha, 25:19, 22
Mary, 25:21
Patience, 25:20
Phebe, 25:21
Polly, 21:179
Richard, 25:26, 27
Robert, 21:114, 142, 143; 22:21;
23:53-55. 234; 25:17
Ruth G., 25:23
Sarah, 23:54; 25:18, 19, 21, 22, 27, 28
Sarah (___), 23:234; 25:17, 19, 21, 22
Sarah (Sanders), 23:53
Tabitha, 25:21
Tabitha (___), 25:20, 21, 27
PILLINER
Peter Lawrence, 21:108
Susie Louise (Bennett), 21:108
PILLSBURY/PILSBURY
___, Capt., 24:99
Abigail, 25:188
Caleb, 25:89
Charles Stinson, 23:51; 25:89
Daniel, 25:188
Elizabeth, 24:232
Elizabeth (Godfrey), 24:232
Esther, 25:43, 89
James, 24:103
John Calvin, 25:52
John Sargent, 23:51; 25:89
Joseph, 24:232
Martha (___), 25:52
Mary (Dennett), 24:103
Moses, 24:232; 25:52
Sarah, 25:52
Sarah (Morse), 25:89
Sarah Ann (Stevens), 24:99
Susannah (Worth), 24:232
PINCHARD
___, Mr., 22:204

PINEL
___, Mrs., 24:195
Philip P., 24:195
PINGREE
___, Mrs., 24:196
Harold, 24:196
PINION
Ruth, 25:9
PINKETT
Francis, 23:147
PINKHAM
Harold A., 21:135; 25:47
PIPER
Fred S., 22:107
Joseph, 25:190, 198
Nathaniel, 22:107
Sarah (___), 25:190
Sarah (Edwards), 22:107
Sarah/Sally (Nichols), 25:189, 190,
198
Walter, 25:190
PITMAN
___, Dr., 21:139
Bethia Chapman, 25:52
Eliza Buffinton, 25:152
Elizabeth, 21:30
John Francis, 25:53
Joseph, 21:137; 25:52
Mark, 25:52, 53, 151, 152
Mary, 25:52
Sophia, 25:52
Sophia (___), 25:52, 53, 151, 152
Susanna Francis, 25:151
PLADSEN
Phyllis J., 25:124
PLOOF, 23:212
PLUMB
Deborah, 21:98
PLUMER/PLUMMER
Aaron, 22:221, 224, 225, 232-234;
25:12, 16
David, 22:225, 227
F., 21:114
Francis, 21:111
Joseph, 23:54, 187
Samuel, 24:217
POLAND
Bethiah (Friend), 22:58
Elizabeth (___), 22:57
J., 24:34
Jemima (Browne), 22:57
John, 22:58, 107; 23:150
Lydia, 22:57
Nathaniel, 22:57
Samuel, 22:57
POLHEMUS
John F., 24:114
POLK
James K., 22:120a
R.L., 24:124
POLLAD
John, 23:150
Mary (___), 23:150
POLLARD
Jonathan, 24:104
Olive (___), 24:104
Thomas, 24:52
POLLEY/POLLY
Elizabeth (___), 25:4
George, 25:4
Susanna, 23:219
POND
Daniel, 21:211
Jemima, 21:44
Nathaniel O., 25:174
Tabitha (Edwards), 21:211

POODNEY
Mary, 24:48
POOL/POOLE, 21:209; 22:113
___, Cornet, 21:211
Abigail (___), 22:111
Abigail/Nabby (___), 25:146
Armitage, 21:210
Belknap, 21:219
Benjamin, 21:217-220
Bethiah, 21:219
Bethiah (Mansfield), 21:219
Bety, 21:215
Bridget, 21:219, 220
Bridget (___), 21:220
Bridget (Fitch), 21:213, 216, 217, 219
Caleb, 22:111
Ebenezer, 22:225, 227-234; 23:159, 165
Eleazer Flagg, 21:219
Elizabeth, 21:213-215, 220, 222
Elizabeth (Eaton), 21:220
Elizabeth (Goodwin), 21:215
Ephraim, 21:214
Esther, 21:219
Esther (Flag), 21:219
Eunice, 21:216
Francis, 22:112
James, 21:214, 216, 219
John, 21:209-222; 22:21, 111, 112; 23:159
Johanna (___), 21:209
Jonathan, 22:112, 225, 229, 230
Joseph, 22:225, 229
Judah (___), 21:212
Judith (___), 21:211, 212, 222
Judith/Judah, 21:213, 215, 220, 222
Margaret (___), 21:209-211, 222
Marke, 22:221, 227
Mary, 21:210, 211, 213, 214, 219, 220, 222
Mary (Gooding/Goodwin), 21:213, 214
Mary (Parker), 21:213, 220
Mehitable, 21:219
Mehittable (Gibson), 21:219, 220
Nathaniel, 21:214
Prudence (Townsend), 21:216
Rebecca, 21:220
Rebecca (Boutwell), 21:213, 221
Rebecca (Williams), 21:220
Rebeckah (Wade), 21:220
Return, 22:111
Samuel, 21:213, 216, 217, 219, 220
Sarah, 21:211, 212, 214-216, 219, 222
Sarah (Eaton), 21:214, 219, 220
Sarah (Townsend), 21:215
Sarah (Woodbury), 22:111
Solomon, 22:225, 230, 231
Susannah, 21:215, 216
Susannah (___), 21:215
Thomas, 21:213, 216, 219-221
Timothy, 21:213-215; 22:77
Unice/Eunice (Green), 21:216
William, 21:213, 216-220, 222
Winthrop, 22:225, 233
Zachariah, 21:219, 220
POOR/POORE, 23:147, 150
Abraham, 24:96
Alfred, 25:198
Alice, 25:56
Anna (Giles), 21:53
Betty (Stevens), 24:94, 100
C. Howard, 25:82
Daniel, 21:195, 199; 24:38, 43, 92
Deborah, 21:213
Dorothy (Kimball), 24:92

Ebenezer, 24:91, 94, 100
Elizabeth, 22:92; 24:96
Elizabeth (___), 24:96
Harriet Victoria (Hatchard), 21:53
Hephziba, 24:94
James, 24:98
Jennie Linde, 21:53
John, 21:53; 24:44
Joseph G., 21:53
Lawrance, 23:150
Margaret (Farnum), 24:38
Mary, 24:38, 40, 43, 84
Mary (Stevens), 24:44
Mehitabel (Osgood), 24:43
O. J., 23:191
Phebe, 24:94
Rebecca, 23:117; 24:103
Rebecca (Stevens), 24:44
Ruth, 21:116; 24:36, 38, 39, 44
Samuel, 24:94
Sarah, 24:44, 88, 92, 96
Sarah (___), 24:44
Sarah (Poor), 24:44
Sarah F., 24:103
Thomas, 21:199
Timothy, 24:44
POPE
___, Mr., 21:13
Charles Henry, 21:37, 49, 89; 23:99, 234, 235
Damaris, 22:216
Elizabeth (___), 22:172
Harriet, 22:237
Henry, 21:222
Jeremiah Lee, 22:171
John, 22:176
Josiah Clark, 22:172
Lois (___), 22:171
Nathaniel, 22:172
Robert G., 21:170; 24:105
Ruth (___), 22:176
Samuel, 22:171, 172, 176
Sarah, 22:236
William, 22:176
PORTER, 21:225; 22:135
Abigail, 23:117
Alice M. (Johnson), 23:127
Dudley, 23:150
Greenleaf, 23:150
Hannah (Dodge), 22:57
John, 22:57, 58
Joseph, 24:78
Joseph G., Mrs., 23:113
Lydia, 21:42
Lydia (Herrick), 22:57
Mary, 21:237; 22:57
Mary (___), 22:58
Rufus, 22:31
Samuel, 22:57
T. C., 22:138
POTTER
"Daughter", 21:51
Abigail, 21:51
Abigail (Wells), 21:51
Benjamin, 22:213
David, 22:45
Edmund, 21:51
Edward, 22:42
Elizabeth, 21:51; 24:99
Hannah, 21:51
Hannah (Patch), 21:51
Jemima (Quarles), 21:51
John, 21:51
Marjorie, 22:170
Mary, 21:51; 24:91
Nathaniel, 21:51

Rebecca, 21:145
Robert, 21:30; 22:209
Sarah, 21:51
Sarah (Graves), 21:51
Susanna, 21:51
William, 21:51, 145
POWERS
Charles L., 23:17
POWTER/POULTER
Elizabeth, 23:223
PRAMBERG
Noreen C., 21:144, 204
PRATT/PRATTE
Betsey (Mansfield), 25:147
Daty, 25:147
Grace, 22:110; 25:156
Joseph, 21:12; 22:171
Lucy, 23:155
Margaret (___), 22:171
Peggy, 22:171
Richard, 22:49; 25:147
Tacy, 25:147, 148
PRENTICE/PRENTISS
Abigail, 21:157
Frances, 21:176
Henry, 23:207
John, 22:225, 230, 231
PRESCOTT, 23:35
John, 24:170
Jonathan, 23:226, 227
Rebecca (Bulkeley), 23:226, 227
Wm. P., 23:56
PRESTON
___, Capt., 23:9, 10
Anna (Leach), 21:41
Belle, 21:156
Betty (Tyler), 21:99
David, 21:41
Elizabeth, 21:41
Elizabeth (Voden), 21:41
John, 21:41
Jonathan, 21:41
Martha, 21:41
Martha (___), 21:40
Mary, 21:41
Mary (___), 21:41
Nanna/Nancy (Tyler), 21:99
Rebecca, 21:39, 41; 22:22
Rebecca (___), 21:41
Rebecca (Nurse), 21:40, 41
Roger, 21:40; 25:132, 133
Thomas, 21:40, 41
PREUSS
Arthur, 23:138
PRICE
___, Capt., 21:92
___, Mr., 23:218
Anna, 24:35
B. T., 23:95
Bartel T., 23:96
Bert, 23:96
Clara D., 23:95
Daniel, 23:95
Daniel D., 23:97
Daniel E., 23:95-97
Dorothy, 23:95, 97
Elizabeth (___), 23:96
Eva, 23:96
Florence, 23:96
Francis, 23:95, 96
George, 23:96
George D., 23:95
John, 23:96
John I., 23:95
John Ira, 23:94-97
Leon, 23:95, 96

Marion (___), 23:95
Marion (Spragg), 23:96
Mary E., 23:96
Mary E. (Lawrence), 23:96
Mary Elizabeth (Skidmore), 23:94-96
Sarah (___), 23:95
Walter, 21:90; 23:96
Walter S., 23:95
PRICHARD/PRITCHARD see also
    PRITCHET
Anne (Hill), 25:92
Anne (Parker), 25:93
Joanna, 24:54
Pearly P., 25:93
William, 21:44
PRIDE
___, Mrs., 24:106
PRIEST
Mary (Parker), 24:49
Phillip, 24:49
PRIESTLEY
James, 23:150
PRIME
Mark, 22:167
PRINCE
___, Dr., 24:194
Betsy, 22:172
Hannah (Stevens), 24:92
John, 21:12; 24:232a
Thomas, 24:92
Walter, 22:172
PRINGLE
Hannah Parsons (Wiley), 21:104
James R., 23:194
PRITCHARD see PRICHARD
PRITCHET/PRITCHETT see also
    PRICHARD
___ (Dennison), 21:44
Benjamin, 21:45
Eleazer, 21:45
Elizabeth, 21:44
Hannah (Perley), 21:45
John, 21:44, 45
Joseph, 21:45
Martha (Gould), 21:45
Mary, 21:45
Paul, 21:45
Samuel, 21:44, 45
Sarah (Harris), 21:44
William, 21:44, 45; 22:159
PROCTER/PROCTOR, 22:25
___, Capt., 22:85, 84
___, Lawyer, 22:84
Abigail, 23:105
Ann (Allen), 23:101, 102, 106
Anne S., 23:102
Benjamin, 23:103-105, 107, 150
Celia (Gallagher), 23:101, 106
Cotton, 25:83
Daniel, 22:172; 23:104
Daniel Epes, 23:102, 103, 106
David, 25:87
Debby, 22:173
Denmark, 23:103; 24:201
Eben, 22:172
Ebenezer, 22:172, 173
Eddie, 23:102
Eliza, 23:103
Elizabeth, 23:103
Elizabeth (___), 25:78
Elizabeth (Bassett), 21:87; 23:105, 169
Elizabeth (Epes), 23:102-104, 106,
    107; 24:201, 204
Elizabeth (Parker), 25:46
Elizabeth (Robbins), 23:57
Elizabeth (Thorndike), 23:105

Elldad, 24:216
Epes, 23:103
Ester (Fletcher), 25:40
Even C., 24:202
Frances Ann, 23:102
Frances M., 23:102
Francis, 23:102
Francis Epes, 23:101, 106
George, 23:101, 106
George H., 24:201, 202
George Henry, 23:101, 106
Grace Carolyn (McEachern), 23:101,
    106
Greenwich, 23:103
Hannah, 23:103, 105
Humphrey, 22:225, 232
I., 24:34
Isaac, 23:150
J. W., 22:85
Jacob, 21:120; 23:57, 58
James Lester, 23:102
Jeams, 25:40
John, 22:58; 23:58, 103-105, 107, 114,
    150, 169; 24:140, 202
John Joseph, 23:101, 106
John L., 23:101; 24:201
John P., 24:202
John W., 22:83
Joseph, 21:120; 22:225, 232, 233;
    23:57, 58, 102, 103, 105-107;
    24:201, 202, 204
Joseph O., 24:201, 202, 204
Lecretia (Stanwood), 23:57
Leland H., 23:107
Lucy (___), 25:83
Lucy (Bray), 21:120; 23:57
Lydia, 23:103, 104
Lydia (Giddons), 23:107
Lydia (Gould), 23:102, 103, 106, 107
Lydia (Waters), 23:103, 104, 107
Mabel B., 23:102
Martha, 23:105
Martha (___), 22:172
Martha (Giddons), 23:104, 105
Martha (Harper), 23:58, 105, 107
Martha (Wainwright), 21:120; 23:58
Mary, 23:103-105
Mary (___), 22:173
Mary (Dennen), 21:120; 23:57
Mary (Parker), 25:45
Mary (Perkins), 23:58
Mary (Whittredge), 23:104, 105, 107
Nancy, 23:103
Nabby, 22:172
Oliver, 25:45, 46
Patty, 22:172
Polly, 22:172; 23:103
Priscilla, 23:104
Prudence, 23:104
Rachel (Parker), 24:216
Rebecca, 25:87
Sarah, 22:57; 23:103-105, 176; 25:87
Sarah (Leatherland), 21:120; 23:58
Sarah (Steele), 23:101, 106
Sylvester, 23:83, 85, 104
Thomas, 21:120; 22:232; 23:57
Thomas M., 22:221, 233
Thorndike, 25:78
William, 22:221, 228, 229; 23:150;
    25:83
William Allen, 23:102
William L., 23:57
PROPER
Donna M., 24:174
PUDNEY/PURDEE, 25:9
John, 25:10

PULSIFER, 24:153; 25:7
PUNCH
Terrance, 25:121
PUNCHARD
Benjamin Hanover, 23:30, 31
John, 25:150
PURCHAS/PURCHIS
Abraham, 25:129
John, 25:129
Oliver, 21:152, 153; 22:208
Ruth (___), 25:129
PURDEE/PUDNEY, 25:10
John, 25:9
PURINGTON
Abbie Sarah, 24:200
Adelaide, 24:200
Alice Greenleaf, 24:200
Anne, 24:200
Charles Sumner, 24:200
Daniel, 24:200
Daniel S., 24:197
Dillwyn Varney, 24:200
Donald Varney, 24:200
Joseph Albert, 24:200
Lydia (Gifford), 24:200
Lydia Marie, 24:200
Sarah (Varney), 24:200
Sarah Abbie, 24:200
Sarah P. (Varney), 24:197
William Sidney, 24:200
Winfrey Stanley (___), 24:200
PUTNAM, 21:10; 22:135; 23:35
"Daughter", 21:42
"Son", 21:42
___, Mrs., 24:196
Abigail, 21:42
Alfred P., 24:196
Amos, 21:42
Ann, 21:41, 44; 23:55
Ann (___), 21:41
Ann (Carr), 23:54
Archelaus, 23:91
Daniel, 22:31
Eben, 22:137
Ebenezer, 21:213
Edward, 21:42, 44
Elizabeth, 21:42
Elizabeth (Hutchinson), 21:41
Elizabeth C., 22:147
F.W., 24:122
George Granville, 21:10, 11
Hannah, 21:42
Hannah (___), 21:42
Hannah (Cutler), 21:41, 42
John, 21:37, 41, 42
Jonathan, 21:41, 51
Joseph, 21:42; 25:58
Joshua, 21:42, 43
Josiah, 21:42
Lydia (Porter), 21:42
Mary, 21:42
Mary (Leach), 21:42
Mary (Veren), 25:58
Merelyn, 21:18
Nathaniel, 21:41, 90
Priscilla, 21:42
Rachel (Buxton), 21:42
Rachel (Goodale), 21:42, 43
Rebecca, 21:42
Robert, 23:138
Ruth (Hutchinson), 21:42
Samuel, 21:42
Sarah, 21:42
Susanna, 21:42
Thomas, 21:41, 42, 90; 25:58

PYNCHON
William, 23:180a
PYNE
Mary Frances, 21:108

QUARLES, 23:212
Elizabeth (Goldsmith), 22:41
Francis, 22:41; 25:164
Jemima, 21:51; 22:57
QUINAN
Peter, 23:150
QUINCY
George H., 21:232
QUINN
Annie, 25:68
Edward W., 23:17
Robert H., 23:18

RADASCH
Arthur, 22:42
RADDIN
Anna (Mansfield), 21:32
Benjamin, 21:32; 23:206
Mary (___), 23:206
RADFORD
Dwight A., 25:121
RAE see also RAY, 23:73
RAINSFORD
Edmund J., 23:18
RAMSDALL/RAMSDELL, 21:150
Allen, 25:184
Anna, 22:46, 47, 54
Anna (Atwell), 22:50
Anna (Chadwell), 22:47
George, 25:184
Hannah, 21:239
Huldah (___), 25:129, 184
Isaac, 21:148
John, 25:9
Jonathan, 22:47
Mary (Batten), 21:239
Nehemiah, 22:50
Noah, 21:239
Tabitha (Atwell), 22:46
William, 25:129, 184
RAND
Abigail, 21:33
Abigail (Carter), 21:28
Alice, 21:28
Alice (Sharp), 21:28
Ann/Hannah/Anna (Ivory), 21:30, 31
Anna, 21:31, 32, 35
Bartholomew, 21:33
Daniel, 21:32-34
Ebenezer, 21:35
Edmund, 21:28
Elizabeth, 21:28, 30-32, 35
Elizabeth (___), 21:29, 30
Elizabeth (Parker), 21:32, 34, 35
Elizabeth (Richardson), 21:31, 33
Elizabeth Simpkins, 21:33
F. O., 21:28, 32
Florence Osgood, 21:28
Francis, 21:28
Haide, 21:33
Hannah, 21:30, 31, 33
Hannaniah, 21:35
Henry, 21:28
John, 21:28, 31, 32, 34, 35
Levinah, 21:34
Lois, 21:31
Margery, 21:28
Martha (Bruce), 21:33, 34
Martha (Nazro), 21:33
Martha (Osgood), 21:35
Mary, 21:30-35

Mary (___), 25:78
Mary (Carter), 21:28
Mary (Gray), 21:33
Mary (Keyes), 21:32-34
Mary (Simpkins), 21:33
Nathaniel, 21:28, 31
Phebe, 21:34
Rebecca, 21:35
Rezinah, 21:34
Richard, 21:32
Robert, 21:28-34, 152; 22:44, 45
Samuel, 21:28
Sarah, 21:30, 34
Sarah (Dudley), 21:32, 34
Sarah (Edenden), 21:28
Solomon, 21:34
Susanna, 21:28, 32-34
Susanna (Cheever), 21:31, 32
Tabitha (Ivory), 21:30, 31
Thankful, 21:34
Thomas, 21:28, 31, 32, 34, 35; 23:150
William, 21:34
Zachariah, 21:29-34
Zachary, 21:31
RANDALL/RANDELL see also
RENDALL
___, Goodwife, 21:112
Elizabeth, 22:86
P. E., 22:177
RANKIN
Edward B., 23:16
Edward P. B., 23:135
RANTOUL
Mary (___), 25:78
Robert, 25:78
Robert S., 24:56a
William, 25:78
RAPAPORT
Diane, 25:3, 7, 8
RATCLIFF
Roselyn, 22:195
RATFORD
John, 23:150
RATHBUN
Joshua, 22:179
Mary (Wightman), 22:179
Susannah, 22:179
Tabitha (Brown), 22:179
Valentine Wightman, 22:179
RATTIGAN
John P., 23:17, 18
RAWSON
___, Mr., 25:18
Edward, 21:112, 185; 22:19, 21
RAY see also RAE, REA, WRAY, 23:73
Alan, 23:193, 194
Mary, 23:139, 193; 24:151

RAYMENT
Hannah, 22:55
RAYMOND
George Willis, 23:155
John, 23:150
Polly (___), 23:150
RAYNOR, 22:30
Henry, 22:101
Johannah (Edwards), 22:101
REA see also RAY, RAE, WRAY
Mary (___), 21:41
See Ray, 23:73
READ see also REED, REID
___, Sister, 24:105
Christopher, 23:222
Dorothy (Fletcher), 25:142
Elizabeth, 23:222
Elizabeth (Pike), 25:18, 22

Esdras, 24:105, 106
John, 25:18
Katharine (___), 23:222
Peter, 25:142
Thomas, 25:87
READING/RIDING see also REDDING
Hannah, 22:225, 227-229
Herbert, 23:150
William, 23:151
REAR
J. M., 21:100
REARDON
Edmund, 23:17
REDDING see also READING
Elizabeth, 24:222; 25:16
Hannah, 22:228
Jeremiah, 24:222
Joseph, 24:222; 25:16
Lucy N., 23:127
Mary (___), 24:222
Thomas, 24:222
REDDINGTON see also REDINGTON
Daniel, 24:41
Elizabeth (Stevens), 24:41
REDFERN
Lydia (Tarbox), 22:50
William, 22:50
REDINGTON see also REDDINGTON
___, Sgt., 23:237
Abraham, 23:236
John, 23:236
Mary (Gould), 23:238
Sarah, 23:117
REED see also READ, REID, 22:135
Bethiah, 21:158
Betsey (Walker), 22:120
Charley, 23:56
Chas. S., 21:104
Ebenezer, 25:18, 22
Elizabeth, 23:151
Emily (Emerson), 21:104
Jacob, 22:27
Jacob W., 22:144
Keziah, 21:239
Mary (___), 21:43
Paul C., 25:95
Rebecca, 22:84
Remember, 21:43
Sheldon C., 24:61
Thomas, 21:43
William, 24:81
REEKS
Lindsay S., 24:49
REID see also READ, REED
Joseph, 24:99
Sarah (Stevens), 24:99
REILLY
John C., 23:139, 159; 24:217
REINHOLD, 21:9
REISINGER
Joy, 22:200
REITWIESNER, 24:69
William Addams, 24:67
REMIC/REMICK
Abraham, 24:162
Peter, 23:151
Ursula (Parker), 24:162
REMINGTON
John, 22:167
Mary, 24:42
RENDA
Wendy Witten, 24:108
RENDALL see also RANDALL
Ann, 24:161
RENICK, 21:9

RENSHAW
Wm. E., 22:79
RENUF
Elizabeth, 23:151
RESTALL
Harriet (___), 22:76
REVERE
Paul, 23:3, 90, 156; 24:127
REYNA
Juana (Manuel), 24:68
REYNER
Humphrey, 22:165, 167
REYNOLDS
Caroline, 25:173
David, 23:151
Hope, 23:233
RHEAULT
Charles, 25:204
RHOADES/RHOADS/RHODES/
DeRHOADES/RORES/RODES/
RHODS/ROADS, 22:202, 23:35
"Daughter", 23:40
"Son", 23:40
Abigail (Coates), 22:210
Abigail (Stanbrough), 23:37
Alphonzo, 23:36
Amey C., 23:49
Amos, 22:208
Amy, 23:45
Ann (Graves), 21:31; 22:210
Anna (Burrill), 22:211
Caroline Elizabeth, 23:46, 49, 50
Eleazer, 22:210-214; 23:38-45, 48
Elizabeth, 22:210, 214; 23:37, 39, 40, 46
Elizabeth (___), 22:208; 23:36, 46
Elizabeth (Burrage), 21:31
Elizabeth (Coates/Coats), 22:211, 214; 23:37
Elizabeth (Coldham), 22:210-212
Elizabeth (Coldham/White/Paul), 22:202, 203, 206
Elizabeth (Paul), 22:46, 214
Elizabeth (Waterhouse), 23:45, 49
Elizabeth (Wyatt), 21:31
Elizabeth Joanna (Barstow), 22:201, 202
Ephraim, 21:31
Eunice, 23:117
Eunice (Atwell), 22:46
Ezekiel, 22:46
Freelove, 23:37, 39, 40
Hannah, 21:40; 23:42-44
Harold, 23:45
Henry, 21:31, 149; 22:46, 202-211, 214; 23:37-40, 44, 46
Hezekiah, 22:46
Hiram Boden, 23:46
Hiram Bowen, 23:46, 49
Howard J., 22:201
Isaiah, 21:35
James, 22:202
James Green, 23:45, 49
Jane (Coates), 22:210
Jane (Durham), 23:46, 50
Joanna (Larrabee), 21:31
John, 22:214; 23:38-40, 45, 151; 25:17
Jonathan, 22:205, 210, 211, 213, 214; 23:37-40, 42-49
Jonathan Stanbrough, 23:46, 50
Jonathan Stanbury, 23:49
Joseph, 22:206, 210, 212-214; 23:36
Joshua, 21:31; 22:205, 206, 210-212, 214
Josiah, 22:205-207, 210-214; 23:37, 38, 40, 44

Lucy, 22:49
Lydia, 23:42-44, 46, 50
Lydia (Shaw), 23:36
Lydia M., 23:49
Lydia Margaret, 23:46, 49
Margeret (Bowen), 23:40-42, 44-46
Martha, 23:42-44
Martha (Coates), 23:37, 40
Martha (Stanbrough), 23:37-40
Mary, 22:214; 23:38-44, 48
Mary (Ballard), 21:31
Mary (Hawkins), 23:40, 42, 43
Mary (Rand), 21:31
Mary (Stoddard), 23:50
Mary (Young), 23:44-49
Mary A. (Stoddard), 23:46
Mary Catherine, 23:46, 49, 50
Morris, 23:47
Obadiah, 23:37, 38
Peter, 23:36
Priscilla (Smith), 22:214
Roland, 25:154
Samuel, 22:205, 206, 210, 212-214; 23:38; 24:79; 25:17
Sarah, 22:45, 54; 23:42-44
Thomas, 21:31
Violetta, 23:46, 49, 50
Walter, 22:201, 202, 211; 23:37, 38, 40, 44, 46
William, 23:41-44
Zachariah, 22:201, 202
Zadoc, 23:46
Zadock Young, 23:45, 46, 49
RICE
Abigail (Clark), 21:157, 160
David, 21:32
Elizabeth (Rand), 21:32
Ezekiel, 21:152
Hannah (Whitney), 21:152
Jason, 21:156, 157
Luther, 25:60a
Susanna (Haven), 21:156
RICH
A. B., 21:226
Hiram, 24:202
James, 23:151
Rachel, 23:151
Robert, 23:151
Shebnah, 25:23
RICHARD
Edith, 22:74
Lydia, 22:236
RICHARDS
Abigail (___), 23:119
Amanda Malvina, 25:54
Ann (Knight), 23:168
Crispas, 22:44
Daniel, 23:169
Edward, 22:203; 23:168, 169; 25:103
Elizabeth (Bassett), 23:169
Hannah Woodbury, 22:237
John, 23:169
Joseph, 22:236, 237; 25:53, 54, 153
Lydia, 22:236
Lydia (___), 22:236, 237; 25:53, 54, 153
M., 24:70
Margaret/Peggy, 23:119
Martha, 22:236
Mary Ann, 21:224
Rebekah, 22:236
Samuel Crowell, 25:153
Sarah Archer, 22:237
Theodore, 23:119
RICHARDSON, 21:216; 23:35
___, Mr., 21:113, 114

Abigail (Kneeland), 24:98
Alice Eliza, 22:119
Alvin Howard, 21:105
Andrew Craig, 22:119
Betsey, 25:78
Caleb, 21:113; 24:98
Charles, 22:237
Charles Mansfield, 22:237
Christian (Outerson), 22:119
David, 23:151
Douglas, 23:222; 24:153; 25:33
Elijah, 21:105
Elizabeth, 21:31, 33
Elizabeth (Atwell), 22:46, 52, 53
Elizabeth (Emerson), 21:105
Elliot, 23:8
Emerson, 21:105
Eunice, 24:195
Eunice (___), 25:78
Frances Adelaide, 21:105
Hannah, 22:72
Hannah (Skidmore), 23:91
Hannah (Stevens), 24:98
Henrietta, 21:105
Henry, 25:83
James, 22:119; 23:151
Jane (Beerworth), 22:119
John, 21:113
Joseph, 22:46, 53
Joshua, 21:112; 25:78
Lydia, 23:227
Mary Elizabeth, 21:105
Nathaniel, 25:78
Nellie, 21:105
Priscilla (___), 25:83
Rebecca, 21:103
Richard, 21:29, 30
Samuel, 23:91
Sarah, 25:85
Sarah (___), 22:237; 25:145
Simeon, 22:225, 227
RICHFORD
Mary, 23:240
RIDDAN
Elizabeth (King), 23:168
Joanna (Hawkins), 21:38
John, 21:38
Thaddeus, 21:38; 23:168
RIDEOUT
Abraham, 21:116
Jemima (Davis), 21:116
Judith (Bedell), 21:116
Nathaniel, 21:116
Nicholas, 21:116
Rowland, 21:116
Susanna, 21:116
Susanna (Spaulding), 21:116
RIDING see READING
RIENER
Sidney, 25:123
RIGGS
Ann (Wheeler), 24:232
Asa, 22:225, 228-230
Hannah, 24:232
John, 25:203
Martha, 21:161
Mary (Millett), 24:232; 25:203
Polly, 21:161
Rachel, 25:203
Ruth (Wheeler), 25:203
Samuel, 22:225, 230-233
Thomas, 24:232; 25:203
RILEY
Bridget, 24:123
Bridget (___), 24:123
Cornelius, 25:73

Cornelius Bernard, 25:73
Cornelius Joseph, 25:73
Daniel, 24:123
Hannah, 22:120
Phil P., 22:32
Thomas, 23:16

RING
Sarah, 21:12

RIORDAN
Thomas, 25:74

RIST
Dorcas, 21:91

RITCHIE
Lawrence T., 23:17

ROACH
Margaret (Ahern), 25:72
Mary, 21:179
Morris, 25:72

ROADS see RHOADES

ROAFE
John, 25:103

ROBBINS, 25:41
Charles L., 22:225, 230
Charlotte (Bray), 22:240; 23:57
Ebenezer, 23:57, 240
Eleanor, 24:53
Elizabeth, 21:120; 23:57
George, 25:169
Hannah (Chandler), 23:240
John, 22:240; 23:57
Mary, 25:143
Mary (___), 25:45
Mary (Brashear), 23:240
Nathaniel, 23:240
Rebecca (___), 23:240
Richard, 23:240
Sarah (Estebrook), 23:57
Stephen, 25:168
Thomas, 21:90; 23:240
Xena Christina (Jackson), 23:240

ROBENS
Mary, 23:151

ROBERTS, 21:9
Allen, 23:138
B. P., 25:106
Charles L., 22:221, 225, 228-233
Hannah, 22:158
Jean Sillay, 22:180a
John, 23:151
Jonathan, 21:77, 191
Levi, 22:221, 227
Nancy, 22:51
P., 24:34
Rick, 21:80
Robert, 25:133
Thomas, 23:151

ROBERTSON
Earton P., 23:158
Irene, 23:109

ROBIN/ROBINS
Nathaniel, 23:140, 151

ROBINSON
___, Mrs., 24:196
Abraham, 23:164, 218
Andrew, 24:218
Ann, 23:164, 179
Ann (Batten), 24:218
Anna, 24:218
Betsey, 22:53
Caroline E., 21:21, 228
Daniel, 22:88
Dean, 25:193
Elizabeth (Stevens), 24:37
Enders A., 21:93
Hannah, 22:88; 24:39, 44
John, 22:37, 88; 24:196, 218

Jonathan, 24:218
Joseph, 24:37
Martha (Gardner), 24:218
Mary, 22:88, 91; 24:218
Mary (Harraden), 23:164
Mary (Silver), 22:86-88, 91
Phebe, 24:41
Robert, 22:87, 88, 91
Samuel, 21:13; 22:88; 25:78
Sarah (___), 24:218
Sarah/Sara, 22:88, 225, 231
Thomas, 22:88
William Ring, 24:218

ROBOTTI
Frances Diane, 22:120a; 23:180a,
240a; 24:56a, 116a, 176a; 25:156a

ROBY
Joseph, 23:116
Rebekah, 25:88

ROCH/ROCHE
Alphonsine, 21:54
Peter H., 23:18
Richard W., 23:16

ROCKEFELLER, 21:79

ROCKWELL, 22:101
Norman, 22:128
S. Forbes, 21:199

RODERICK
George Holmes, 24:70
Louise Almira (Huston), 24:70
T. H., 24:61, 65, 72
Thomas H., 24:59, 70, 114

RODES see RHOADES

RODGERS
Robert H., 23:51, 52

RODMAN
Harold, 24:223
Roberta (Pandolfini), 24:223

ROFE/ROFF/ROFFE/ROFFES
___, Goody, 25:100, 101
___, Mrs., 25:101
John, 25:96, 101-105
Mary (Scullard), 25:96, 97, 101-105

ROGERS, 22:135
___, Mr., 24:105
___, Mrs., 24:197
Abigail (Gould), 23:174
Abigail/Nabby, 21:239; 23:174
Anna, 21:238
Bethia, 21:170
Daniel, 22:225, 227, 229, 230; 23:227
Eliza Georgeanna (Clague), 21:179
Elizabeth (Carr), 22:120, 239
Esther (Ordway), 22:239
Eunice, 24:50
Ezechiel, 21:170; 22:164-167; 25:9, 10
George C., 24:197, 200
George H., 22:225, 234
George Henry, 21:179
Grace, 23:174
Grace (Rogers), 23:174
Herbert, 22:76
Herbert George, 21:179
Jane, 23:119
Jane (___), 23:151
Joan (Hartopp), 22:165
Joan (Wilson), 22:165
John, 21:5, 66, 169, 170; 22:225, 229,
230, 239; 23:174; 24:26
Joseph, 21:71
Josiah, 24:172
Lydia (Hobart), 21:179
Lydia Marie (Purington), 24:200
Maria Louisa (Doty), 21:179
Mary, 23:174
Mary (___), 22:165

Mary (Toothaker), 23:174
Mary (Whiting), 23:227
Nathan, 21:179; 22:120, 239
Nathan Jefferson, 21:179
Nathan John, 21:179; 22:239
Nathaniel, 21:169, 170; 22:137, 164,
165; 24:26, 140, 168; 25:12, 167
Polly (Pike), 21:179
Richard, 21:170; 22:164
Richard Carr, 22:120, 239
Robert, 22:239; 25:102
Ruth (Brown), 22:239
Ruth (Parker), 24:206
S. G., 22:231
Samuel, 21:83, 84; 22:225, 228-231;
23:174
Sarah, 21:170; 23:174
Sarah (Currier), 21:144
Shubael G., 22:221, 225, 231-233
Susanna (___), 22:239
Thomas, 21:169, 170; 22:239; 23:174
Thomas Jefferson, 21:179
Timothy, 22:225, 232; 24:206
William, 23:151, 174; 25:188

ROLANDSON
Thomas, 22:151, 153

ROLF/ROLFE
___, Goodwife, 25:98
Esther, 21:146
Ezra, 22:151
Henry, 21:114
Hester, 23:230-233
John, 21:146; 23:233, 234; 25:95, 98
Marie/Mary (Scullard), 21:146; 25:95,
96, 99
Mary, 22:86

ROLINGS
Elephalet, 25:45
Patey (Sargent), 25:45

ROLLE
Richard, 21:162

ROLLINS
John, 22:225, 227, 228; 23:151

ROONEY
Mickey, 25:108

ROOSEVELT
___, Pres., 23:114
Franklin D., 21:138, 139

ROOTEN
Richard, 22:206

ROPER
Sarah, 22:109
Stephen J., 21:199

ROPES
___, Mrs., 24:196
Benjamin, 21:10; 22:175
David Nichols, 25:151
Elizabeth Grant, 25:151
George, 21:10; 25:151
Hannah, 22:174
Hannah (___), 22:174-176, 235
Hardy, 22:174-176, 235
Henry, 25:151
J. Bertram, 24:196
Joseph, 22:175; 25:151
Joseph Elson, 22:176
Mary Ann, 25:151
Samuel, 22:235
Sarah, 22:235
Sarah (___), 25:151
Sarah Grant, 25:151
Thomas Holmes, 25:151
Timothy, 25:151

RORES see RHOADES

ROSE
Ernestine J., 22:195

Ernestine June, 22:170
ROSEAR
  Richard, 23:151
ROSENCRANTZ, 23:212
ROSS/ROSSE, 23:70
  ___, Mrs., 21:114
  Alexander, 23:72, 74, 76
  Elizabeth, 23:73
  Elizabeth (Wallace), 23:72, 74, 76
  Fenill, 25:8
  Gilicrest, 25:8
  Increase, 23:42
  James, 25:6
  Jeremiah, 23:151
  John, 25:8
  Katharine, 22:169
  Mary, 21:145, 146
  Robina, 23:68, 69, 72-75
  Seeth (Holman), 25:6
  Theodore A., 23:138
  Thomas, 25:6
ROSSNAGLE
  John, 22:77, 79
ROTHMAN
  Sheila M., 25:107
ROTUNDO
  Barbara, 25:204
ROUNDS/ROUND
  John, 21:6
  Jonathan, 21:7
  Richard, 23:41
ROUNDY, 23:212
  Deborah (Plumb), 21:98
  Eliza Ann, 25:153
  George, 21:108; 22:78
  Mary, 21:98
  Mary Smith (Wilson), 21:108
  Nathaniel, 23:189
  Robert, 21:98
  Ruth Smith, 21:108
  Samuel Goodwin, 25:54
  Thomas, 25:54, 153
  William, 22:78
ROUNTY
  George C., 23:210
ROW
  Isaac, 22:231
  James, 21:208
  Zebulun, 23:151
ROWE/ROW, 22:113
  Albert E., 24:230
  Charlotte (Webb), 24:230
  Daniel, 24:171
  Ebenezer, 22:221, 227
  George F., 24:230
  George Franklin, 24:230
  Isaac, 22:225, 231
  John, 22:112; 23:151
  Mary, 24:232
  William, 22:112
  William D., 24:230
  William H., 24:230
  William Henry, 24:230
  William Hutchinson, 22:43
ROWELL
  Anne (___), 21:117
  Hannah, 22:236, 237
  Hannah (___), 22:236, 237
  Johannah, 22:55
  John, 22:236, 237
  Mary, 25:25
  Philip, 21:117
  Sarah (Barnes), 22:55
  Thomas, 22:55
  Thomas Pitman, 22:237
  Valentine, 22:56

ROWLANDS
  John, 25:124
  Sheila, 25:124
ROWLANDSON
  Martha, 21:88
ROY
  Thomas Sherrard, 23:138
ROYSON
  John, 22:225, 229, 230
RUCKE
  Hannah, 25:8
RUDDOCK/RUDDUCKE
  Emma, 24:230
  John, 25:6
RUGG
  Hepsibah, 21:157, 160
  Jonathan, 21:157
  Mehitable, 21:156
  Sarah (___), 21:157
RUGGLES
  ___, Mr., 23:224
  Benjamin, 23:222
  Dorcas/Doriks (Whiting), 23:222
  Dorothy, 23:224
  Elisabeth (Whiting), 23:222
  Elizabeth, 23:224
  Lucy (___), 25:91
  Samuel, 23:221, 222, 224
RUNDLE
  Elizabeth, 22:179
RUNNELS, 22:135
  Geo., 21:103
  Mary E. (Tyler), 21:103
  Samuel, 21:96
  Stephen, 22:144
RUPTON see also UPTON
  John, 21:115; 25:9, 10
RUSS
  John, 21:195
  Sarah, 21:116
  Willis R., 23:56
RUSSELL/BUSSELL see also
    BUSHNELL, 24:99; 25:190
  Andrew, 23:108
  Donna Valley, 25:42
  Dorcas (Chester), 23:221
  Elizabeth (Pitman), 21:30
  James, 24:43
  Jason, 23:89
  Jemima, 24:43, 90, 91
  John, 21:212
  John C., 23:188, 189
  Joseph, 21:213
  Marsha, 22:86
  Mary, 24:43
  Mary (___), 23:108
  Miriam, 23:209
  Priscilla (Osgood), 24:43
  Richard, 23:221
  Robert, 21:199
  Sarah, 21:43
  Tabitha, 23:210
RUSSELS
  Mary, 22:179
RUST, 24:149, 150
  Benjamin, 22:221, 225, 227-229, 232, 233
  Mary, 23:154
RUTMAN
  Darrett B., 23:135
RYAN
  Edward, 23:16
  James G., 25:121
  John, 23:10
  Mamie, 23:56
  Nancy, 22:149

Thomas, 23:17
  Virginia M., 25:187
RYNE
  William, 25:184
RYSKAMP
  George R., 25:123

SABIN
  Martha (Haven), 21:157
  Thomas, 21:157
SACHEM
  Joshua, 21:149
SACHSEN, 24:68
  Magdalena (___), 24:68
SACKETT
  Elizabeth (Kirtland), 21:30
  Richard, 21:30
SADDLER/SADLER, 21:217
  John, 23:151
  Mary Ann, 24:173, 174
  William, 23:151
SADIE
  Elizabeth (Peters), 21:88
SADLER see SADDLER
SAFFORD
  Charlotte, 21:106
  O. J., 23:113
SAGE
  Abigail, 24:72
  Allen, 24:71
  Comfort, 24:72
  David, 24:71
SALDANA
  Richard, 21:7
SALLARD
  John, 22:103
SALMON
  Anna (Thompson), 23:120
  Peter, 23:120
  Sarah, 23:120
SALTER
  Matthew, 25:25
SALTONSTALL
  Leverett, 24:232a
  Nathaniel, 21:49
  Richard, 22:69; 23:180a; 24:109, 112
SAMBON
  Solomon, 21:13
SAMPSON see also LAMPSON
  John, 23:148, 151
  William, 23:151
**SANBORN/SANBORNE/SANBURN/
    SANDBURN**
  Benjamin, 22:177; 23:117
  George, 23:77
  George F., 22:99, 110; 25:121
  George Freeman, 22:177
  Hannah (Thorne), 23:117
  James, 22:218
  John, 23:54
  Levi, 22:225, 228-230
  Mary, 22:177
  Melinde, 21:183; 22:59, 134
  Melinde (Lutz), 22:177
  Melinde Lutz, 22:99, 110
  Molly (Dimond), 22:218
  Nathan P., 24:79
  Sarah (Worcester), 22:177
  Sarah Dimond, 22:238
  Solomon, 21:13
SANDERS
  Abigail, 23:232
  Alice (___), 23:234
  Ann, 23:235
  Ann (___), 23:233
  Ann (Holmes), 23:235

Barbara B., 23:231
Barbara Brett, 23:229
Benjamin, 23:235
Elizabeth, 23:233, 235
Elizabeth (Grafton), 23:230, 231
Grace, 23:232
Hannah, 23:235
Hannah (Pickman), 23:231
Hope (Reynolds), 23:233
James, 23:235
John, 23:229-235
Joseph, 23:232
Josiah, 23:235
Judith, 23:234
Lea, 23:234
Martin, 23:234, 235
Mary, 23:232, 235
Mary (Farley), 23:235
Mary (Munjoy), 23:235
Nathaniel, 23:151
Paul, 23:109
Rachel (____), 23:234
Rachell, 23:235
Ruth, 23:231
Sarah, 23:53, 232
Susanna (Tomson), 23:235
Thomas, 23:233
SANDERSON, 22:48
____, Rev., 21:22
E., 21:17
Edward Frederick, 21:227
Howard K., 21:215
Howard Kendall, 22:47, 49
SANDS
Henry, 22:167
SARGEANT/SARGENT/
SERGEANT/SERGENT, 22:109,
135; 24:8
____, Mrs., 24:196
Abigail (Clark), 24:16, 175, 231
Benjamin, 22:178
Charles, 22:225, 233
Christopher, 22:145
David, 22:225, 227
Eunice, 22:178
Fitz E., 22:225, 234
Francis, 23:8
Gartret (Davis), 22:178
Gustavous, 22:225, 226, 228-233
Jacob, 22:178
John, 21:216; 25:45
Joseph, 23:151
Judith, 24:16, 175, 231
Judith (Parsons), 24:16, 175, 231
Lydia, 25:190, 194, 200
Martha, 22:97, 98
Mary (Colby), 25:200
Mary (Tewksbury), 22:97
Nathaniel, 24:16, 175, 231
Patey, 25:45
Patty (____), 23:151
Phillip, 22:97
Phineas, 25:190
Rachel, 25:44
Ruth (Moulton), 22:178
Samuel, 22:225-230; 23:151
Selina, 23:129
Sarah (Harvey), 22:178; 24:16, 175,
231
William, 24:16, 175, 231; 25:200
William A., 23:162
William Denny, 24:196
SARTON
May, 22:169
SAUCE
Abigail (____), 23:151

Nicholas, 23:151
SAUNDERS, 22:25
Anne (Parker), 25:91
Henry, 22:27
Joseph, 23:151
Levi, 23:195
Sarah, 23:229
Tobias, 23:109
William, 25:91
SAUR
K.G., 24:135
SAVAGE, 21:37; 22:159
Ephraim, 21:216
Hannah, 21:216
James, 21:30, 89, 148; 22:101, 109
Mary, 23:219
SAVILLE
Thomas, 22:221, 233, 234
William, 22:225, 232-234
SAWYARD/SAYARD/SAYWARD/
SAYWOOD
Daniel, 22:225, 228-230
James, 22:221
James S., 22:229, 230
Jonathan, 23:151
SAWYER, 21:173
Charles, 22:225, 232, 233
Edward, 22:167
Thomas, 22:167
William, 21:217
SAYARD see SAWYARD
SAYERS
Samuel, 21:172
SAYWARD/SAYWOOD see
SAWYARD
SCALES
Wm., 22:167
SCALISI
Marie, 25:198
Marie Lollo, 22:178; 25:187
SCANLON
Larry, 24:224
SCANNELL
Henry, 24:131, 132
SCENTER
Sarah (Parker), 24:162
SCHAAF
Elizabeth, 22:82, 108
SCHAFFNER
W., 24:70
SCHAPHFER
Guss, 24:174
SCHIDMORE see SKIDMORE, 23:87
SCHLINTING
Alexander, 24:55
Anna E. (____), 24:55
Helen, 24:55
John Andrew, 24:55
SCHMID
Jean Parker, 24:153; 25:33
John Carolus, 24:153; 25:33
SCHNEIDER
Eva, 22:80
SCHOEFFEL
Agnes (Booth), 23:56
John B., 23:56
SCHUKNECHT
Patti Gottschall, 22:179
SCHULTZ
Caroline, 23:129
SCIDMORE see SKIDMORE, 23:87
SCOT/SCOTT
Darius B., 22:76, 79
Hew, 23:86
J., 24:34
Robert, 21:169

Samuel, 25:177
Ursula, 22:58
SCRIBNER
Elizabeth, 22:178
Hannah (Welch), 22:178
Thomas, 22:178
SCRIPTURE
Abigail, 25:35
SCRIVEN
William, 22:43
SCUDAMORE/SCUDDAMORE/
SCUDIMORE see also
SKIDMORE, 23:87
Richard, 23:88
Thomas, 23:88
John, 23:151
SCULLARD
Betty, 25:99
Marie, 25:96, 105
Mary, 21:146; 25:95-97, 99, 101-104
Rebecca (Kent), 25:95
Samuel, 25:95
Sara, 25:96
Sarah, 25:99
SCULLER
Sarah, 25:95
SEARL/SEARLE/SEARLES/SEARLS
____, Miss, 22:84
Beth/Betsey, 22:47, 54
Eliza, 24:93, 102
Elizabeth, 24:102
Esther, 24:70
Hannah, 21:159
Jabez, 24:70
Joseph, 22:78
Phebe (Ames), 24:93, 102
Thankful (Topliff), 24:70
SEATON
James, 21:145, 146
Mary (Ross), 21:145, 146
Rebecca (Adams), 21:145, 146
SECCOMB/SECOMB, 22:25; 23:212
Eben, 23:210
Hannah (Bessom), 23:210
SEDMORE see SKIDMORE, 23:87
SEGARS/SEGER/SEGERS
Henry, 22:109
Sarah (Bishop), 22:109
William, 22:225, 227, 228; 23:140,
142-149, 152-154
SELAH
Matthew, 23:151
SELMAN
Archibald, 24:79
SELZNICK
David O., 25:81, 202
Irene Gladys (Mayer), 25:81
SENTER
Abigail (Parker), 25:45
John, 25:45
Rebecca (Parker), 24:163
Reuben, 24:163
Sary (Parker), 24:163
SERGENT/SARGEANT see
SARGEANT
SEROLE
John, 24:77
SEROTE see also SOUTH, SOUTHARD
John, 24:77
Stephen, 24:77
Susanna, 24:77
SESSIONS, 24:85
Anna (Cole), 21:94
Josiah, 21:94
SEWALL
____, Judge, 21:172

Phillis, 23:58
Rebekah, 25:164
Samuel, 23:3
SEXTON
Ann, 22:169
SEYMOUR
William, 23:56
SHACKLEFORD
William, 23:151
SHACKLEY
Charles Henry, 21:109
Lydia Ellen (Bryant), 21:109
Mabel Elizabeth, 21:109
Myrtle Rebecca, 21:109
SHAKESPEARE, 23:56
SHANNON
Catherine B., 23:18
SHARKEY
Patrick, 23:16
SHARP
Alice, 21:28
Elisabeth (Cook), 23:223
SHATSWELL
Mary, 21:172, 198
Richard, 25:104
SHATTOCK/SHATTUCK
Grace (___), 23:239
Hannah, 24:83, 93
Hannah (___), 25:129
Henry Lee, 23:8
Joanna (Chandler), 24:93
Joseph, 24:93
Lemuel, 23:226
Mary, 25:92
Mercy, 23:239
Patience, 25:129
Retire, 25:129
Samuel, 22:216, 217; 23:239; 25:129
Sarah (___), 25:129
SHAW
Elias, 23:151
Elizabeth, 23:152
Elizabeth/Eliza (Mauger), 22:119
John, 22:119, 120
Lydia, 23:36
Margaret (Aitkin), 22:119
Marion (Dickson), 22:120
Mary Marion, 22:119
Moses H., 22:221, 233, 234
Sophia Louisa, 25:197
Thomas, 22:119
SHAY/SHEA, 22:123; 23:41
Jonathan D., 25:122
Joseph J., 23:17
SHEATH
Thomas, 23:141
SHED
Joseph, 22:84
Sarah, 23:224
SHEEHY
Alfred C., 23:17
Richard W., 23:17
SHELDON
Rebecca, 23:117
SHENBERG
Hyman, 25:81, 202
Margaret, 25:81
SHENNE see MASON
SHEPARD/SHEPERD/SHEPHERD,
   21:10
Bee, 22:168
Elizabeth, 25:54
Elizabeth (___), 22:235
Jeremiah, 21:35; 22:235
Michael, 22:235
Stephen Webb, 22:235

SHEPARDSON
Lydia, 24:156
SHEPERD/SHEPHERD see SHEPARD
SHERBORN
James, 21:50
Sarah (Gray), 21:50
SHERIN see SHERWIN
Ebenezer, 21:96
SHERMAN
Angeline Lydia/L.A., 22:120
Thomas, 21:199
SHERRY
P. P., 22:72
SHERWIN/SHERIN
Ebenezer, 21:95-97
Hepzibah (Cole), 21:95-97
Susannah (Howlett), 21:97
SHILL
Peter, 23:125
SHILLABER
Benjamin, 22:27
Robert, 22:27
SHILLETTS
George, 23:210
Sarah (Bessom), 23:210
SHILLITO, 23:212
SHINGLETERY see SINGLETARY
SHOLES
Cyrus, 23:152
SHONTEE
___, Mdm., 23:152
SHOPE
John, 23:152
SHORE
Abigail, 21:38
SHORT
Anthony, 21:114
Henry, 21:111-114; 25:103
SHOVE
G. H., 22:27
Margaret, 22:167
SHUMWAY, 23:212
SHURTLEFF
Nathaniel B., 21:144
SIBBALDS
Mary, 23:159, 174
SIDMAN
Roberta Marie, 21:18
SIKES
Elijah, 25:168
SILLAY
Frank, 22:180a
SILSBE/SILSBY
Hannah, 21:37
Henry, 21:29; 22:47
SILVA
___, Mayor, 23:193
SILVER
___, Mrs., 25:101
"Child", 22:90
"Daughter", 22:87
Abigail, 22:94
Adelaide, 22:95
Anne, 22:94
Benjamin, 22:96
Daniel, 22:94, 96
Elizabeth, 22:87, 90, 94, 96
Elizabeth (Caton), 22:96
Eunice, 22:98
Hannah, 22:87, 89, 91, 92, 94, 96
James, 22:94
Jemima (Kimball), 22:97, 98
John, 22:86, 87, 90, 93, 94, 96, 98
Katherine (___), 22:86-90, 99
Marie Adelaide, 22:94
Martha, 22:87, 88, 91, 98

Martha (Sargent), 22:97, 98
Mary, 22:86-88, 90, 94-96
Mary (___), 22:90, 97
Mary (Pecker), 22:94
Mary (Thomas), 22:86, 87
Mary (Williams), 22:89, 92-96, 99
Mary Adelaide, 22:96
Mehitable, 22:90, 94, 98
Mercy, 22:90
Peter, 22:90, 96, 99
Ruth, 22:90, 97, 98
Samuel, 22:86, 87, 90, 94, 96-98
Sarah, 22:87, 88, 90-94, 97, 98
Sarah (Colby), 22:90, 97, 98
Sarah (Keyser), 22:93, 94
Sary, 22:88
Susanna, 22:94
Thomas, 22:86-99, 101; 25:104
Timothy, 22:98
William, 22:96
SIMANAINEN
J., 24:70
SIMES
Wilton, 25:9
SIMMONS
Elizabeth (___), 25:184
Frances, 21:224
Frances R., 21:229, 230
John, 21:229
Mary (Lockwood), 21:229
Thoms, 25:184
SIMMS
Anngret, 25:122
SIMONDS, 23:212
Benjamin, 23:41
SIMPKINS
Mary, 21:33
William, 21:33
SIMPSON
Stephen, 23:172
William, 23:152
SINGER
Rachel (___), 24:220
SINGLETARY/SHINGLETERY
Amos, 21:144
Benjamin, 21:144
Eunice, 21:144
Jonathan, 21:144, 145, 147
Lydia, 21:144
Mary, 21:146
Mary (Bloomfield), 21:144, 145
Mary (Stockbridge), 21:144
Nathaniel, 21:144
Richard, 21:144
Sarah (Belknap), 21:144
Sarah (Currier), 21:144
Susannah (Cooke), 21:144
SINGLETON
Joanna, 23:152
Mary, 23:7
SINNOTT
Mary, 25:201
Walter, 25:201
SKELTON
Mary, 22:23
Samuel, 22:23; 23:180a; 24:232a
Susannah, 22:23
Thomas, 22:187
SKERRY, 21:12
Francis, 23:112
Henry, 22:208
Samuel, 21:13, 14

SKIDMORE/SCHIDMORE/
   SCIDMORE/SEDMORE see also
   SCUDIMORE/SCUDAMORE/
   DeSCUDAMORE, 23:87
   Ann E., 23:94, 97
   Betsey, 23:92
   David, 23:92
   Elias, 23:89, 91
   Elizabeth M. (___), 23:97
   Ellen Augusta, 23:94
   George F., 23:94
   George Franklin, 23:97
   Hannah, 23:91
   Hannah (Luscomb), 23:91
   Henry, 23:95, 97
   Henry Felton, 23:93, 94
   Henry W., 23:94
   Herbert Ramsdell, 23:97
   James, 23:93
   Jane M., 23:94
   Jemima, 23:88, 91, 92
   Jemima (Gould), 23:87, 88, 90
   John, 23:93
   Joseph W., 23:94
   Katy (Patrick), 23:91
   Keziah, 23:87, 88
   Louisa F., 23:94
   Martha Jane, 23:93
   Mary (Berry), 23:97
   Mary (Fisk), 23:93
   Mary B. (Berry), 23:94
   Mary E. (Berry), 23:95
   Mary E. W., 23:94
   Mary Elizabeth, 23:94-96
   Mary S., 23:93
   Nancy, 23:92
   Phebe (Felton), 23:92, 94
   Phebe Felton, 23:90
   Phebe/Phebea F., 23:92, 93
   Polly, 23:91, 92
   Polly/Molly, 23:88
   Rachel, 23:92
   Rachel (Wilkins), 23:88, 89, 91
   Rebekah, 23:88, 91
   Richard, 23:87-95
   Robert, 23:95
   Sarah, 23:92, 93
   Sarah F., 23:93
   Stephen F., 23:93
   Susannah/Sukey (Carey), 23:93
   Thomas, 23:87, 88
   William, 23:91, 93
   Zele/Zeal, 23:91
SKILLING/SKILLIN/SKILLINGS
   John, 23:161, 162
SKINNER
   Lydia (___), 24:156, 157
   Susan (Parker), 24:210
SLADE
   Temperance, 21:180
SLATE
   Elizabeth (Abbe), 21:37
   William, 21:37
SLOSSER
   Gaius J., 22:79
SMALL
   Ann (___), 21:40
   John, 21:40
   Mary, 21:40, 43
SMALLEY
   Alice, 25:20
   Ann (Cash), 25:21
   Benjamin, 25:21
   Francis, 25:20
SMART
   Paul F., 23:85

SMETHURST
   Gamaliel, 23:211
   Rebecca (Bessom), 23:211
SMITH, 21:70; 22:135; 23:65; 24:7, 126
   ___, Bishop, 23:32
   ___, Wid., 23:152
   Abigail, 23:117; 24:114; 25:52
   'Children', 25:159
   Anna (___), 22:172-175
   Anna (Hill), 21:105
   Anne S. (Procter), 23:102
   Benjamin, 21:98; 22:174, 175
   Betsy, 22:172
   Catherine, 22:24; 25:53
   Charles, 22:221, 226, 228-233; 23:152
   Daniel, 25:52, 56
   David, 22:172, 173
   Deborah (Wilcomb), 25:56
   Edward, 22:237; 24:137
   Elizabeth, 21:215; 22:179; 25:52
   Elizabeth (___), 25:52, 53
   Elizabeth (Goodale), 21:39
   Elizabeth (Tisdale), 21:52
   Ephraim, 22:49, 50, 172-175
   Ethel Farrington, 21:153; 22:53
   Francis, 21:217
   Franklin Carter, 25:121
   Fred, 21:105
   George, 21:27; 24:226
   George G., 22:226-228
   George Girdler, 23:152
   Hannah, 22:51
   Hannah (Cheney), 25:56
   Hezekiah, 22:145
   Hue, 22:175
   Hugh, 22:167, 173
   Isaac, 21:214
   Jabez, 25:53, 169
   Jacob, 23:152
   James, 21:98; 23:152
   Janet, 21:137
   Jeremiah, 25:52
   Jesse, 22:236
   Joanna, 25:52
   Job, 23:142
   Joel, 24:79, 80
   John, 21:39, 52, 154, 210, 211, 214;
     22:167, 179, 215, 216, 226, 231;
     23:38, 112, 152; 24:8-10, 52, 129,
     220
   John Kimby, 25:53
   Joseph, 22:226-228-231, 234; 23:152
   Kate, 21:138
   Lois (___), 22:49, 50
   Lucena (Gale), 22:180
   Lydia, 21:239
   Lyman Brown, 21:104
   Margaret, 21:98, 239
   Margaret (Buffum/Thompson), 22:215,
     216, 218
   Martha (Emins), 23:164
   Mary, 21:52, 71, 158; 22:226-228;
     25:52
   Mary (___), 22:175; 25:52
   Mary (Currey), 22:179
   Mary (Davis), 23:162, 164, 179
   Mary (Harris), 22:179
   Mary (Mitchell), 24:226
   Mary (Roundy), 21:98
   Mary Anderson, 25:53
   Mary Eden, 22:237
   Mary Jane, 24:226
   Mehitable, 22:237
   Millet, 25:192
   Moses, 21:180; 25:56
   Nabby, 22:236

   Nancy, 25:195
   Nanny, 22:172
   Nathan Praster, 25:52
   Nathaniel, 23:152
   Nelda Virginia (Haszard), 21:18
   Patience (Shattock), 25:129
   Peggy, 22:175
   Peter, 23:159; 25:12
   Phebe, 23:38
   Phyllis Courchene, 21:141
   Priscilla, 22:214
   Ralph, 22:190
   Rebecca (___), 21:98
   Rebecca (Adams), 21:146
   Rebecca Cleaves, 23:210
   Richard, 21:146, 157; 23:16, 157, 162,
     179; 25:56
   Robert, 24:134
   Robert C., 21:199
   Ruth, 21:180; 22:173; 23:57; 25:56
   Ruth (___), 22:173
   Ruth (Little), 21:180; 25:56
   Ruth Dodge, 21:105
   S., 24:34
   Sally (___), 25:192
   Sally (Bryant), 21:104
   Samuel, 21:67; 22:237; 24:105; 25:52,
     53, 151
   Sarah, 21:52, 21:240a; 22:236
   Sarah (___), 22:236, 237; 23:172
   Sarah (Coher), 21:98
   Sarah (Haven), 21:157
   Sarah (Saunders), 23:229
   Sarah G., 22:52
   Silas, 22:27; 23:152
   Sullivan, 22:180
   Susan (___), 25:53, 151
   Susanna, 25:151
   Susannah (___), 21:215; 22:237; 25:53
   Susannah (Wiley), 21:214
   T., 21:114
   Theodore Daniel, 21:18
   Thomas, 21:29, 98; 22:151; 23:164,
     168; 24:137
   Thomas B., 21:231
   Timothy H., 22:226
   William, 21:104; 22:27; 23:152
   William Bryant, 21:104
   William Burgis, 25:52
   William Castle, 23:152
   William E., 24:202
SMOLENYAK
   Megan, 23:20; 25:185
   Megan (Smolenyak), 25:185
SNELL
   Calvin, 22:200
SNELLING
   John, 21:14
SNODDY
   James, 23:152
SNOW
   Ann, 25:21
   Bethiah (Parker), 24:49, 50
   John, 25:21
   Mermedeke, 23:152
   Richard, 24:49, 50
SOLART
   John, 22:40, 103
   Mary, 22:106
SOMERBY
   Abiel, 21:47
   Anthony, 21:113, 185; 25:102
SOMES
   Abagiel (___), 23:152
   Benjamin, 22:221, 227, 228
   Benjamin F., 22:226, 234

Elizabeth (Kendall), 24:70
Icabod, 23:152
John, 22:221, 227
Morris, 24:70
Patience, 24:70
SOUSA
John Philip, 23:173
SOUTER, 23:72, 75
Ann (Wilson), 23:65, 66, 77
David, 23:65
David Hackett, 23:64
James, 23:64-66, 77
John, 23:66
Mary (Mitchell), 23:66
SOUTH/SOUTHARD/SEROTE/
SOTHEARD/SOUTHERD/
SOUTHER, 24:77
"Child", 24:78, 81
Abraham, 24:77-82, 108
Amaziah, 24:78, 81
Amos, 24:79, 81
Amos P., 21:53; 24:79, 108
Betsey, 24:78, 81
Charles Harold, 21:53; 24:108
Cyrus, 24:78, 79, 81, 82
Earnest George, 21:53; 24:108
Emme, 22:172
George, 22:172
George Edward, 21:53; 24:108
Geraldine Agnes (Akeley), 21:53
Hannah, 21:53
Isaac, 24:79, 81, 108
Jennie Linde (Poor), 21:53
Jennie/Jane (Lambert), 24:77, 78, 81
John, 21:213; 24:78, 81, 108
Joseph, 24:79, 81
Judith A., 24:17
Judith Ann, 21:53; 24:108
Mary (Parker), 21:213
Mary Alice (Pattee), 21:53
Ruth (Tozer), 21:53
Sarah, 24:108
Sarah (___), 22:172
Sophia (Gulliver), 21:53
Stephen, 24:79, 81
Susannah (Paris), 24:77, 79, 81, 82
Susannah/Sukey, 24:79, 81
Thomas G., 21:53; 24:108
SOUTHWICK
Cassandra, 24:108
Cassandra (___), 22:215, 216
Cassandra (Burnell), 22:22-24
Daniel, 21:27; 22:23, 24, 217
George, 22:25, 27
Hannah, 22:23
John, 22:22, 23
Joseph, 22:23, 24
Josiah, 22:216, 217
Lawrence, 22:22-24, 215, 216; 24:108
Mary (Trask), 22:23
Mercy, 23:155
Provided, 22:23, 217
Rebekah, 25:52
William, 22:27
SPAFFORD
Judith, 24:85
SPARHAWK
Esther, 24:158
John, 23:226
Joseph, 23:226
Nathaniel, 22:78; 23:226
Patience (Newman), 23:226
Samuel, 23:225, 226
Sarah (Whiting), 23:225, 226
Thomas, 23:226

SPARKS
Elizabeth, 25:201
John, 25:201
Mary (Sinnott), 25:201
SPARROW
Jonathan, 25:21
SPAULDING
Andrew, 21:117
Anna (Parker), 24:215
Benoni, 21:116
Edward, 21:116
Gideon, 25:83
Hannah (Jefts), 21:117
Isiah, 25:83
John, 24:163; 25:37, 88
Lydi (Parker), 25:37
Lydia, 25:83
Mary, 21:101
Noah, 24:215
Orlando, 24:172
Rachel (___), 25:88
Rachel (Parker), 24:162, 163
Rebeckah (Stearns?), 21:116
Simeon, 24:159
Stephen, 23:38
Susanna, 21:116
Susannah (Crosby), 21:116
Thaddeus, 22:77
Zacheus, 25:83
SPEAR/SPEARS
Barbara, 22:170
Carolyn M., 23:111
Eva Clough, 22:163
SPENCER, 21:114
Garrard, 21:29
John, 21:111, 112
Marcy, 22:179
Wilbur D., 25:18
SPILLER
Cora, 21:225
Francis, 21:228
Francis Cleaves, 21:225
Nancy Augusta (Lefavour), 21:19, 21, 225, 228
SPINNER, 25:123
SPOFFORD, 24:89
Abigail, 24:39
Abigail (Stevens), 24:89
Hannah, 24:89
John, 22:167
SPOKESFIELD
Sarah Parker, 21:104
SPRAGG
Marion, 23:96
SPRAGUE, 22:25
Dorothy, 24:209
Ebenezer, 22:27
Jemima (Burditt), 21:237
Phineas, 21:237, 239; 24:41
Sally/Sarah (Fuller), 21:239
Sarah, 24:36, 40, 41
Sarah (Hasse), 24:41
Sarah Ann, 21:239
SPRIGG
June, 24:186
SPRING
___, Dr., 25:60a
SPRINGER
___, Dr., 21:17, 228
ST. JOHN
Elizabeth, 23:219
Oliver, 23:219
Sarah (Bulkeley), 23:219
ST. LAWRENCE
Joseph, 23:15

STACEY see also STACY
Eli, 22:226, 228, 231, 234
Francis, 23:214
Joseph, 23:214
Mary, 23:214
Rachel (Brown), 21:180
Rebecca, 23:214
Rebecka (Bessom), 23:214
Timothy, 21:180
STACHIW
Myron O., 24:217
STACKHOUSE, 22:157
Richard, 23:112; 25:108a
STACY see also STACEY
E. H., 25:13
Eli, 24:220, 228-233
Elizabeth, 24:37
Jean, 22:55
Nymphas, 23:148
STAINWOOD
Jane (___), 25:55
Philip, 25:55
STAMFORD
Daniel, 22:226
STANBOROUGH/STANBROUGH
Abigail, 23:37
Martha, 23:37-40
STANDISH
___, Capt., 21:24
STANDLEY
Benjamin, 22:55
Bethiah (Lovett), 22:55
George, 22:55
Hannah (Rayment), 22:55
Hannah (Wells), 22:55
Hannah (Woodbury), 22:55
Jean (Stacy), 22:55
Joanna (Allen), 22:55
Matthew, 23:120
Ruth (Andrews), 23:120
Titus, 22:55
STANLEY
Elizabeth, 24:40, 84
Samuel, 21:207, 208
STANTON
Lydia, 23:117
Margaret, 22:167
Richard H., 23:17
STANWOOD
David, 23:165, 179
Deborah, 24:219
Dorcas, 24:220
Dorothy (Davis), 24:220
Ebenezer, 23:57
Ebenezer, 23:153; 25:55, 57
Eunice (Hodgkins), 23:57
Frances M. (Procter), 23:102
Hannah, 24:218-220
Hannah (Warner), 25:55, 57
Isaac, 23:57; 25:57
John, 24:220
Jonathon, 21:180; 23:57; 25:55, 57
Lecretia, 23:57
Martha (Burnham), 23:57
Mary, 23:179
Mary (Nichols), 25:55, 57
Ruth (Smith), 21:180; 23:57
Sarah, 23:57
Sarah (Stanwood), 23:57
Sarah (Wilcomb), 25:55, 57
Susanna (Davis), 23:165, 179
STAPLES
Geo., 21:207
Martha (Davenport), 24:20
Paulina, 25:190
Thomas Warren, 24:20

John, 21:116, 199; 23:189; 24:35-44, 83-103, 116
John Abbott, 24:100
John F., 24:103
John Varnum, 24:89, 98
Jonas, 24:89
Jonathan, 24:36, 38, 40, 42, 43, 83, 86, 88, 90-93, 95, 101-103
Joseph, 21:199; 22:226, 232, 233; 24:35-38, 40, 42, 43, 83, 84, 88, 89, 91, 96-98, 102, 103
Joseph L., 25:13
Joshua, 24:35, 36, 39, 40, 44, 54, 83, 84, 92, 93, 101, 102
Judith (Spafford), 24:85
Leonard, 24:94, 100, 103
Lizzie, 23:212
Louisa (Flowers), 24:98
Louise, 24:92
Lucretia, 24:97, 100
Lucy, 24:85
Lucy (Butterfield), 24:102
Lucy (Osgood), 24:97
Lydia, 24:38-40, 44, 84, 89, 91, 97, 101
Lydia (__), 24:92, 101
Lydia (Brown), 24:95
Lydia (Felch), 24:43, 90, 91
Lydia (Frye), 24:41, 88
Lydia (Gardner), 24:97
Lydia (Gray), 24:40, 84
Lydia (Huse), 24:83, 93
Lydia Farnum (Holt), 24:103
Maria, 24:37
Maria (Mooars/Morse), 24:43
Martha, 24:38-40, 44, 54, 85, 88, 92, 101, 102
Martha (__), 24:83, 93, 101
Martha (Cross), 24:87, 95
Martha (Hale), 24:96
Martha (Mooar), 24:95, 103
Martha (Phelps), 24:83
Martha (Stevens), 24:40, 44
Mary, 24:35, 37-40, 42-44, 90-92, 98, 116
Mary (__), 24:87, 91, 95
Mary (Barker), 24:36, 43, 95
Mary (Blunt), 24:100
Mary (Chandler), 24:100
Mary (Flanders), 24:103
Mary (Frye), 24:36, 39, 40
Mary (Haskell), 24:89
Mary (Ingalls), 24:35, 37, 38
Mary (Kimball), 24:102
Mary (Mooar), 24:93, 97, 101, 102
Mary (Noyes), 24:98
Mary (Parker), 24:92, 100
Mary (Phelps), 24:43, 89, 90
Mary (Poor), 24:38
Mary (Poor), 24:40, 43, 84
Mary (Remington), 24:42
Mary (Stevens), 24:39
Mary (Treat), 24:42
Mary Butler (Noyes), 24:100
Mary Walker, 24:102
Mary Walker (Stevens), 24:102
Mehitabel, 24:37, 43, 87, 101
Mehitable (__), 24:85
Mehitable (Farnum), 24:41, 87
Mehitable (Harris), 24:92, 101
Mehitable Hunt, 24:101
Molly, 24:84, 92
Moses, 24:95, 96
Moses T., 24:35
Myra (Kittredge), 24:101
Nabby, 24:94

Nabby (Johnson), 24:84, 94
Nancy, 24:94, 100
Nancy (Symonds), 24:103
Nathan, 21:199; 24:35, 36, 39, 40, 44, 84
Nathaniel, 23:115; 24:37, 44, 96, 102
Nehemiah, 24:94
Noah, 24:83, 93
Oliver, 23:152; 24:96
Osgood, 24:103
Pamelia, 24:101, 102
Pamelia (Stevens), 24:101, 102
Patty, 24:99, 100
Persis, 24:100
Peter, 24:84, 92, 94, 100
Phebe, 24:39-43, 86, 89-93, 98, 101
Phebe (Ames), 24:93, 102
Phebe (Bodwell), 24:40, 83
Phebe (Frye), 24:89, 90, 98, 99
Phebe Kimball, 24:99
Philip, 24:92
Phineas, 24:41, 44, 83, 87, 95, 101
Pliny, 24:101
Polly C., 24:101
Polly Mehitabel (Chandler), 24:93, 102
Priscilla, 24:38, 39
Prudence, 24:84, 92
Prudence (Hardy), 24:44, 92
Rachel, 24:44
Rebecca, 21:30; 24:44, 92, 98, 101, 103; 25:25
Rebecca (__), 24:44, 91, 103
Rebecca (Barnard), 24:39, 44
Rebecca (Farnum), 24:95, 103
Rebecca (Holt), 24:98
Rebecca (Hunt/Kent), 24:83, 92
Rebecca (Mansur), 24:102
Rhoda, 24:95, 103
Richard, 24:90
Ruth, 24:38, 90
Ruth (Buxton), 24:97, 98
Ruth (Poor), 21:116; 24:36, 38, 39, 44
Sally, 24:86, 96
Sally (__), 24:103
Sally (Townsend), 24:96
Samuel, 23:142, 149, 152, 153; 24:35-37, 40, 44, 83, 84, 93, 94, 97, 101, 102, 206
Samuel Ingalls, 24:99
Sarah, 23:207; 24:35, 37-39, 41-44, 83, 84, 87, 88, 90, 92-95, 97, 99-101, 103
Sarah (__), 24:83, 92, 93
Sarah (Abbott), 24:35, 37, 88, 90, 96, 99
Sarah (Bailey), 24:89, 98
Sarah (Davis), 24:35, 37
Sarah (Farrington), 24:95
Sarah (Gray), 24:43, 90
Sarah (Hardy), 24:92
Sarah (Ingalls), 24:90, 99
Sarah (Lynde), 24:38, 42
Sarah (Peabody), 24:43, 88
Sarah (Poor), 24:88, 92, 96
Sarah (Sprague), 24:36, 40, 41
Sarah (Stevens), 24:87, 95
Sarah (Varney), 24:41, 87
Sarah Ann, 24:99
Sarah Jane (Low/Lowe), 24:97, 102
Sarah/Sally (__), 24:100
Serena, 24:98, 102
Simeon, 24:44, 87, 92, 95, 100, 101
Simeon, 24:100
Solomon, 24:91, 95, 103
Susan, 24:100, 102
Susan (Stevens), 24:102

Susann (Bragg), 24:88, 95
Susanna (Manning), 24:93, 102
Susanna (Wardwell), 24:92, 100
Susannah, 22:50; 24:40, 84, 90, 95
Susannah (Symms), 24:36
Susanne, 24:88, 101, 103
Susanne (Abbott), 24:91, 99
Susanne (Noyes), 24:95, 102
Susanne (Stevens), 24:101
Susanne (Symms), 24:35
Tabatha (Parker), 24:206
Tabitha, 24:94
Tabitha (Farnum), 24:41, 85, 86
Tabitha (Holt), 24:84, 94
Theodore, 24:43, 89, 90, 97
Thomas, 24:42, 43, 90, 99
Timothy, 23:222, 223; 24:35-39, 42, 44, 88, 92, 94, 96, 100
Timothy Chandler, 24:102
Uriah, 24:94
Varnum, 24:97
Warren, 24:97, 102
William, 22:226, 234; 24:35, 83, 87, 91, 93, 95, 96, 98, 190
William Frye, 24:98
Z., 23:152
Zachariah, 23:152
Zacharius, 24:88
Zachary, 23:148
STEVENSON
  Andrew, 25:5
  Constance Louise, 21:18
  David, 23:86
  Noel C., 22:200
  Rebecca, 25:5, 6
  Wendy B., 23:86
STEWARD
  Mary, 21:52
  Robert, 21:52
STEWART see also STUART
  Duncan, 25:8, 9
  John, 25:9
  William, 23:15; 25:9
STGACY
  Eli, 24:219
STICKNEY
  Anna (Whiting), 23:223, 224
  Daniel, 25:141
  Matthew Adams, 22:42
  Sm., 22:167
  William, 23:223, 224
STILES
  Hannah (Lovejoy), 24:38
  Henry Reed, 22:106
  Hezekial, 24:38
  Phinehas, 23:152
STILSON
  Agnes, 21:37, 38
  Grace (__), 21:37
  Vincent, 21:37, 38
STIMSON
  Hannah (Haven), 21:158
  James, 21:36
  Patience (Cook), 21:36
  Stephen, 21:158
STINNES/STINNESS, 23:212
  Ruthy (Bessom), 23:210
  Samuel, 23:207, 210
STIRLING see also STERLING
  Earl Of, 22:65
STOCKBRIDGE/STOCKBRIG
  L. R., 25:194
  Lyman, 25:193, 195
  Mary, 21:144
  Mary (__), 23:152
  Sarah (Nichols), 25:195

Sarah J. (___), 25:193
Sarah Jane (Nichols), 25:194, 195
STOCKER, 22:212; 25:184
James, 25:129
Mary (___), 25:129
Samuel, 22:44
Sarah, 22:53
STOCKWELL
William, 23:152
STODDARD
___, Mr., 25:41
Mary, 23:50
Mary A., 23:46
STODDER, 21:10
STOKELY
Robert, 23:152
STOKES, 23:212
STONE, 21:50; 24:126, 131
A., 24:70
Abbie Ellen, 23:211
Anne (Haven), 21:155
Anne (Parker), 25:93
Anne Maria (Merrill), 23:211
Archelaus, 21:177
Asa Blaney, 23:211
Daniel, 21:177, 178
Ebenezer, 21:159
Edwin M., 23:118
Elizabeth, 25:170
Eunice, 21:177
Hanah (___), 25:129
Hannah (Searle), 21:159
John, 22:27; 23:111; 25:108a
Josiah, 21:155
Lucy, 21:159
Lucy P., 24:196
Mary, 21:159; 22:47, 52, 54
Mary (Haven), 21:159
Mary (Trowbridge), 21:159
Patience (Goodwin), 21:177
Robert, 25:129
Samuel, 21:159
Sarah, 21:177
Sarah (Jenkins), 21:177, 178
Sarah (Weston), 21:177
Thomas, 25:93
William, 23:152
STONEKING
M., 24:71
STOONE
Benjamin, 25:129
STOREY see also STORY
Alexander, 25:78
Elinor, 25:78
Sally, 25:78
Sally (___), 25:78
STORRER
Jeremiah, 23:152
Joseph, 23:152
Mary (___), 23:152
STORY see also STOREY, 21:208
Dana, 24:144, 151
Elizabeth, 24:165
Isabel, 22:40
James, 23:152
John, 23:152
Lydia, 23:57
William, 22:152, 154, 159; 24:28, 151; 25:132
STOVER
Abigail, 21:59
Elizabeth, 21:59
George, 21:59
Jerusha (___), 21:59
Joseph, 21:59
Lucy, 21:59

Martha, 21:59
Sarah (___), 21:59
STOWE
Anna, 21:159
Anna, 21:160
STRATON/STRATTON
Eugene Aubrey, 22:200
James, 23:153
Margerit (___), 25:35, 39
STRAW
John, 25:200
Lydia (Sargent), 25:200
STREETER
Esther, 21:158
Experience (Haven), 21:157
Samuel, 21:154, 157
Sebastian, 24:115
STREETS
David H., 25:121
STRIBLE
Ann (Morrissey), 23:228
John, 23:228
Mary, 23:228
STRICKLAND/STRICTLAND, 21:115
Allan, 23:117
George W., 21:106
George Warren, 21:106
Maria Louise (Knapp), 21:106
Sarah, 21:102, 115, 163, 164; 22:218
Sarah (Woodbury), 23:117
Elizabeth Obear (English), 21:106
STRIKER
Samuell, 23:153
STRONG
George, 23:209
Jane (Misservy), 23:209
Mary, 23:209
Susanna, 23:209
Susanna (Bessom), 23:207, 209
William, 23:207, 209
STROUT, 25:23
Christopher, 25:18, 20, 21, 27
Elizabeth, 25:22
Joanna, 25:18
Mary S. Lang, 25:23
Sarah, 25:18
Sarah (Picke/Pike), 25:18, 21, 22
Thomas, 25:22
STUART/STUARTS/STEUART see also STEWART
___, Miss, 22:22
Alexander, 22:78, 79
Ellenor, 21:38, 52
Margaret, 23:86
William, 21:84
STUDLY
Joseph, 25:160, 161
STURGEON
___, Mrs., 21:17, 19
May, 21:17
Stanley S., 21:17
SULLIVAN, 25:63
Charles S., 23:17
Daniel, 23:126
Edward, 21:139
J., 23:56
James, 21:140
James T., 23:17
Johanna, 25:63
John F., 23:17
John J., 23:17
K., 24:69
Michael H., 23:17
Michal, 23:153
SUMNER
Charles, 22:120a, 148

Harrison G., 24:138
Jane, 22:211
Sarah T. (___), 24:138
Thomas, 22:167
SURRIAGE
Agnes, 22:20
SUTTON
___, Mr., 23:29
Eben, 23:115
Richard, 21:199
SUTWIFF
Michal, 23:153
SWAIN/SWAINE/SWAYNE
___, Maj., 21:213
___, Mr., 21:220
Jeremiah, 21:216; 22:206, 212
John, 21:220
SWALLOW
Hannah, 24:53
Jonathan, 24:53
Phebe, 24:53
SWAN
Elizabeth (Parker), 25:138
Elizabeth (Stacy), 24:37
Ellen, 23:157
Hannah (Stevens), 24:35, 37
Hannah (Stevens), 24:37
Henry, 25:138
Marshall, 22:112, 113
Marshall W. S., 23:165
Richard, 22:167
Robert, 24:35, 37, 39
SWANBACK
Alice Alvira 'Vera', 24:19-21
Charlotte (Davenport), 24:17-22
Elisha, 24:19-21
Emily, 24:19, 20
John, 24:17-22
Joseph, 24:20
Joseph Bancroft, 24:19
Ruth (Kennedy), 24:19, 21
SWANSON
William, 23:153
SWANT
Scott T., 24:186
SWAYNE see SWAIN
SWEATE
Stephen, 25:102
SWEENEY
Joan, 22:23
Joan M., 21:24
Mary (Parker), 24:49
SWEET
Lucy, 22:226, 231
SWEETSER
Lucy (Danforth), 21:239
Lydia (Smith), 21:239
Sally, 21:239
William, 21:239
SWETT, 25:191
Benjamin, 23:54
SWIFT
___, Mr., 21:158
John, 21:156
Nathaniel, 24:97
SWINERTON/SWINNERTON
___, Dr., 21:92
Hannah (___), 25:79
John, 25:79
Mercy (___), 25:79
SWITCHER
James, 23:153
SYKES
___, Mr., 23:28
B., 24:70
Bryan, 24:71

Mary, 23:26-28, 31-33
SYMMES/SYMMS
   ___, Mr., 21:197
   Susannah, 24:36
   Susanne, 24:35
   William, 21:196, 198
   Zechariah, 22:165
   Zachary, 24:35
SYMONDS, 22:25
   Abigail, 22:236
   Catherine, 23:236
   Elizabeth, 25:129
   Elizabeth Masury, 25:184
   Hannah (___), 25:184
   John, 23:236
   Nancy, 24:103
   Ruth, 23:176; 24:16, 136, 175, 231
   Ruth (___), 23:236
   Samuel, 21:113; 23:153, 236; 24:26;
     25:102
   Sarah (Hunt), 25:184
   Thomas, 25:184
SZUCS
   Loretto Dennis, 24:228; 25:122

TAFT
   Margaret, 23:240
   Margaret (Milner), 23:240
   Nicholas, 23:240
TAILOR see also TAYLER/TAYLOR
   Abigail, 22:226, 228
   Thomas, 21:212
TAINNER/TAINOR see also TAYNOR
   Ann, 25:25
   Elias, 25:25
   Elizabeth, 25:25
   Elizabeth (Condy), 25:25
   Joanna, 25:25
   Josias, 25:25
   Thomas, 25:25
TALLEN/TALLON
   James H., 23:16
   Nathaniel, 23:153
TAPIO
   Rick, 25:122
TAPLEY, 23:60a
   Betsy Lunt (Stevens), 24:98
   Harriet Silvester, 22:27
   William, 24:98
TAPPAN/TAPPIN see also TOPPAN
   James, 22:221, 226-232, 234; 23:153
TAPPING
   Joseph, 25:164
TARBELL
   Anna/Anne, 24:52; 25:41, 88
   Elizabeth, 24:176
   Hannah (___), 21:35
   John, 21:35, 40
   Mary, 21:40
   Sarah, 22:187
TARBOX
   ___, Mr., 21:31
   ___, Mrs., 21:151
   Anna, 22:50
   Ben, 23:140-150, 152-154
   Benjamin, 23:153
   Deborah (Gray), 21:50
   Dolly R. (Hill), 22:50
   Dorothy (Gray), 21:50
   Ebenezer, 21:31, 32, 151
   Elizabeth (___), 21:151
   Hannah, 21:151
   Jacob, 21:31
   John, 21:32, 150, 151; 22:50, 204
   Jonathan, 21:151
   Joseph, 21:151; 22:50

Lydia, 22:50
Lydia (Atwell), 22:50
Mary, 21:151; 22:50
Mary (Bell), 22:50
Mary (Brean), 21:32, 151
Mary (Haven), 21:149, 151
Mary (Rand), 21:32
Nathaniel, 21:151
Robert, 21:31
Sally L. (Newhall), 22:50
Samuel, 21:151; 22:50
Sarah, 21:151
Susanna, 21:151
Susannah (Stevens), 22:50
William, 22:50
TARR see also FARR, 22:113
   Abigail (Stevens), 24:88
   Ada, 21:162
   Addison, 21:161
   Addison F., 21:162
   Adelaide/Adeline G. (Norwood),
     21:161
   Adeline, 21:162
   Alden, 21:208
   Amanda, 21:162
   Benjamin, 22:21, 112, 226, 228-230;
     23:165
   Betsy, 21:161
   Charles, 22:226, 233
   Charles H., 21:162
   Clarence H., 21:162
   David, 22:226, 228-230, 234; 24:88
   David P., 21:161; 22:226, 230, 231
   Edward, 21:162
   Eliza, 21:161, 162
   Elizabeth, 23:165, 179
   Elizabeth (___), 22:111
   Ellis, 21:161
   Francis, 22:226, 234
   Franklin A., 21:162
   Frederick, 21:162
   Henry, 22:226, 229, 230
   Howard, 21:162
   Jabez, 22:226, 232, 233
   Jacob, 24:88
   Mabel B. (Procter), 23:102
   Martha (Harvey), 21:161
   Martha (Riggs), 21:161
   Mary, 21:161
   Nathaniel, 22:226, 233, 234
   Polly (Riggs), 21:161
   Richard, 22:111, 112; 23:159
   Washington, 22:226, 234
TARROT
   Abigail, 21:36
TATMAN, 21:217
TAYLER/TAYLOR see also TAILOR,
   22:135
   ___, Mr., 21:155
   Abigail, 22:228, 229
   Abigail (___), 22:230
   David, 25:145
   Edward, 21:210
   Elizabeth, 24:77, 78; 25:108
   George, 22:206
   Isabell, 24:48
   James, 21:151, 214; 25:9
   Joseph, 22:59
   Lydia, 22:93
   Mary, 21:43; 23:153; 25:156
   Mary (Davis), 22:188
   Oliver Alden, 22:146
   Penelope (Favor), 22:59
   Robert, 21:149
   Ryan, 25:121
   Sarah (___), 25:145

Thomas, 23:153
Timothy, 22:188
William, 22:213
Zachary, 22:131; 23:185, 186
TAYNOUR/TAYNOR/TAINOR see
   also TAINNER
   Elias, 25:25, 28
   Elizabeth, 25:24, 25, 27, 28
   Joanna (___), 25:25
   Mary, 25:26, 28
   Mary (Rowell), 25:25
   Thomas, 25:25
TELBE
   Anna, 23:51, 59
TEMPLE
   Joanna (Prichard), 24:54
   Richard, 24:54
   Sarah, 24:54
TENNEY
   David, 21:103
   Elizabeth, 23:176
   Esther (Miller), 21:103
   Marinda, 21:103
   Seth, 21:103
   Thos., 22:167
   Wm., 22:167
TEPPER
   Michael, 21:89
TEWKSBURY see also TUCKESBARY
   Mary, 22:97
THACHER/THATCHER
   ___, Rev., 24:202
   Anthony, 21:200, 202, 203
   Bethiah, 21:203
   Edith, 21:202
   Elizabeth (Jones), 21:203
   James, 21:203
   John, 21:203
   Judah, 21:203
   Mary, 21:201
   Peter, 21:201-203
   Thomas, 21:202
   William, 21:202
   William Vincent, 21:203
THAYER
   Huldah, 22:161
   Jane, 25:151
   Jane (___), 25:151
   John, 21:204
   Mary (Butterworth), 22:161
   Nancy, 22:169; 25:52
   Oliver, 22:236
   Rebekah (___), 22:236; 25:52
   Sally, 25:52
   Samuel, 22:161
   Sarah, 22:178
   Stephen, 22:236; 25:52
THIBAUT I
   Rey, 24:67
THODE
   Ernest, 25:123
THOMAS
   Amy (Rhodes), 23:45
   Archibald, 23:15
   George, 21:227
   L. J., Mrs., 23:114
   Martha (Rhodes), 23:42, 43
   Mary, 22:86, 87
   Ray, 25:154
   Samuel B., 23:46
   Spencer, 23:153
THOMPSON see also TOMPSON,
   24:61, 141, 148, 150, 152
   Anna, 23:120
   Benjamin, 21:180a; 23:184
   Daniel, 24:208, 209

James, 23:153
John, 22:215
Margaret, 22:215, 216
Neil D., 21:48
Rebecca (Parker), 24:208, 209
Sarah, 21:38; 22:22
Savile, 23:153
Susan Emerson, 21:104
Susanna, 24:160, 207
Tamosin/Thomasine/Tomasin (Ward),
    22:215
Thomas, 23:49, 153
William, 24:30
THOMSON
George, 22:29, 30
William O., 21:137
THORLEY
Richard, 22:167
THORNDIKE/THORNDYKE/
    THORNEDICK
___, Mr., 22:102
Elizabeth, 23:105
Israel, 21:135, 136
Jeremiah, 21:165
Larkin, 21:100
Paul, 22:103
Sarah, 24:97
THORNE
Hannah, 23:117
THORNEDICK see THORNDIKE
THORNELL
Joanna, 21:146
THORNER
Elizabeth, 23:213
Elizabeth (Bisson), 23:213
William, 23:213
THOROLD
George, 21:71
THORPE, 21:148
THRASHER
Benjamin, 24:115
Emma Eliza, 24:115
Hannah (Edgcomb), 24:115
THRELFALL
John Brooks, 23:51
THURSTON
Daniel, 22:221, 226, 232, 233; 23:54;
    25:44, 45, 139
Elizabeth, 24:221
Hanah (Parker), 25:44
Hannah (Parker), 25:45
THWING
___, Mrs., 23:124
TIBBETTS
Agnes, 22:56
Charles S., 25:25
Walter, 22:56
TILLINGHAMS
Betsey (Atwell), 22:48
Nicholas, 22:48
TILLINGHAST
Amos Atwell, 22:48
TILTON
Cephas, 25:192, 194
Elizabeth, 25:193
Harriet (___), 25:192
Harriet (Nichols), 25:193, 194
Pheobe, 22:99
Rebecca A., 25:193
William, 21:29
TIMMINS
Edward F., 23:17
TINGLEY
Guilford Solon, 22:161
Martha Pamelia (Meyers), 22:161
Raymon Meyers, 22:161

TINNEY
Rebecka (Haven), 21:157
Samuel, 21:157
TIPPEN/TIPPIN
Mary, 23:153
Mary (McHoney), 23:153
Thomas, 23:149, 153
TISDALE
Elizabeth, 21:52
Elkanah, 21:194
Sarah, 21:52
TITCOMB/TITCOMBE
Elizabeth (Bidfield), 21:49
Joane (Bartlett), 21:49
William, 21:47, 49, 172, 185
TITTLE, 21:232
TITUS
Lydia, 21:36
TODD
Frank/Bill, 22:166
James, 24:222
John, 22:166; 24:222
Mary, 24:222
Mehitable, 24:222
Phyllis Adele (Gilbertson), 22:162
Robert M., 22:226, 234
Ruth, 24:222
Samuel, 24:222
Timothy, 24:222
TOISH see also MACKINTOSH
John, 25:9
TOLAND
Michael A., 23:17
TOM
Joan, 21:80
TOMKINS
Mary, 21:142; 23:54
TOMLINS
Edmond, 22:204
Edward, 22:213
Timothy, 22:209
TOMPSON/TOMSON see also
    THOMPSON, JAMESON
Alexander, 25:8
Alice, 25:43, 137, 138
Andrew, 25:8, 9
George, 25:9
James, 25:9
Susanna, 23:235
William, 25:137
TOOMEY
John J., 23:135
TOOTHAKER
Mary, 23:174
Roger, 23:174
Sarah (Rogers), 23:174
TOPLIFF
Patience (Somes), 24:70
Samuel, 24:70
Thankful, 24:70
TOPPAN see also TAPPAN, 22:135
A., 21:114
Abraham, 21:112
Christopher, 21:114; 22:143
James, 22:228
TORREY, 24:168; 25:26
Clarence Almon, 21:198, 213; 22:101,
    107; 23:160, 220
Samuel, 23:29
TOTINGHAM, 21:220
TOWER see also TOWNE, 22:237
Hannah (___), 22:237
Jacob, 22:237
Susanna Phippen, 22:237
Thomas, 25:9

TOWLE
Henry, 22:177
Marie Antoinette, 22:177
Susan/Sukey (Pierce), 22:177
TOWNE/TOWN/TOWNS see also
    TOWER, 22:135; 23:237
Bethiah (Reed), 21:158
Catherine (Symonds), 23:236
David, 22:146
Edwin Eugene, 21:158
Elijah, 21:158
Elizabeth, 21:45
Elizabeth Lefavor, 25:53
Elizabeth Safford, 25:53
Esther, 21:154, 158
Esther (Gould), 21:45
Foster, 24:172
Hannah, 22:237
Hannah (___), 22:237; 25:52-54, 151,
    153
Israel, 21:155, 158
Jacob, 22:237; 23:236, 237; 25:52-54,
    151, 153
Joanna (Blessing), 23:236-238
John, 21:158; 25:54
Jonathan, 21:45
Joseph, 21:158; 22:146; 23:237
Joseph Hardy, 25:52
Joshua Goodale, 25:52
Loina, 25:52
Lois, 21:158
Lucy Boardman, 25:153
Lydia, 22:238; 25:53
Lydia (___), 25:52, 53, 152
Lydia (Lock), 21:158
Martha Ellen, 25:152
Mary, 21:158; 22:215; 23:238; 25:151
Mary (Smith), 21:158
Mary Ann, 25:52
Mehitable, 21:158
Moses, 21:158
Naomi (Stebbins), 21:158
Peter, 23:117
Phebe, 21:45
Rebecca, 21:40, 41; 22:22, 23, 215;
    23:238
Rebecca (Sheldon), 23:117
Sarah, 23:238
Solomon, 25:52, 53, 152
Susanna, 21:155, 158
Susanna (Haven), 21:158
William, 21:158; 23:236, 238
TOWNSEND, 23:218
Ebenezer, 24:54
Elizabeth (Berry), 22:44
Hannah, 22:44
Hannah (___), 25:79
Hannah (Foster), 22:44
Henry H., 22:44
Jacob, 22:44
Jerusha, 22:44
Johanna (___), 24:54
John, 21:214, 221; 24:54
Joseph, 22:43, 44
Judith (Woodman), 22:44
Mary (Davis), 22:44
Mary (Newgate), 24:54
Moses, 25:79
Olive, 24:54
Priscilla, 22:43, 44
Prudence, 21:216
Sally, 24:96
Sarah, 21:215; 22:44
Sarah (___), 22:44
Sarah (Atwell), 22:43, 44
Sarah (Boutall), 21:221

Sarah (Pearson), 24:54
Thomas, 22:44; 24:54
Timothy, 22:44
TOZER
Ruth, 21:53
TRACY
Hannah, 23:8
Patrick, 23:7, 11
TRAPANI
Minne, 23:47
TRASK/TRASKE, 21:27; 22:25
___, Capt., 21:25, 26
Abagail (Parkman), 23:239
Christian (Woodbury), 23:239
Edward, 23:239
John, 21:25, 26; 23:239
Mary, 22:23, 216; 23:239
Mercy (Eliot), 23:239
Nicholas, 21:27
Richard, 22:28; 23:35, 200
Sarah (___), 21:25
Susannah, 22:24
William, 21:24-26; 22:23, 24
William Blake, 21:25, 26; 22:41
TRAVERS
H., 21:114
TRAVETT see TREVETT/TREVITT
TRAVIS
Elizabeth, 21:152, 156, 160
John, 21:156
TREADWELL
Esther, 25:156
Jas. W., 23:56
John, 22:49, 52
Mary (Taylor), 25:156
Thomas, 25:156
TREAT/TREATT see also TREVITT
Henry, 25:17
Mary, 24:42
TREFETHEN
Abigail Grace Elkins, 21:224
TREFREY/TREFRY
Henry, 23:189
James, 23:208
Susannah M. (Blaney), 23:208
TRELAWNY, 22:43
TRENT
Robert, 21:171
TRETA
Samuel, 25:20
TREVETT/TREVITT/TRAVETT/
    TREAT/TREATT, 21:34, 25:25,
Hannah, 25:19, 20, 22, 24-27, 58
Henry, 25:19, 25
Martha (___), 25:28
Martha (Jackson), 25:25
Mary (___), 25:19, 25
Richard, 25:24, 25, 27, 28
TRIPP
Anne, 25:202
Emma Armina, 24:70
Julius, 24:70
Matilda (Benson), 24:70
TROMMSDORFF
M., 24:70
TROWBRIDGE
Lydia, 21:159
Mary, 21:159
Thankful, 21:159
TRULL
John, 24:48
Mary, 24:48
Sarah (French), 24:48
TRUMBLE/TRUMBULL
Benjamin, 25:53, 54
Charles, 22:236

Hannah (___), 22:174-176, 235, 236
John, 22:167, 175
Mary, 22:176
Myer, 22:176
Nathaniel, 22:174-176, 235, 236;
    25:53, 54
Phebe, 25:93
Richard, 22:174
Sarah (___), 25:53, 54
Sarh Ann, 25:53
William, 22:235
TRUSLER
Thomas, 21:90
TRYON
Mary, 21:37
TUCK
Elizabeth, 24:224
TUCKER, 22:25, 135; 24:91
___, Capt., 24:79
Andrew, 22:237; 25:53, 54, 153
Andrew Hardy, 25:54
Eben, 22:237
Eleanor, 22:196
Elizabeth (Bessom), 23:210
Eunice, 22:235
George, 23:153
Gidson, 25:53
Henry, 22:237
John, 22:27, 147, 237; 23:210
John C., 23:16
John Henfield, 25:153
Jonathan, 22:237; 24:207
Lydia, 22:237
Martha, 22:237; 25:53
Martha (___), 22:237; 25:53, 54, 153
Martha (Bessom), 23:210
Mary, 21:116
Mary Widger, 23:187
Nancy (___), 22:235
Nicholas, 25:17
Ralph, 25:204
Robert, 22:235
Samuel, 22:237; 24:80
Thomas, 22:235
William, 22:235
TUCKERMAN
Francis, 24:232a
S. P., 22:60a
TUCKESBARY see also TEWKSBURY
Henry, 23:153
Philip, 23:153
TUDOR
Frederick, 24:125
TUFT/TUFTS, 22:135
Asa, 24:208, 209
Betsy (___), 24:138
Elizabeth, 25:137
Elizabeth (Parker), 24:208, 209
Gardiner, 22:147
Ivory, 24:138
John, 23:12; 24:208
Mary (___), 25:166
Peter, 25:166
TULLY
G., 24:69
TURBAT
Peter, 23:232, 233
Sarah (Sanders), 23:232
TURK
Marion G., 23:215
TURNER, 24:91
___, Capt., 21:212
Catherine (Fields), 22:179
Chloe, 22:179
Elias, 23:214
Experience (Benton), 22:179

George S., 21:108
Hannah, 23:214
Hannah (Penfield), 22:179
Isaac, 23:214
James, 23:214
Joanna (Goodridge), 24:55
John, 22:179; 23:25, 153, 214
Margaret, 23:214
Mary, 23:214
Mary (Bessom), 23:214
Mary Wilson, 21:108
Obadiah, 23:120a, 218
Robert, 21:148
Ruth Ella (Wilson), 21:108
Samuel, 23:214
William, 24:55
TUTT
Hannah, 23:212
TUTTLE
___, Mrs., 25:54
Barnet Woodbury, 21:179
Betsey Elizabeth, 21:179
Betsy F. (Atwell), 22:49
Elizabeth, 25:54
Jonathan, 22:49
Maria Elizabeth (Hickok), 21:179
Mary (Woodbury), 21:179
Nathl, 25:54
Warren, 21:208
William Thomas, 21:179
TUTTY
Hannah, 23:58
TWISS
Eunice, 24:207
TWIST
Benjamin, 21:50
Robert, 21:50
TYBBOTT/TYBOTT
Agnes, 23:177
Mary, 24:16, 175, 231
TYGNE
Elizabeth, 23:162
TYLER, 23:212
Abby (Colton), 21:101
Albert, 21:103
Almana M., 21:103
Betty, 21:99
David C., 21:103
Deborah, 21:99
Eli S., 21:103
Elizabeth (Parker), 25:44
George F., 21:103
Hannah, 21:99, 100
Hannah M., 21:101
Jacob, 24:85
James, 22:226-228
Jason C., 21:103
Jephthah, 21:99, 101, 103
Job, 25:44
John, 22:180
Lucy C., 21:101
Lydia (___), 24:85
Lydia W., 21:101
Mary, 23:153
Mary (Briant), 21:99
Mary B., 21:101
Mary E., 21:103
Molly/Mary, 21:99, 101
Nanna/Nancy, 21:99
Parrley W., 21:101
Rebecca (Gould), 22:180
Sally (Wilmot), 21:101
Sarah, 21:99
Sarah C., 21:101
Wm. N., 21:103

TYNGE
Edward, 23:162

ULILINO
Angelina, 25:113
ULLMANN
Helen, 22:183
Helen Schatvet, 22:200
ULRICH
Mary, 21:116
UNCAPHER
Wendy K., 25:123, 124
UNDERHILL
Joanna (Healey), 22:177
John, 22:177
Mary/Molly, 22:177
UNDERWOOD
Joseph, 21:220
Mary (Poole), 21:220
UPDIKE
John, 21:82; 22:169
UPHAM
Charles, 21:37, 41, 42
Charles W., 21:143
Charles Wentworth, 24:232a
Mary, 24:160, 207, 209, 211
William P., 23:160
UPTON see also RUPTON, 22:24, 25,
    30; 25:9, 10
___ (Stuart), 22:22
Abigail (___), 21:39
Abigail (Frost), 21:39
Amos, 22:31
Ann, 21:39
Caleb, 21:52
Ebenezer, 22:30
Eleanor, 21:38
Ellenor (Stuart), 21:38, 52
Ezekiel, 21:39, 41; 22:22
Ezra, 21:43
Francis, 21:39
Gardner, 22:29
George, 21:43
Hannah, 21:36, 43
Issabbel, 21:39
James, 21:38; 22:22
John, 21: 38, 52, 115, 214; 22: 22, 29,
    30, 32
Jonathan, 22:175
Joseph, 21:39, 214
Ken, 22:29
Mary, 21:38, 39
Mary (Maber), 21:39, 52
Mary (Steward), 21:52
Paul, 21:43
Phebe (Goodale), 21:43
Rebecca, 21:52; 22:22
Rebecca (Preston), 21:39, 41; 22:22
Robert, 22:175
Ruth (Marsh), 21:39
Samuel, 21:39, 214; 22:22
Sarah (Thompson), 21:38; 22:22
Susanna (Whipple), 21:43
Susannah, 25:148
William, 21:38, 39, 52, 214; 22:22
URIEN
Peter, 23:141
URIN
Ellinor, 25:55
UTERMANN
G., 24:70
UTTAM
Marianne, 22:170

VACCA, 22:99

VAIL/VAILL
___, Rev. Mr., 21:21
Susanna, 21:157
VALPEY
Abraham, 24:96
Elizabeth (Abbott), 24:96
Mary (___), 24:96
Samuel S., 24:96
VAN DERLIP
W. C., 23:56
VAN GALEN
Margaret, 21:146
VANDERBILT, 21:79
VANE
Harry, 22:240a; 23:240a
VARILL see VARREL
VARNEY
Dorothy, 23:153
George Dillwyn, 24:200
Sarah, 24:41, 87, 200
Sarah (Whittier), 24:200
Sarah P., 24:197
VARNUM
Dolly (Stevens), 24:89
Hannah, 24:43, 89
John, 24:89
Jonathan, 24:89
Parker, 24:215
Phebe (Parker), 24:89
VAROL see VARREL
VARREL/VARILL/VAROL
Mary, 23:153
Richard, 23:153
Sarah, 23:153
Susanna, 23:153
VASSALL
Judith, 21:43
Samuel, 23:180a
VAUGHN
William Preston, 23:170
VEALY
Marcy, 21:92
VERDI
Giuseppe, 25:106
VEREN/VERIN
Hilliard, 21:91, 92; 22:208, 209, 240a;
    23:177; 25:17, 129
Jane, 21:33
Joshua, 22:240a
Mary, 25:58
Mary (Conant), 23:177
Philip, 22:240a
Sarah, 23:177
VERNON
___, Adm., 23:87
Anne C., 22:126
VERRIEL
Samuel, 23:153
VERRY
David, 23:91
Jemima (Skidmore), 23:91
VERSAILLES
Elizabeth Starr, 21:238; 24:217
VERY, 21:10; 22:25; 23:35
Abigail (___), 22:173, 175
Amos, 23:108
Elizabeth, 22:171
Elizabeth (___), 22:171, 172
Jacob, 22:171, 172
John Crowninshield, 22:173
Jonathan, 22:175
Jones, 22:27; 24:232a
Joseph, 23:36
Nabby, 22:175
Patty, 22:172
Samuel, 22:173, 175

VESEY
William, 23:235
VICK
Douglas F., 21:49
VICKERY
David, 21:177
Hannah, 21:177
Hannah (Parker), 21:177
Jonathan, 21:178
Mary, 21:177
Mary (___), 21:178
Sarah (Stone), 21:177
VICTORIA
Duchess, 24:68
Queen, 21:81; 24:67, 69
VICTORIA ALBERTA
Princess, 24:69
VILES
Bowman, 22:79
VINCENT
Elizabeth, 25:79
Elizabeth (___), 25:79
Joseph, 25:79
Lydia (Nowell), 25:79
Mary (Brown), 24:175
Matthew, 25:79
Sarah, 24:16, 175, 231
Sarah (___), 25:79
Timothy Laitila, 25:122
VINSON
Sarah, 23:228
VODEN
Elizabeth, 21:41
Mary, 21:41
Mary (Ormes), 21:41
Moses, 21:41
VOICE, 23:150
William, 23:153
VON RHODEN, 22:133
VON WILLIBRAND, 24:63
VOYE
Nancy S., 24:217

WADE, 24:85
Jonathan, 25:8, 131, 140
Rebeckah, 21:220
Thomas, 24:148
WADSWORTH
Lydia, 24:116
WAINRIGHT/WAINWRIGHT
Francis, 23:58
Hannah, 23:153
Martha, 21:120; 23:58
Mary, 22:89
Mary (Williams), 22:89, 95
Phillis (Sewall), 23:58
Sarah, 23:58
Simon, 22:89, 95
Thomas, 23:153
WAIT/WAITE/WAITT see also
    WAYTE
Aaron, 22:172, 175
Benjamin, 24:217
Elizabeth (___), 22:172, 175
Hannah (___), 21:153
Harriet, 22:175
Isaac, 23:153
Jonathan, 21:153
Martha (___), 21:159
Mary (Parker), 24:154
Thomas, 24:154
William, 22:50; 23:109, 207
WAKEFIELD
Caleb, 21:209
Comfort (Clark), 25:155
Hannah (Emmons), 25:155

John, 25:155
Nathaniel, 25:155
Wm., 23:232
WALCOTT
___, Mrs., 21:41; 24:196
Samuel, 24:196
WALDO
___, Mr., 24:32
Cornelius, 24:28, 30; 25:132
WALDRON
___, Maj., 21:142; 23:54
E. T., 23:90
WALKER, 21:152; 22:115; 24:146-150;
25:134
Abner, 23:153
Betsey, 22:120
David, 25:151
Elizabeth, 23:169; 25:86
Hannah, 21:159, 160
Henry, 22:153; 24:143
John, 23:93
John Ives, 25:151
Liz, 22:169
Martha, 21:151, 158, 160
Martha (___), 21:158, 159
Martha (Howe), 21:155
Mary, 21:155, 160
Mary (___), 25:151
Nathaniel, 24:104; 25:189
Patrick, 23:15
Richard, 21:29, 210
Samuel, 23:93; 24:104
Sarah (Skidmore), 23:93
Stephen, 23:93
Tabitha, 23:169
Thomas, 21:155, 158, 159
WALKES
Joseph A., 23:170
WALL
Bartholomew, 21:148
John, 21:148
WALLACE/WALLES/WALLIS,
24:148
Ann (Whyte), 23:74
David, 22:226-231
Dennison, 22:27
Elizabeth, 23:72, 74-76
Elizabeth (Ross), 23:73
Ella (___), 23:126
George, 23:76, 153
Jacob T., 24:170
James, 23:69, 76
James Campbell, 23:76
Jane (Campbell), 23:76
John, 23:73, 76, 126, 161
Lydia (English), 21:100
Mary (Hogg), 23:74
Robina, 23:73
Robina (Pender), 23:68, 69, 72, 77
Robina (Ross), 23:75
Sophia Mary, 21:120, 22:218
William, 23:68, 69, 72, 74-76, 153
WALROTH
Joanne Ruth, 21:144
WALSH
Jane, 25:11
Michael J., 23:17
Nathaniel, 23:15
WALTON
Samuel, 22:45
WARD
___, Maj., 22:37
Benjamin, 22:49
Betsy, 22:171
Betsy F. (Atwell), 22:49
Buffum, 22:218

Caroline (Reynolds), 25:173
Ephraim, 21:159
Experience (___), 22:171
George, 22:221, 231, 232
Hitty, 22:171
John, 21:195; 22:20; 23:26
Joshua, 22:171; 23:186
Martha (___), 22:174
Mary, 21:28
Mary (Haven), 21:158, 159
Mary (Stone), 21:159
Miles, 22:171
Olive A., 21:54
Oliver, 22:171
Richard, 21:159
S. H., 23:88
Sally, 22:171
Sarah (___), 22:37, 171
Tamosin, 22:215-217
Thankful (Trowbridge), 21:159
Thomas Ian, 22:174
William, 22:174
WARDELL
Lydia, 21:112
WARDEN
Amanda (___), 22:185
Andrew, 22:185, 193
Charles, 22:185, 186
Emilianne, 22:185
Emily, 22:185, 186, 193
Mary (___), 22:185
Sanders, 22:185
WARDWELL
___, Judge, 24:195
___, Mrs., 24:195
Claire Marjorie, 24:226
Clarence Milton, 24:226
Dorothy (Wright), 21:88
Eliakim, 21:85, 88
Elizabeth, 21:88
Elizabeth (___), 21:85
Joshua, 24:92
Lydia (Perkins), 21:85
Mercy, 21:86, 87
Nathan, 24:90
Peter, 24:100
Phebe (Stevens), 24:90
Rebecca, 21:87
Returne (Ellinwood), 21:88
Ruth (Bragdon), 21:88
Samuel, 21:85-88
Sarah (Hooper), 21:85-87
Sarah (Stevens), 24:92
Susanna, 24:92, 100
Susanna (___), 24:100
Thomas, 21:87
Thomas, 21:85, 87
William, 21:85, 88
Zemira Aureta (Paine), 24:226
WARE
Hannah, 21:157, 160
Hannah (___), 21:157
Joseph, 21:157
WARNER
Abigail, 22:56; 25:201
Abigail (Baker), 25:201
Caleb, 25:152
Caleb Henry, 25:152
Daniel, 25:55
Edward, 25:152
Frederick, 21:44
Hannah, 22:179; 25:55, 57
Hannah (Davis), 25:55, 57
John, 25:55, 57, 210
Mary Pearson, 25:152
Nathaniel, 24:218

Philemon, 23:140
Saml, 23:144
Sarah (Dane), 25:55
Susan, 25:152
WARREN/WARRIN, 23:153
Christopher, 23:46
Elisha, 25:84
Elizabeth, 24:159, 205, 206
Ephraim, 25:83, 84
Joseph, 23:153; 24:159; 25:84, 88
Marah/Mary (Parker), 25:84
Mary, 25:83
Paula Stuart, 24:227, 229
Ruth, 21:99
Sarah, 25:94
Sarah (Abot), 25:84
Sybil, 25:86
Tabitha (Parker), 24:159
Violetta (Rhodes), 23:46
WARSHALL
Stephen, 25:11
WASHINGTON
___, Gen., 21:180a; 24:80
___, Pres., 21:136
George, 23:11, 12; 24:79
WASTOL/WESTOL
John, 21:149
Susanna (___), 21:149
WATERHOUSE, 23:47
Elizabeth, 23:45, 49
J. L., 23:50
John, 23:46, 49
Lydia (Rhodes), 23:50
Lydia Margaret (Rhodes), 23:46, 49
WATERMAN
Florence (Eaton), 23:158, 178
WATERS, 22:159; 23:234
Henry F., 21:148
Lydia, 23:103, 104, 107
Mary (Hawkins), 21:38
Samuel, 21:38
T. Frank, 24:150
T.F., 24:140
Thomas F., 22:161
Thomas Franklin, 24:25, 26
WATKINS
Andrew, 25:54
Betsey (___), 25:54
Walter Kendall, 24:168
WATSON
Abraham, 25:79
Elizabeth, 24:96
Elizabeth (___), 25:79
John, 24:96
Joseph, 25:202
Josephine, 21:54
Louis, 23:17
Marjory, 25:202
Robert, 23:153
WATTS, 22:21
John, 22:49
WAYTE/WAYTT see also WAITE,
24:153
Abigail, 24:156
Benjamin, 24:156
Chas., 21:166
Isaac, 24:156
Jacob, 24:156
John, 24:153, 156
Mary, 24:156
Mary (Hills), 24:156
Mary (Parker), 24:156
Rachel, 24:156
Sarah (___), 24:153
Thomas, 24:156

WEATHERALL
Bob, 24:27, 33
Robert K., 24:23
WEAVER
Caleb, 25:153
Joan, 22:170
Mary (___), 25:153
William, 25:153
William L., 21:36
WEBB
___, Mr., 21:148
Benjamin, 22:171, 172, 174-176
Charlotte, 24:230
Elizabeth, 22:174, 175
Hannah, 25:151
Hannah (Allen), 21:14
John, 21:71
Jonathan, 22:176
Mary, 22:171
Mary (___), 22:171, 172, 174-176
Mary (Hallowell), 21:71
Priscilla, 22:172
William, 21:14
WEBBER/WEBER
Daniel, 23:154
Ignatius, 22:226, 230
James, 24:221
Lois, 25:108
Martha Ann (Batten), 24:221
Mary (___), 25:18
Richard, 25:18
Sarah (Strout), 25:18
Thomas, 25:18
William, 24:221
WEBSTER, 22:203
___, Mrs., 21:173
Betie, 25:100, 101
Daniel, 23:185, 186, 188
Edith (Kimball), 21:120
Elizabeth, 21:112; 25:96, 101, 103-105
Elizabeth (Emeri), 25:96-98
Elizabeth (Parker), 25:91
Elizabeth (Whiting), 23:227, 228
George Pearl, 21:120
Grace Pearl, 22:238
James Henry, 22:238
John, 21:172
Lorenzo D., 24:171
Mary, 21:172, 212
Mary (Shatswell), 21:172, 198
Moses, 25:91
Nathan, 25:98
Noah, 25:160
Ruth Mehitable (Pearl), 22:238
Samuel, 23:227, 228; 25:167
Sarah Dimond (Sanborn), 22:238
William W., 22:238
WEDGWOOD
Mary, 21:89
WEED
Ann, 21:177
WEEDEN
Mary Louisa, 25:196
WEEKS
Mary T., 21:108
WELCH
George N., 23:17
Hannah, 22:178
Moses, 23:154
Walter, 23:16
WELD/WELDE/WELDS see also
WELLS
___ (Whiting), 23:219
___, Dr., 21:92
Daniel, 21:157; 23:219
Dorithy/Dorothy, 23:219

Dorothy (Whiting), 23:219
Edmund, 23:219, 220
Elias, 25:189
Elizabeth (White), 23:219
Elizabeth (Wilson), 23:219
Joanna (Haven), 21:157
John, 23:219
Joseph, 23:219
Margaret (Deresleye), 23:219
Margreat, 23:219
Mary (Savage), 23:219
Samuel, 23:219
Susanna (Polley), 23:219
Thomas, 23:219
William Addison, 23:220
WELLCOME
Elizth. (___), 25:80
Thoms., 25:80
WELLES see WELLS
WELLINGTON
Benjamin, 23:223, 224
Mary (Whiting), 23:223, 224
WELLMAN/WELMAN
Abraham, 21:92, 95
Sarah (Wyatt), 21:14
T. B., 22:74
Thomas, 21:29, 95; 23:120a, 158
Thomas B., 21:215
Timothy, 21:14
WELLNER
Ruth Quigley, 22:3
WELLS/WELLES see also WELD,
21:157
Abigail, 21:51
Abigail (Warner), 22:56; 25:201
Charles B., 23:56
Elida Raymond, 23:155
Elizabeth, 25:201
Hannah, 22:55
Johannah (Rowell), 22:55
John, 21:26, 81; 22:108
John Andrew, 22:27
Mary, 22:59
Mary (Perkins), 22:55
Thomas, 22:55, 56, 184; 25:135, 201
Titus, 22:55
WENDELL
Mercy, 22:60a
WENTWORTH
___, Gov., 23:11
John, 21:135
Thomas, 23:180a
WESLEY
John, 23:24
WESSELS
Tom, 22:161
WESSON
Ephraim, 21:220
Esther (Miles), 23:180
Hannah (Mansfield), 23:180
James, 23:180
John, 21:156, 210, 213, 216
Martha (Haven), 21:156
Nathan, 23:180
Samuel, 21:156
Thomas, 21:217
WEST
B., 23:150
Benjamin, 22:226-228; 23:154
Elizabeth (Jackson), 23:239
John, 22:37; 24:147; 25:135
Ruth, 23:239
Thomas, 23:239
WESTALL see WESTOL
WESTCOTT
John, 23:40

WESTOL/WESTALL/WESTOLL
John, 21:149, 152, 154
Susanna, 21:151, 152, 160
Susanna (Kirtland), 21:149
WESTON
Eliza, 23:156, 158
Elizabeth (Browne), 21:177
John, 21:211
Joseph, 21:177, 178
Joshua, 25:167
Samuel, 23:174
Sarah, 21:177
Sarah (___), 21:177, 178
Sarah (Rogers), 23:174
Thomas, 21:177, 217
WETHERBEE
John, 23:99
WHEELER/WHELLER, 22:212;
24:149
___, Goodman, 22:204
Aaron, 22:226, 228
Abigail (Allen), 24:232; 25:203
Abigail Jane, 25:152
Ann, 24:232
Anne (Yoeman), 25:203
Charles, 22:226, 234
Daniel, 22:221, 226, 229-234
Elizabeth, 23:169
George, 22:56
Henry, 24:232; 25:203
Joanna, 22:55; 23:176
John, 22:55; 23:176; 25:203
Jonathan, 22:240
Joseph, 25:152
Katherine (___), 22:56
Mary, 21:179
Mary (___), 21:29; 22:240
Rebecca, 23:226
Sarah (Larkin), 22:55; 23:176
Susan (___), 25:152
Thomas, 21:29; 22:204, 208, 209
WHEELOCK
Sarah (Rand), 21:34
Timothy, 21:34
WHEELWRIGHT, 22:135
Andrew Cunningham, 22:148
John, 21:85; 23:54
Martha (Moyce), 23:54
Sarah Cabot, 22:148
WHELLER see WHEELER
WHERETT
Helen 'Peg', 24:224
WHIPPLE
Elizabeth, 25:201
Elizabeth (Hawkins), 25:201
Henry, 24:121
Jacob, 21:159
Jennet (___), 23:120
Jerusha, 21:159
Jerusha (___), 21:159
Job, 23:154
John, 22:151, 166; 23:120, 154
Mathew, 21:186; 22:226, 230, 232;
24:52; 25:201
Rose (___), 21:186
Sarah, 21:39
Susanna, 21:43
WHITAKER
Abigail, 24:48, 51
David, 24:50
Nathaniel, 25:150
WHITCHER, 24:18
Benjamin, 24:180, 187
Dolly, 22:47, 54
WHITCOMB
William C., 22:77, 78

WHITE/WHYTE, 23:215
  Abigail (___), 25:80
  Ann, 23:74
  Anne (___), 21:114
  Beatrix (Holton), 21:43
  Benjamin, 23:154
  Da'el Joseph, 23:154
  Dinah (Kenney), 21:43, 44
  Donald A., 23:85
  Elizabeth, 22:202, 203, 206; 23:219;
    25:52
  Elizabeth (___), 24:195
  Freeman, 24:183
  Hannah, 21:43
  Helen Marilyn, 21:18
  Henry, 23:154; 25:80
  Hugh, 23:154
  J. T., 21:233
  Jeremiah, 23:154
  John, 23:210; 24:164; 25:80
  Joseph, 21:43, 154
  Josiah, 21:43
  Judith (Vassall), 21:43
  Mary, 21:43; 22:161; 23:154
  Mary (Taylor), 21:43
  Nicholas, 23:161
  Peregrine, 21:43
  Phebe (___), 25:80
  Philip H., 23:210
  Remember (___), 23:154
  Remember (Reed), 21:43
  Resolved, 21:43
  Richard, 22:186
  Ruth (Emery), 24:164
  Samuel, 21:43, 44; 22:27
  Sarah, 21:43
  Sarah (Gardner), 21:43
  Solomon, 23:154
  Susana (___), 21:43
  Thomas, 22:36
  William, 21:43; 23:154
WHITEHOUSE
  Elizabeth, 23:117
WHITERIDGE/WHITERIDGES
  see WHITRED
WHITFORD
  Rebekah, 25:80
  Rebekh. (___), 25:80
  Samll, 25:80
WHITING/ WHYTING/
    WHYTYNGE, 21:66
  ___, Mr., 21:148; 22:206
  "Daughter", 23:220
  "Son", 23:219, 220
  Alice, 23:223
  Alice (Cook), 23:222, 223; 24:37, 43
  Ann (___), 21:160
  Anna, 23:223, 224
  Anna (Danforth), 23:223
  Anne, 23:227
  Anne (Frie), 23:224
  Audrey, 23:218
  Benjamin, 23:223-226, 228
  Charles, 21:65
  Daniel, 21:159
  Deborah (Hill), 23:224
  Dorcas/Doriks, 23:222-224; 24:104
  Dorcas (Chester), 23:220, 221
  Dorothy, 23:219, 221, 224, 226, 228;
    24:50
  Dorothy (Crosby), 23:224
  Ebenezer, 23:226, 228
  Eleazer, 23:223, 224; 24:50
  Elizabeth, 23:220-222, 226-228;
    24:104
  Elizabeth (Bradford), 21:65

  Elizabeth (Brown), 23:223
  Elizabeth (Powter/Poulter), 23:223
  Elizabeth (Read), 23:222
  Elizabeth (St. John), 23:219
  Esther (___), 23:220
  Eunice, 23:223
  Fannie, 23:223
  Hannah (Haven), 21:159
  Isabel, 23:218
  Isabel (___), 23:218
  Isaiah, 21:159
  James, 23:218, 225
  John, 23:218-227; 24:104
  John Roger Scott, 23:218
  Jonathan, 21:159; 23:223; 24:104
  Joseph, 23:219, 220, 222, 225, 226,
    228; 24:104, 176
  Katharine, 23:222
  Leonard, 23:222
  Lydia (___), 23:227
  Lydia (Parker), 23:227
  Margaret, 23:218
  Mary, 23:221-224, 227; 24:104
  Mary (___), 23:225
  Mary (Cotton), 23:226
  Mary (Lake), 23:227
  Mary (Whiting), 23:222, 223
  Mehitable (Haven), 21:159
  Nathaniel, 23:218
  Oliver, 23:221-223; 24:104
  Rebecca (___), 23:220, 225, 226;
    24:104
  Rebecca (Bishop), 24:176
  Rebecca (Bulkeley), 23:226, 227
  Samuel, 21:210; 23:218-226, 228;
    24:87
  Sarah, 23:225-227; 24:104
  Sarah (Danforth), 23:220, 225
  Sarah (Hunt), 23:224
  Sarah (Stevens), 24:87
  Stephen, 23:227
  Thomas, 23:226, 227
  Unis, 23:225
  William, 23:218; 24:104
WHITLOCK
  Rose, 25:33, 34
WHITMAN, 22:117
  Eliza, 21:28
  Robert, 25:133
WHITMARSH
  Natalie, 25:11
WHITNER
  Elizabeth, 21:81
WHITNEY
  Elinor (___), 21:152
  Elizabeth, 21:151
  H. O., 24:223
  Hannah, 21:152
  James, 21:151
  John, 21:151, 152, 158, 159
  Jonathan, 21:151
  Lydia, 21:152, 158, 160
  Lydia (Jones), 21:151
  Margaret, 21:54
  Martha (Walker), 21:151
  Mary, 21:151
  Mary (Hapgood), 21:151
  Sarah (Haven), 21:150-152, 159
WHITRED/WHITREDG/
    WHITRIDGE/WHITREDGE/
    WHITRIGE/WHITERIDGE/
    WHITERIDGE/WHITTEREDD/
    WHITTERIDGE/
    WHITTERREGE/WITTREGE,
    22:114, 115, 117; 24:28, 110, 111
  ___, Goodman, 22:152, 153, 159

  Abigail, 22:155, 158, 160
  Caroline (Patch), 22:161
  David, 22:151, 159; 24:136; 25:131
  David A., 22:114; 24:27, 109, 139
  Elizabeth, 22:155, 158
  Elizabeth (___), 22:151, 152, 155, 158,
    160
  Florence (___), 22:158
  Frances (___), 22:155, 156, 158, 160
  Hannah (Roberts), 22:158
  John, 22:155, 158, 160
  Livermore, 22:160
  Mary, 22:155, 158, 160; 23:104, 105,
    107, 177
  Richard, 22:158, 160
  Samuel, 22:155, 158, 160
  Susanna, 22:155, 158, 160
  Susanna (___), 22:155, 156, 160
  Susanna, 22:160
  Susanna (___), 22:160
  William, 22:160
  Thomas, 22:151, 154-158, 160
  William, 22:114, 118, 151-156,
    158-160; 24:28, 109, 111, 142, 151;
    25:133
WHITTAKER
  Abigail, 24:50
  John, 24:50
WHITTEMORE
  Elizabeth, 21:32
  Joel, 21:34
  Rezinah (Rand), 21:34
  William, 22:50
WHITTEREDD/WHITTERIDGE/
    WHITTERREGE see WHITRED
WHITTIER, 24:169; 25:91
  Dearborn, 24:170
  John Greenleaf, 21:82, 142; 22:94;
    23:54; 24:108
  Mark, 24:170
  Sarah, 24:200
WHITTINGHAM
  John, 22:153
WHITTRED/WHITTREDGE/
    WHITTERREGE/
    WHITTRIDGE/WHITTRIGE see
    WHITRED
WHYTE see WHITE
WHYTING/WHYTYNGE see
    WHITING
WICOM
  Richard, 22:167
WIGGIN, 23:231
WIGGLESWORTH
  Edward, 25:188
  Mary, 25:172
WIGHTMAN
  Mary, 22:179
WIIKNIKAINEN
  Marsha Ann, 21:18
WILCOMB
  Charity (Dodd), 25:55, 57
  Deborah, 25:56
  Ellinor (Urin), 25:55
  Ridchard, 25:55
  Sarah, 25:55, 57
  Sarah (Moore), 25:55-57
  William, 25:55, 57
  Zecceus, 25:55-57
WILD see also WILDES
  William, 22:167
WILDER
  Mary, 21:215
WILDES see also WILD
  Ephraim, 23:238
  John, 23:237, 238

Priscilla (Gould), 23:238
Sarah, 23:237
Sarah (Averell), 23:237, 238
WILEY
Benjamin, 21:213
Chloe (Holt), 24:44
David, 24:44
Hannah Parsons, 21:104
John, 21:211, 214
Lydia, 21:214
Mary, 21:214
Mary (Nichols), 21:213
Mary (Poole), 21:214
Nathaniel, 21:214
Phineas, 21:214
Rebecca (Emerson), 23:155
Ruth (___), 22:76
Susanna, 21:214, 220
Timothy, 21:214, 216, 217, 219, 220
WILJANON
Linda Lee, 21:18
WILKES
Robert, 21:92
WILKINS
Bray, 21:211; 23:91
Esther (Stevens), 24:40
Hannah, 24:43
Hannah (___), 24:89
Israel, 23:88
John, 21:40
Margaret (Case), 23:88
Martin, 24:89
Mary, 23:147, 154
Mary (Goodale), 21:39
Rachel, 23:88, 89, 91
Thomas, 24:40
WILL
Black, 23:168, 169
WILLARD, 22:75
John, 21:42
Sarah, 24:158
Simon, 24:159
WILLCUTT
John, 23:54
WILLET/WILLETT
"Daughter", 22:88
Elizabeth (Lowle), 22:91
Francis, 22:86, 88, 91
Hannah, 22:88, 91
Jackman, 21:111
Joanna/Johannah, 22:88
John, 22:88
Joseph, 22:88
Judith, 22:91
Martha, 22:88
Martha (Silver), 22:87, 88, 91
Mary, 22:91
Mittens, 23:56
Ruth, 22:91
Sara/Sara, 22:88
Thomas, 22:88
William, 22:88
WILLIAM
Conqueror, 21:186; 22:201
Duke, 24:68
King, 22:123; 23:162
WILLIAMS, 24:121
Abigail, 21:33, 41; 25:52
Abigail (___), 22:171-174, 176
Angeline Lydia/L.A. (Sherman),
Anne, 25:204
Benjamin, 21:120; 23:180
Betsey (Walker), 22:120
Dorithy/Dorothy (Weld), 23:219
E. A., 21:207
Elizabeth, 22:237

Henry, 22:171-174, 176; 23:36
Henry L., 22:120
Isaac F., 24:171
Jane Cooper, 22:180a
John, 21:220; 22:89, 176; 23:44, 45
John Dorand, 23:180
Joseph Warren, 22:171
Katy, 22:171
Loretta, 23:170
Lucian, 22:120
Lydia, 22:173
Lydia W., 25:194
Mary, 21:33; 22:89, 92-96, 99
Mary (___), 23:36
Mary (Lovell), 21:120; 23:180
Melzer A., 23:36
Rebecca, 21:220
Rebecca (Colby), 22:89
Rebeckah (Pearson), 21:220
Roger, 22:240a; 23:240a; 24:232a
Ruth, 25:53
Samuel, 23:219
Sarah, 22:237; 23:154
Thomas, 21:220
Thomas Russel, 22:172
Willard, 22:174
William, 22:236, 237; 25:52
WILLINGTON
Benjamin, 24:37
Elizabeth (Stevens), 24:37
WILLINK
Wilhelm, 23:48
WILLIS, 23:161, 162
Mary, 24:157
Thomas, 24:157
Timothy, 21:213
William, 23:159
Willie, 23:178
WILLISTON
Nancy, 23:208
WILLOUGHBY
Abigail (___), 25:78, 80
Abigall, 25:78
Nehemiah, 25:78, 80
WILLSON see also WILSON
Edmund Burke, 24:232a
Elizabeth (Atwell), 22:46
Henry, 22:221, 232
Lydia (Johnson), 22:162, 163
Samuel, 22:46, 163
WILLY
___, Mr., 21:219
WILMERDING
John, 25:11, 12, 14
WILMOT
Sally, 21:101
WILSON see also WILLSON,
21:9, 163, 232
___, Aunt, 21:164
___, Mr., 21:195; 22:152
A.C., 24:71
Andrew, 25:9
Ann, 23:65, 66, 77
Ann (Crighton), 23:66
Anna, 21:102
Asad Experience, 25:160
Bessie Pushee, 21:108
Betsey (Briant), 21:102
Deborah (Buffum), 22:215, 217
Dorothy (Stevens), 24:85
Edith Smith, 21:108
Elizabeth, 21:102; 23:219; 24:211
Esther (Haven), 21:158
Hannah (Swallow), 24:53
Henry, 22:219, 220, 227, 232, 233
Jacob, 21:158

Joan, 22:165
John, 21:102, 105, 108, 158; 22:165;
23:66; 24:211
John Chester, 21:108
Joseph, 21:102, 105
Joseph Austin, 21:105
Joshua, 24:85, 96
Lois (Towne), 21:158
Lydia Ann, 21:105
Mary, 21:240; 23:176; 24:16, 136, 175,
231
Mary Frances (Pyne), 21:108
Mary Smith, 21:105, 108
Mehitable, 22:48, 54
Mehitable/Hattie, 22:47
Rebecca, 21:102, 105
Robert, 22:215
Robert G., 23:56
Ruth Dodge (Smith), 21:105
Ruth Ella, 21:105, 108
Samuel, 24:53
Tabitha, 24:160, 211, 212
Theophilus, 23:231
William, 23:172
WILT
John, 22:212
WIMAN see also WYMAN
John, 25:4, 5
WINBORNE
John, 21:152, 153
WINCH
Sampson, 21:67
Samuel, 21:155
Sarah (___), 21:155
Silence, 21:155, 160
WINCHESTER
Elizabeth (___), 23:224
John, 23:154
William D., 22:221, 233
WINDOW
Ann, 23:176
Elizabeth (Bennett), 23:176
Richard, 23:176
WINGATE
Jennet, 21:52
WINNING
Alexander, 23:34; 24:51
Betsy/Betty (Parker), 24:214
Deborah (Parker), 23:34; 24:51
John, 24:214
WINSHIP
Abigail, 25:39, 45
Edward, 25:6
WINSLOW
Dena, 24:18
Edward, 21:43; 22:69
Susanna (___), 21:43
WINSOR, 23:87
WINTER
Addison, 22:227
Ignatius/Eylacius, 25:12, 13
Sarah Ann (Lane), 25:12
WINTHROP, 22:240a; 23:135; 24:126
___, Gov., 21:209; 22:60a, 165;
23:110, 167
Henry, 24:176a
John, 21:195; 23:110, 180a, 231, 236;
24:176, 176a; 25:156a
Lucy, 25:203
Mary (Browne), 21:240a
Wait, 21:240a
WISE
Alice, 22:188, 189
George, 22:188
John, 22:20; 24:140-142, 147, 151
Mary (___), 22:188

Richard, 22:188
Thomas, 23:154
WITBEE
Eunice, 21:54
WITCHER
Chase, 22:51
Curt B., 25:121
Dolly, 22:51
Hannah (Morrill), 22:51
WITHAM
Deborah (Stanwood), 24:219
Henry, 22:112
John L., 22:227, 231
Rebecca, 24:218, 219
Samuel, 24:219
WITHERBEE/WITHERBY
John Keyes, 21:34
Levinah (Rand), 21:34
Sarah (Brown), 23:99
WITHINGTON
Mary, 23:225
WITHROP
___, Miss, 25:156
WITT
Elizabeth, 21:40
John, 22:206
Mary (___), 21:31
Olive, 23:154
Thomas, 21:31
WITTEN
Ruth Southard, 24:108
WITTER
Elizabeth (Wheeler), 23:169
Josias, 23:169
William, 23:168, 169
WITTREGE see WHITRED
WOBAND
Robert, 22:117
WOBURN
___, Mr., 22:209
WOLF
Freeborn, 23:179
WOLTERS
Lenore, 23:87
WOOD see also WOODS, 24:222
Charles P., 22:227
Daniel, 25:133
Elizabeth (Boutel), 21:215
Eugene, 21:50
Hannah, 21:159
Israel, 24:84
John, 21:215; 24:170
Jonathan, 23:117
Joseph, 23:154
Mary (Davis), 23:164, 179
Rebecca, 23:117
Ruth (___), 24:162
Samuel, 23:164, 179
Sarah, 22:218
Sarah (Redington), 23:117
Sarah (Stevens), 24:84
WOODBERRY/WOODBERY see
WOODBURY
WOODBRIDGE
Benjamin, 21:195
Benjamin Ruggles, 22:48
Dorcas (___), 25:80
Dudley, 25:80
Hannah Shattuck (Stevens), 24:102
John, 21:111, 113, 195
Mercy (Dudley), 21:113
Osgood, 24:102
WOODBURY/WOODBERRY/
WOODBERY, 21:24, 225
"Child", 21:224
Abigail (Allen), 22:55

Agnes (___), 22:58
Alice Ray, 21:106
Andrew, 22:227-230
Ann (Window), 23:176
Anna (Bennett), 23:117
Asa, 22:227, 231-233
Augustus, 21:102
Azariah, 21:223; 23:117
Benjamin, 21:223
Christian, 23:239
Clara, 21:106
Ebenezer, 23:176
Edward, 22:55
Eleanor (Ellingwood), 22:55
Elisha, 21:224
Elizabeth (Hunger), 23:239
Elizabeth (Hunter), 22:55, 56; 23:176;
24:136
Elizabeth (Tenney), 23:176
Florence, 21:224
Hannah, 22:55, 175, 227, 228
Hannah (Dodge), 22:55; 23:176
Hepzibah (Ober), 22:218
Humphrey, 22:55, 56; 23:176, 239;
24:136
Jerusha, 22:57
Jesse, 22:175
Joanna (Wheeler), 22:55; 23:176
John, 21:24; 22:58, 172; 23:176, 240a
Jonathan, 22:55
Joseph, 21:223; 22:218
Joshua, 22:227, 231
Josiah, 22:172, 175
Josiah Perkins, 22:172
Lydia, 23:176
Lydia Obear (English), 21:106
M. Lizzie, 21:224
Margaret (___), 22:172, 175
Mary, 21:179
Mary Ober (Lefavour), 21:224
Nancy, 21:223; 22:238
Nathaniel, 22:227-229, 233
Nicholas, 21:223
Patty, 22:172
Peter, 22:57, 103
Priscilla (Woodbury), 23:176
Rebecca, 22:49
Rebecca Briant (English), 21:102
Sarah, 22:55, 111; 23:117
Sarah (Dodge), 22:57
Stephen, 21:106
Susanna, 23:176
Thomas, 22:55; 23:176
William, 21:223; 22:55, 172; 23:176
WOODCOCK
Sarah, 22:47
Welthea, 22:48
WOODEN
John, 22:38
WOODERD
Ezekiel, 22:107
Sarah (Edwards), 22:107
WOODIER
Grace, 23:239
WOODLAND
Mary, 21:148
WOODMAN, 21:172; 24:28, 146, 149
___, Mr., 21:112; 25:101
A., 21:114
E., 21:114
Edward, 21:111, 113, 114; 25:102
Elizabeth, 24:36
Elizabeth (Stevens), 24:35
Joshua, 24:35
Judith, 22:44
Mary, 21:173

WOODROFFE/WOODRUFF
Charity, 25:55, 57
Frederick Orr, 21:36
John, 25:55
Lettice (Ackhurst), 25:55
WOODS see also WOOD
___, Dr., 25:60a
Mary (Parker), 25:36, 37
Samuel, 25:36, 37
Thomas A., 23:170
WOODTOR
Dee Parmer, 25:121
WOODWARD, 22:42
Ann (Beamsley), 25:202
Deborah (Tyler), 21:99
Ezekiel, 22:39, 40, 107; 25:202
John, 21:214; 22:41
Margaret (Lawrence), 25:202
Mary (Goldsmith), 22:41
Nathaniel, 25:202
Prudence, 25:202
Sarah (Edwards), 22:107
Sarah C. (___), 23:127
WOODY
Richard, 22:44
WOOLRICH
Mary, 21:116
WOOLSON
Elizabeth, 21:154
WORCESTER
___, Dr., 25:150
___, Mr., 21:195
Jonathan, 25:167
Moses, 25:167
Samuel, 25:60a
Sarah, 22:177
Susanna (___), 22:177
Timothy, 22:177
WORDEN
Abigail, 21:175
Hopestill (Holloway), 21:176
Mary (Brown), 21:175
Samuel, 21:176
Sarah (Butler), 21:175
Thomas, 21:175
WORMWALL
Elizabeth, 21:150
WORTH
Susannah, 24:232
WRAY
See Ray, 23:73
WRETLIND
Eric, 23:135
WRIGHT, 21:50
___, Gov., 24:80
Audrey (Whiting), 23:218
Dorothy, 21:88
Eliphalet, 23:38
Elizabeth (Parker), 24:162, 163
Elizabeth (Peters), 21:88
George, 25:108a
John, 21:87; 24:41
Martha (Cummings), 21:240
Mary, 25:80
Mercy (Wardwell), 21:87
Peter, 21:240
Rachel (___), 25:87
Rachel (Parker), 24:206
Robert, 23:218
Samuel, 25:87
Susan, 24:43
Susanna (Johnson), 21:87
Thomas, 24:163
Walter, 21:87, 88
William, 21:240
Zaccheus, 24:206; 25:145

WYATT
 Elizabeth, 21:31
 Sarah, 21:14
 Willm., 25:80
WYER
 Elizabeth (Johnson), 25:5
WYLIE, 21:220
WYMAN, 23:59; 25:26
 Francis, 22:187
 Thomas, 21:28
 Thomas Bellows, 22:45; 23:52;
  24:155, 158; 25:7, 93, 137

YATES
 Deborah (Kendrick), 21:52
 John, 21:52
YEATS
 Marcy, 21:52
YELLINGS
 Elizabeth, 25:165
YOEMAN
 Anne, 25:203
YORK
 Bell, 21:175
 Deborah (Bell), 21:175
 Hannah, 21:175
 Isaac, 24:94
 James, 21:175
 Joannah (___), 21:175
 Lucy (Palmer), 21:175
 Mary (Brown), 21:175
 Phebe (Stevens), 24:94
 Ruth (Main), 21:175
 Thomas, 21:175
YOUNG, 21:9; 23:215
 Abigail, 21:237
 Alexander, 21:202
 Amy (Green), 23:44
 Ann (Snow), 25:21
 Annie/Amy (Green), 23:45
 Barnabas, 25:21
 Betsey, 24:116
 Catherine, 23:46
 Daniel, 22:227
 Elizabeth/Betsy, 23:119
 Epes, 22:227, 232, 233
 Francis, 23:119
 George Henry, 21:206
 Hannah (Rhodes), 23:42, 43
 Jeremiah, 23:42, 43
 Jeremiah Smith, 23:23
 John, 25:21
 Judith (Fuller), 23:45
 Margaret (Kelloch), 23:119
 Mary, 21:240a; 23:44-49, 154; 24:217
 Mary/Polly, 22:48
 Mercy, 22:41
 Nathan, 23:45
 Phebe, 23:42, 43
 Rebecca, 25:21
 Rebecca (Young), 25:21
 Ruth (Cole), 25:21
 Wm. J., 21:208
 Zadock, 23:44, 45, 49
YOUNGLOVE
 Samuell, 22:159

ZARELLA, 25:113, 114
ZOLO
 Richard P., 23:89
ZOUCH, 21:26

www.ingramcontent.com/pod-product-compliance
Lightning Source LLC
Chambersburg PA
CBHW050715100426
42735CB00041B/3306